HOW TO AIR CONDITION YOUR CAR

Timothy Remus
and Jack Chisenhall

First published in 1993 by Motorbooks International Publishers & Wholesalers, PO Box 2, 729 Prospect Avenue, Osceola, WI 54020 USA

Motorbooks International books are also available at discounts in bulk quantity for industrial or sales-promotional use. For details write to Special Sales Manager at the Publisher's address

Library of Congress Cataloging-in-Publication Data Available

ISBN 0-87938-765-3

On the front cover: A sampling of vehicles fitted with aftermarket air conditioning systems includes a street rod, classic American car, Corvette, and vintage pickup truck. *Timothy Remus*

On the back cover: Air conditioning components in place, and air conditioning installation in progress, *Timothy Remus*; also, final installation of a system in a sharp red '32 Ford. *Dennis Clark*

Printed and bound in the United States of America

Contents

Chapter 1

Basics of Air Conditioning

The first automotive air conditioners appeared in American luxury cars after the second world war. Like the cars, those early air conditioning systems were considered very much a luxury. As each year passed however, more and more cars offered the novelty of air conditioning and eventually cars like Cadillac and Lincoln considered air conditioning to be "standard equipment."

Owners of these cars enjoyed the cool fresh air and the lack of fatigue after a long day on the highway. Business men and women reported that the cool air emitted from the dash vents made it easier to look fresh when making summer sales calls. By the same token, Mom, Dad and the kids were now able to take summer vacations in the car and arrive with family harmony intact.

We have come a long way since those early days. Today, air conditioning is standard equipment, not just on Cadillacs, but on most of the cars offered for sale. There aren't many new automobiles that don't offer air conditioning as

70° AIR TEMPERATURE

125°F

Heat always moves toward an area that is cooler. Thus your coffee gets cold because the heat in the cup moves to the cooler surrounding air. Vintage Air

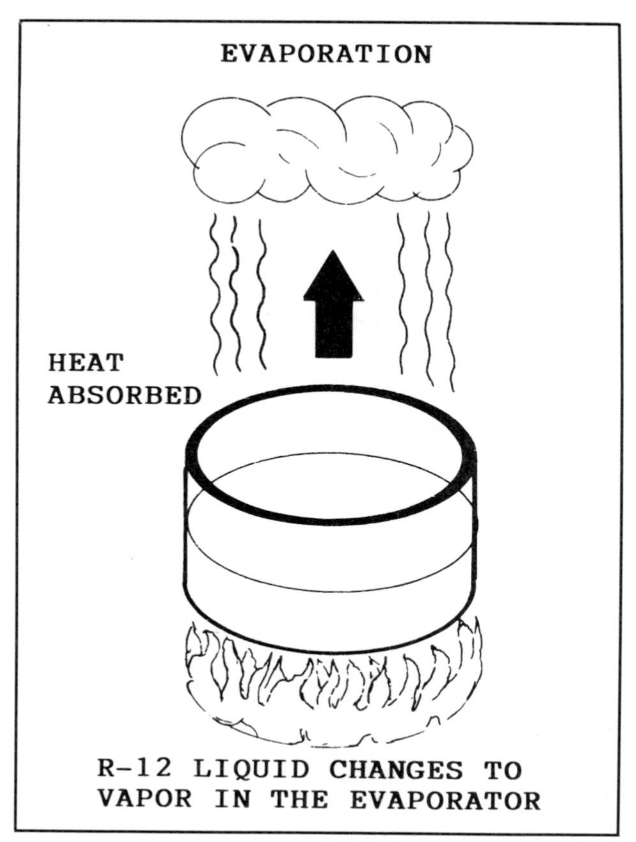
EVAPORATION
HEAT
ABSORBED
R-12 LIQUID CHANGES TO
VAPOR IN THE EVAPORATOR

When you boil water much of the energy put into the pot is used to change the water from liquid to vapor—evaporation. When the refrigerant "boils" in your car's evaporator, a great deal of heat energy is absorbed from the car's interior. Vintage Air

standard equipment or as an option. A new car without air conditioning has become the exception rather than the rule.

Most of the cars on the street carry air conditioning and we've all come to appreciate the cool air that flows from the vents. The trouble comes when we buy or build something old and unusual. A Deuce street rod, a 427 Cobra, a '53 Chevrolet, or a '66 Chevy pickup truck.

Your new hobby vehicle may be fast and exciting, but it probably doesn't have air conditioning (unless the previous owner took care of the problem).

You shouldn't panic—air conditioning can be installed in nearly any vehicle and in most cases that installation can be done in your own garage. Though the procedures are simple and straightforward, it truly helps to understand the laws governing air conditioning before you jump in—cutting holes in firewalls and bolting on compressors. Without a general knowledge of *why* the air conditioner works, you may do a less than ideal installation. If you want the system to look neat and operate at peak efficiency, you need to understand what the heck is going on.

Understanding the Physics of Air Conditioning

In order to understand automotive air conditioning, it's necessary to understanding the principles of refrigeration.

First, consider these properties: hot, cold, and heat transfer. There is no such thing as "cold," only the absence of heat. Creating "cold" is accomplished by removing heat and this is affected by a physical law: Heat always travels from hot to cold. The greater the temperature difference, the faster the heat moves. Your coffee gets cold because the heat of the liquid travels to the cooler atmosphere of the room. This loss of heat from the cup will continue as long as the coffee is hotter than the air in the room.

The second principle we need to understand is one governing vaporization and condensation, sometimes called "Latent Heat of Evaporation." The simplest way to understand this phenomenon is to consider a pan of hot water on the stove. You turn up the heat (adding heat, measured in BTUs as you do so) and the temperature of the water rises to 212 degrees Fahrenheit. You continue adding heat to the water and a funny thing happens. The water starts to vaporize but the

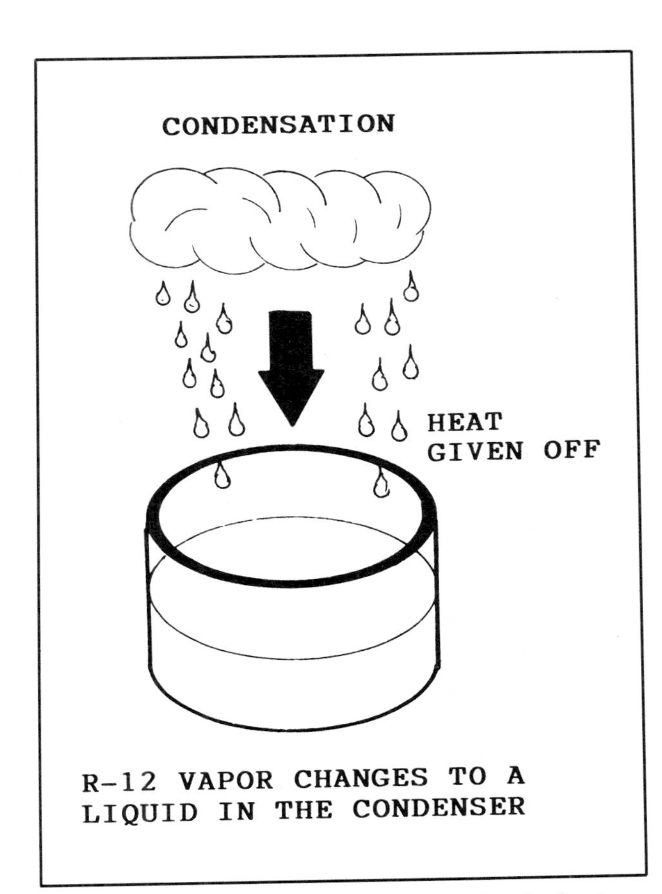

When the water vapor changes form again, the heat energy used to make the water evaporate is given off to the surrounding area. When the refrigerant condenses back into a liquid in your car's condenser, heat is given off to the surrounding air.

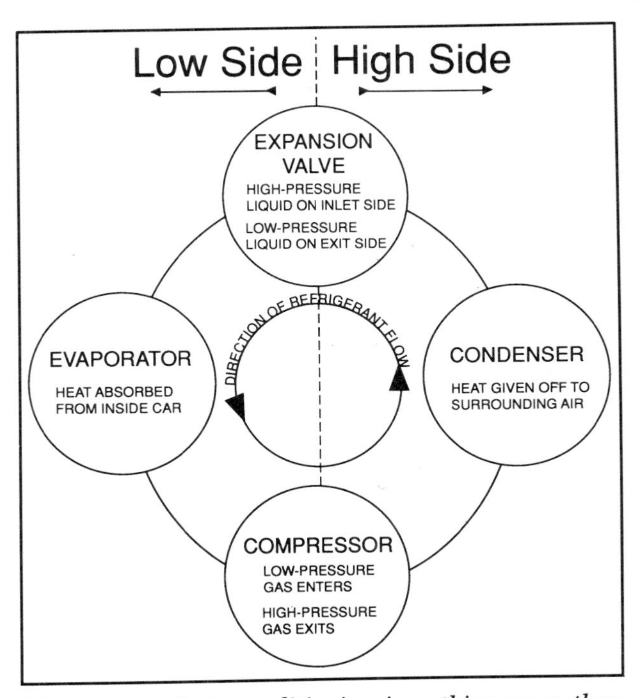

The process of air conditioning is nothing more than an endless repetition of evaporation and condensation cycles. When the refrigerant evaporates, it absorbs heat from inside the car. When it condenses, it gives up that heat to the air flowing past the condenser.

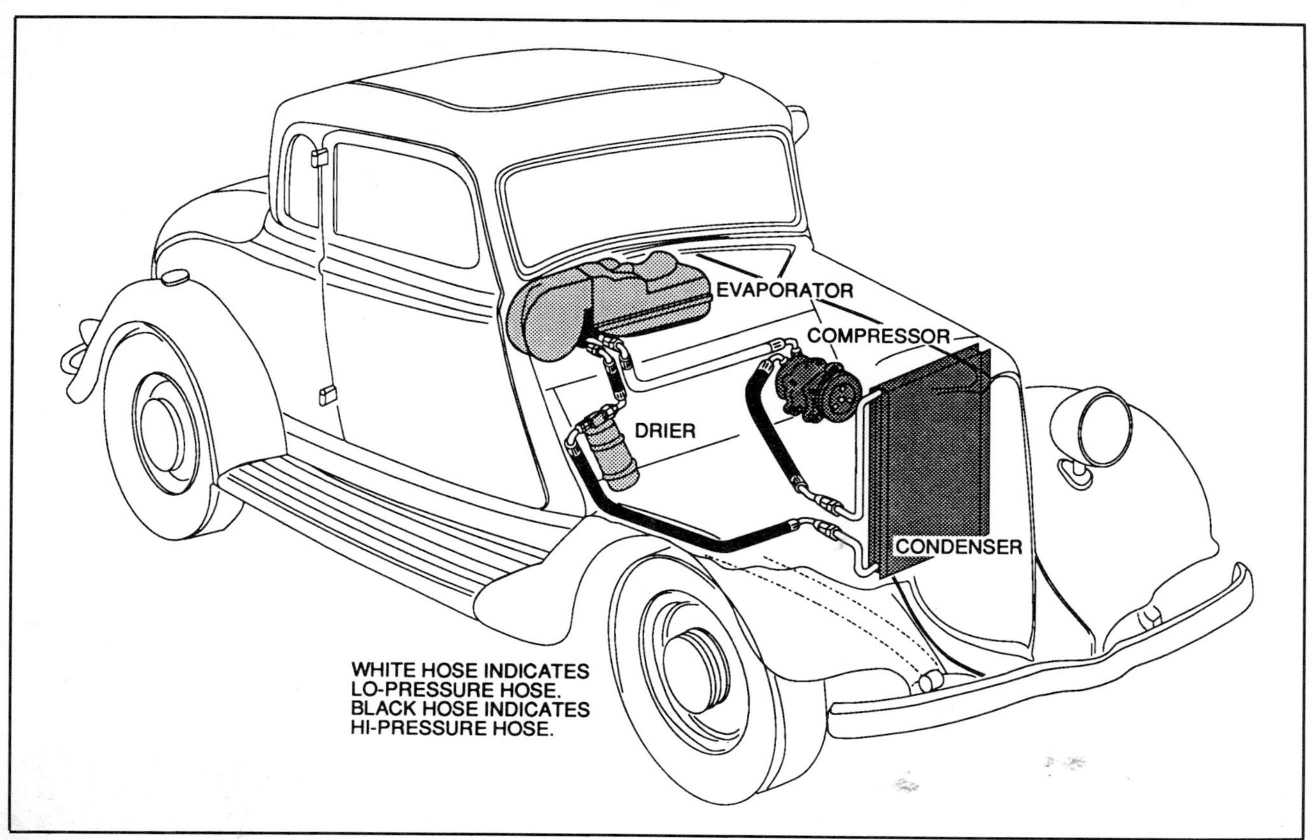

The typical automotive air conditioner is broken up into two sides, the high side, from the compressor to the expansion valve, and the low side, from the expansion valve to the compressor.

temperature remains at 212 degrees (this is a sea-level experiment). What is happening is that most of the heat being added to the water is being used to convert the water from a liquid to a gas. This change of state takes enormous amounts of energy—energy that can't be measured with a thermometer.

Air conditioning uses this same principle. Refrigerant in the car's air conditioning system is encouraged to evaporate—or change state from liquid to a gas—in the evaporator (the unit under the dashboard). As the refrigerant evaporates, heat is absorbed from the interior of the car.

The best example of this Latent Heat business is the chill you feel when you come out of the lake after a swim. Most of that chill is caused by the water evaporating off your body, taking tremendous amounts of heat along with it, as the water changes state from liquid to gas.

The third law we need to consider is Pressure's Effect on Vaporization. (For our discussion, "vaporization" will include vaporization and condensation.) We all know that water boils at 212 degrees Fahrenheit, but that is only true when the water is at a pressure equal to atmospheric pressure at sea level. By increasing the pressure on the water in a sealed container, we can raise the boiling point by two or three degrees for each pound of pressure. The higher the pressure, the higher the boiling point of this water. This is why your radiator is pressurized—to increase the boiling point of the coolant.

The refrigerant in our air conditioner works the same way. Refrigerant CFC-12 boils (or changes state from liquid to gas) at –21 degrees Fahrenheit. (We will talk about the new HFC-134A refrigerant a little later.) Therefore, CFC-12 at sea level will be a gas at most of the temperatures your car will encounter—except that pressure comes into play. As we explained, pressure applied to a liquid will raise the temperature at which it changes its state from a liquid to a gas. By controlling the pressure within the air conditioning system, we can regulate whether the refrigerant is a liquid or gas, and when it changes state.

Essentially, the liquid refrigerant is contained in a closed system divided into two different pressure areas. By moving the refrigerant from the high-pressure side of the system to the low-pressure side, its state is changed from liquid to gas.

When the refrigerant vaporizes in the evaporator (the unit under the dashboard), it absorbs heat from the interior of the car. When that refrigerant is changed back from a gas to a liquid in the condenser (the unit in front of the radiator), it gives that heat off to the atmosphere.

Addressing Safety Basics

Before we jump into the specifics of the air conditioner in your car, we need to back up a little and discuss basic safety. The refrigerant used in most cars and trucks since the early 1950s is CFC-12, a chlorofluorocarbon. (Freon is a trade name owned by the DuPont company.) Starting in 1992, some cars are being offered with a new refrigerant, HFC-134A.

Refrigerant CFC-12 boils at a very low temperature, like –21.7 degrees Fahrenheit. Refrigerant (whether it's CFC-12 or HFC-134A) escaping from the air conditioning system or a container can and will cause severe frostbite of any part of your anatomy it comes into contact with.

Anyone working on an air conditioning system should always wear goggles to protect their eyes and gloves to protect their hands. Also, they should never expose a container of refrigerant to direct heat or sunlight. Even under the pressures normally found in these containers, if heat is added, the refrigerant will boil. This could raise the pressure inside the can to an explosive level.

Service information is included in this book so the owner of the air conditioning system knows what to expect when he or she takes the car in to have it serviced. We recommend that only certified air conditioning technicians charge and service air conditioners.

One last caution, when CFC-12 is exposed to an open flame or to hot metal, poisonous phosgene gas is formed. This was used during WW I as "nerve gas," so keep CFC-12 away from any open flame. A couple of symptoms of phosgene poisoning include headache and dizziness.

How Air Conditioning Works in Your Car

Most automotive air conditioner systems are made up of seven components–along with the hoses and fittings through which the refrigerant

This is a fairly typical aftermarket air conditioning installation showing the compressor, the condenser, and the receiver-drier.

travels between components. The seven components are:

Compressor
Compressor mounting bracket
Condenser
Receiver-drier
Expansion valve
Evaporator
Hose and fittings

The easiest way to explain how the air conditioning works in your car is to trace the refrigerant as it flows through a typical system.

As we described earlier, the air conditioning system is split into two "sides," the low-pressure side and the high-pressure side. The two points that separate the sides are the compressor reed valves and the expansion valve. Let's start our discussion of flow within the air conditioning system at the compressor.

The compressor is a pump, and like most pumps it has a pressure side and a suction side. The suction side of our air conditioner is pulling refrigerant in gas form—refrigerant that has stored enormous amounts of latent heat. The refrigerant leaves the compressor at high pressure and goes next to the condenser. Note: The oil that lubricates the compressor is carried in suspension with the refrigerant and circulates through the system.

The condenser is really just a heat exchanger. A device mounted in the airstream in front of the radiator (in most cases) where it can transfer the heat stored in the refrigerant to the air moving over the coils and fins. The combination of high pressure and the heat loss that occurs in the condenser means the refrigerant is converted from a gas to a mix (when the system is working properly) that is approximately ninety percent liquid.

This mix of mostly liquid refrigerant leaves the condenser and pours into the receiver-drier. The receiver-drier is a metal canister with three functions—to separate refrigerant liquid from a mix of gas and liquid, to filter the refrigerant and to dry the refrigerant. The receiver-drier has a tube that extends almost to the bottom of the cannister. As the refrigerant pours into the canister, the liquid goes to the bottom of the can and the gas rises to the top. Refrigerant leaving the receiver-drier must move out through the tube that extends almost to the bottom, thus only liquid refrigerant (assuming the system is properly charged) will leave the receiver-drier.

Because the refrigerant must be kept extremely clean and dry, most receiver dryers contain both a filter and a desiccant bag to absorb impurities and moisture as the refrigerant circulates through the system.

Most receiver-driers contain two more fea-

Each component should be mounted in an advantageous position so it can do its job. Here the condenser is mounted where it will receive good airflow, making it easy for the unit to cool and condense the refrigerant.

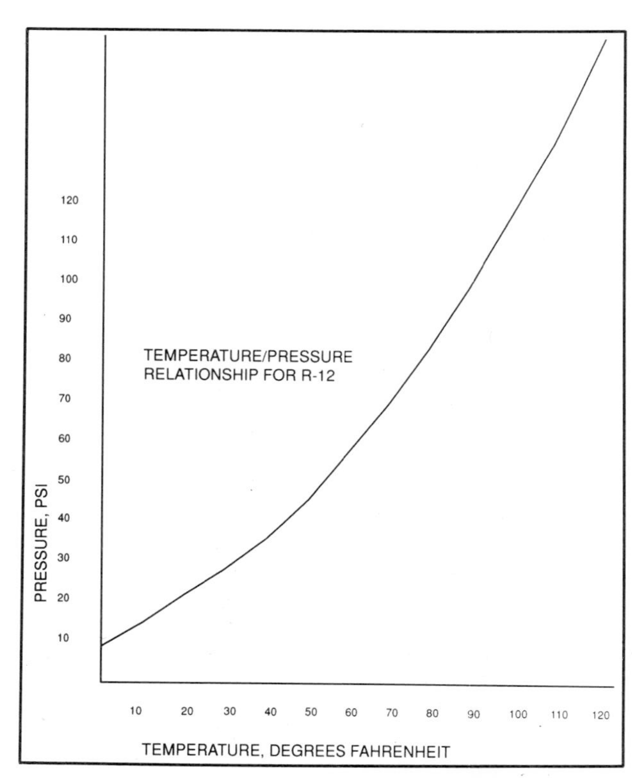

The temperature and pressure of CFC-12 refrigerant almost follows a one-to-one relationship. If you know the pressure, you also know the temperature. This chart shows the relationship in the lower temperature/pressure ranges.

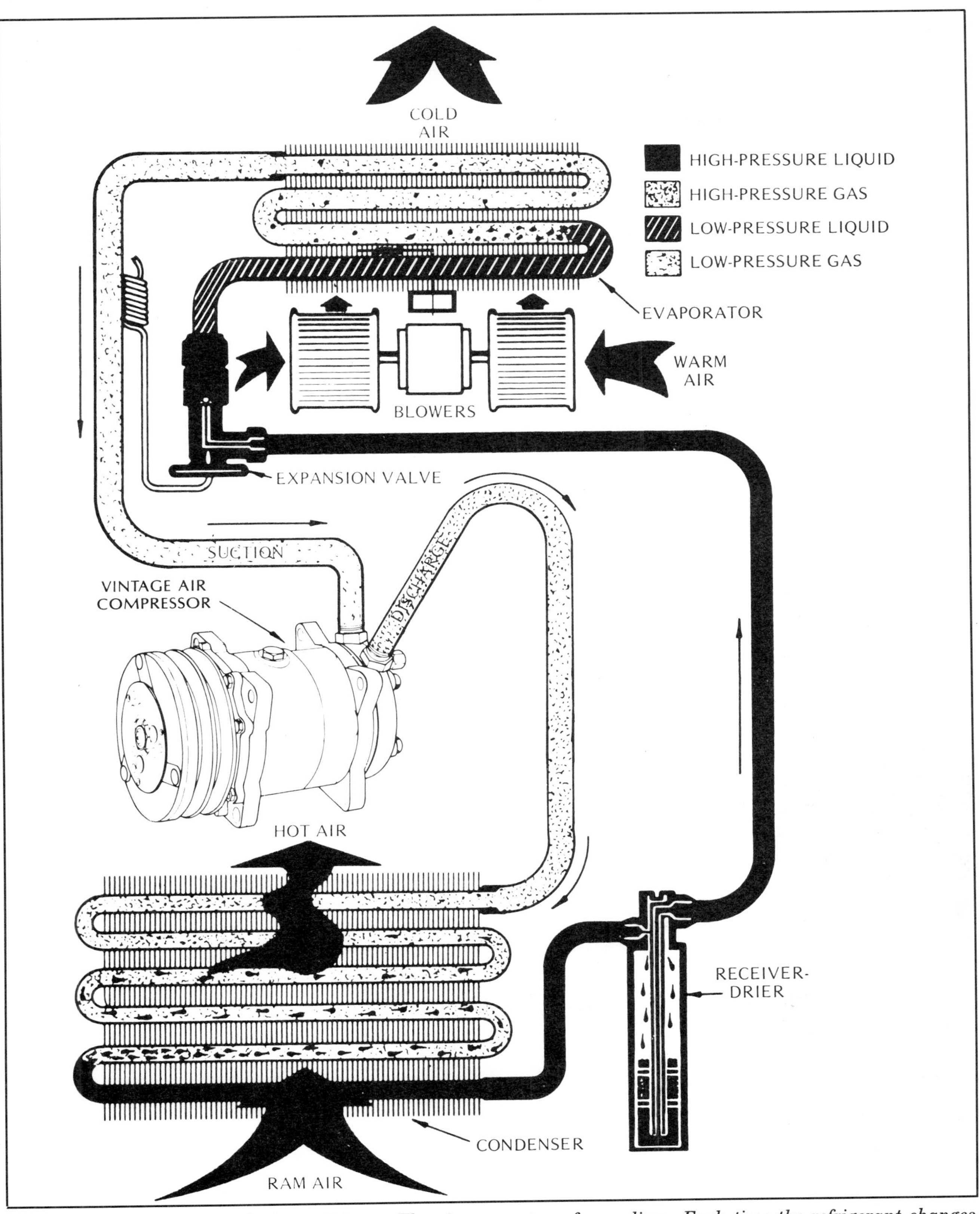

Another look inside a typical air conditioner. The air conditioner doesn't really create cool, it just moves heat from the interior to the exterior using refrigerant as the transfer medium. Each time the refrigerant changes state it either absorbs heat or gives it off. Vintage Air

tures. Most have a sight glass that looks down into the passage or tube leaving the receiver-drier. The cloudy or clear appearance of the refrigerant in the sight glass is a major indicator of whether the system is correctly charged or low on refrigerant. (Note: In HFC-134A systems the sight glass is often eliminated because a window in a HFC-134A systems won't necessarily appear clean when the system fills with refrigerant.) The other feature offered on many receiver-driers is a safety plug, designed to release the refrigerant in the system if the underhood temperature gets too high or the pressure in the system rises too far.

When the refrigerant leaves the receiver-drier of a properly operating system it has: been pressurized by the compressor; cooled and converted into mostly liquid by the condenser; and separated into pure liquid refrigerant by the receiver-drier. This high-pressure liquid refrigerant moves next to the expansion valve.

The expansion valve is one of the two separators between high pressure and low pressure in the air conditioning system. Though there are different types of valves in use, you can think of the expansion valve as a very small orifice with high-pressure liquid refrigerant on one side, and low-pressure liquid droplets—rapidly changing to a gas—on the other side.

The expansion valve is located on the inlet side of the evaporator. As the high-pressure liquid refrigerant moves through the expansion valve, the pressure drops and the refrigerant moving into the evaporator starts to vaporize. And as we know, when a material changes state from liquid to gas, a tremendous amount of heat is absorbed (a thousand times more energy than if there were no change in state).

The evaporator is another heat exchanger, and looks like a small radiator. The refrigerant moves through the tubes while an electric fan moves cabin air over the multiple fins that surround the tubes. As the refrigerant, now at low pressure, moves through the tubes, warm air is constantly moving over the fins, causing the refrigerant to continue vaporizing and to continue absorbing the heat of the air passing over the fins.

Because cool air carries less moisture than hot air, the evaporator functions as a dehumidifier as well. Moisture that collects on the fins of the evaporator is collected in the tray or evaporator housing and runs to a tube that exits outside the car.

Most expansion valves have a capillary tube that runs from the valve to the outlet of the evaporator. As the temperature at the outlet of the evaporator becomes cooler or warmer, this refrigerant charged capillary tube, working through a diaphragm attached to the valve itself, can open or close the valve and thus control the temperature. A more thorough discussion of the various types of expansion valves is included later in the book.

Low-pressure refrigerant leaving the evaporator travels to the suction side of the compressor, the starting point of our discussion.

Summary

Automotive air conditioning relies on three basic laws of nature: Heat transfer from hot to cold, the latent heat of vaporization, and the effect of pressure on vaporization.

By controlling when the refrigerant in your air conditioning system changes from liquid to gas, you effectively move the heat from inside the car to the outside airstream very quickly. When the refrigerant boils in the evaporator, heat is absorbed from inside the car. When that same refrigerant is compressed and passes through the condenser, the heat is given off to the airstream as the refrigerant condenses back into a liquid.

Only when the air conditioning system is well designed, well matched to the job at hand, and correctly installed, can it do the job of removing the heat from inside the cabin of your car or truck. In this book, we will explain what a good system consists of, how to install it in your type of vehicle, and how that system should be serviced and maintained.

Chapter 2

The Components

In the first chapter we discussed how an air conditioning system works and the laws of nature that it relies on for its operation. In this chapter we will discuss the various systems that are available for automotive use, their advantages and disadvantages and some things to look for as you shop for a system to install in your car or truck. Unless noted otherwise, all comments made in this chapter refer to systems using CFC-12 refrigerant.

The Three Basic Systems in Common Use

Though all automotive air conditioners work in basically the same way, there are three types of systems in common use today. The difference is in how the refrigerant flow is controlled. The three types of systems are cycling clutch expansion valve (CCEV), cycling clutch orifice tube (CCOT), and pressure regulating expansion valve.

1. Cycling Clutch Expansion Valve—CCEV

This is the system most commonly used in aftermarket air conditioning applications. The CCEV is a simple system that controls the temperature of the evaporator through the operation of the expansion valve and a thermostatic clutch control switch. Unless otherwise noted, all systems discussed in this book will be the CCEV style of air conditioning.

2. Cycling Clutch Orifice Tube—CCOT

This is an air conditioning system often used by OEMs (original equipment manufacturers), one that uses a fixed orifice instead of a true expansion valve. Control of the evaporator temperature (and preventing evaporator icing) is accomplished by a temperature sensing switch on the outlet of the evaporator. Remember that refrigerant pressure and temperature follow a predictable graph, thus if you control the pressure in the evaporator you also control the temperature.

This style of system "floods" the evaporator with refrigerant and as a result, some of the refrigerant may not fully evaporate. To prevent liquid refrigerant from reaching the compressor suction side (definitely a no-no), an accumulator is used between the evaporator outlet and the compressor suction side. Like a receiver-drier in reverse, the accumulator prevents any liquid refrigerant from reaching the compressor.

The CCOT system is rapidly becoming the most common original equipment (used by both Ford and GM) type system. It is inexpensive to

A comparison of the three types of condensers available. On the bottom is the most efficient, a parallel-flow condenser. On the right is a serpentine, and on the left is the well-known tube-and-fin design.

produce, largely because its fixed orifice metering device is molded plastic with no moving parts, compared to the expansion valve's relatively costly construction. The disadvantages include a lack of precision in the control of the system and a high power requirement for a given amount of cooling. In response, some new car manufacturers are switching to CCEV type of air conditioning.

3. Pressure Regulating Expansion Valve

These systems use both a true expansion valve and a pressure sensitive valve (known by acronyms such as STV, POA, and VIR) on the evaporator outlet to control evaporator temperature and to avoid icing. Again, if you control the pressure in the evaporator you also control the temperature. Instead of cycling the compressor on and off to control the evaporator pressure, these systems run the compressor constantly and use a pressure sensitive valve on the outlet side of the evaporator to control the temperature and avoid evaporator freeze up. There are a number of variations on this basic theme, some use an accumulator while others use a receiver-drier. Few new cars carry systems that run the compressor constantly, however, because of greater fuel usage and increased system complexity.

In cases where the space is tight, a radiator with an integral condenser can be purchased. Shown are two solutions to air conditioning a '39 Ford. On the left is a serpentine condenser mounted to the Ford radiator while on the right is an integral radiator and condenser from Walker radiator.

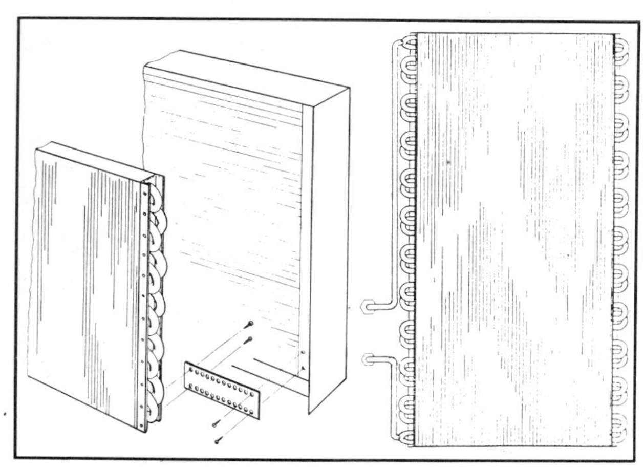

Some condensers (like these tube-and-fin models) have a perforated edge making it easy to attach brackets to the radiator saddle or support. Be sure to design the brackets to leave an air space between the radiator and condenser. Note that the tubes are always run in a horizontal direction (in CFC-12 systems).

Component Selection

The major components of any air conditioning system include the condenser, compressor, hoses and brackets, receiver-drier, evaporator, and controls and fans. The most misunderstood and often mismatched of all the components is the condenser, so let's start our discussion there.

The Condenser

Condensers come in three varieties: tube and fin, serpentine, and manifold style.

Tube and fin are by far the most popular of the designs used in the aftermarket, though that will change as we move into the age of HFC-134A. The tube and fin style of condenser has one, two, or three rows of copper tubing surrounded by fins of sheet aluminum. These copper tube and aluminum finned condensers have the advantage of being inexpensive and easily modified with a torch and silver solder.

The serpentine condensers use a flattened tube that winds its way back and forth (in a serpentine manner) across the fins. In some designs the fins are actually part of the tube. These newer serpentine condensers are finding use in the aftermarket (they have been used for some time on new cars, where space is limited and efficiency must be high). Serpentine condensers are generally made from extruded aluminum with the fittings welded on each end of the tube. Though more expensive than the old standby tube and fin condenser, the serpentine design generally packs more cooling ability into a given package size. (Note: Recent research indicates that the serpentine designs are not useful in HFC-134A systems.)

The manifold (or parallel flow) type of condenser is the newest, most efficient and most expensive of the three designs currently on the market. This design passes the refrigerant through the condenser's manifold, through the multiple micro tubes, then back into the second manifold and back through the second set of tubes. The result is a very efficient design, one that ensures that all the refrigerant actually makes contact with the primary cooling surfaces for maximum cooling in a given package size.

A variety of compressors can and have been used on aftermarket air conditioning installations. The old Frigidaire A-6 is a good choice only if you are cooling a very large vehicle or one with two evaporators. This is a view under the hood of a street-rodded limousine.

This design also features minimal restriction to the passage of refrigerant.

Because HFC-134A systems tend to need more condenser capacity than similar CFC-12 systems, look for more manifold type condensers on the new systems. The tooling for these condensers is completely new however, so there may be a lag time before these are commonly available.

Specifications for a condenser include: the number of fins per inch, cubic inches of mass, and also the cubic feet per minute (CFM) of air that will be moving past the condenser. As you add tubes to a condenser you increase the condenser's ability to dissipate heat, though there is a loss of overall efficiency. Specific guidelines for condenser specifications for particular types of applications (street rods, pickup trucks, etc.) will be included in later chapters.

In general, a larger condenser is almost always better. The idea is to remove heat from the car's interior. Heat and pressure within the A/C system are directly related. The more heat we remove, the lower the pressure within the high side of the system and the better we've done our job. This lowered pressure/temperature requires less horsepower to run the compressor and creates less vibration, the most common cause of compressor mount breakage.

As a rule of thumb, a CFC-12 system using tube and fin condenser and evaporators should have a condenser with about twenty-five percent more capacity than the evaporator.

Each year the aftermarket adds new condenser models, making it easier and easier to find the right condenser or condenser/radiator combination for the job. Though it might not be as visible as the compressor, remember that the condenser is a critical part of your air conditioning system. Spend some time here making sure the condenser is correctly matched to the rest of the system and located so it receives plenty of fresh air.

Note that HFC-134A systems need a high-capacity condenser, either a serpentine or manifold style. With HFC-134A, it's more important than ever to remember the adage that applies to condenser size: "When in doubt, go for more capacity."

The Compressor

What should you look for in a compressor? You will need to make sure that it is properly sized to your system and will perform well and reliably. Appearance is another factor to consider because it is located in your vehicle's engine compartment, an area that is often designed for good appearance as well as good function.

Compressors are considered the heart of the A/C system and most people assume that more is better—but this is not the case. Some air conditioning experts have long been proponents of larger condensers and smaller compressors, but not until industrial and home air conditioner manufacturers began building low-energy air conditioners did the practice gain widespread acceptance. That is the major reason a "low energy condensing unit" is low in energy consumption—because of the larger condenser-to-compressor ratio. The greater heat dissipation ability of the larger condenser means lower pressure, requiring less torque and energy to pump the refrigerant. So when you choose your compressor, avoid the temptation to "max out."

Compressors are sized in cubic inches per revolution. Most automotive applications call for a compressor capacity of five to nine cubic inches per revolution. Specific recommendations will be found in later chapters. Again, just remember that bigger isn't always better. Generally speaking, if your compressor is oversized, relative to the condenser, it will create excess pressure and heat, placing extra loads on the engine and leading to premature compressor and mount failure. Lack of compressor capacity will normally result in reduced performance, but you would normally only notice it at a stoplight or in a traffic jam. This might end up being a blessing, however, as you would also be adding less heat to the radiator in those situations.

The Sanden / Sankyo model 508 is a good choice for many vehicles, offering a lot of compressor in a small, neat package. The round shape makes it easy to mount in a tight engine compartment, and the axial design helps minimize vibration.

Instead of installing one that is bigger than you need, the compressor should be just right, or even "just a little undersized."

With size behind us, let's take a look at what is available to fill your compressor needs. The round, axial designs have become the compressors of choice both for Detroit and aftermarket applications. It's simply hard to argue with their compact size, minimal vibration, and good appearance.

What brands should you consider most seriously?

Jack Chisenhall of Vintage Air feels that: "In my experience, the Sanden (previously Sankyo) is a hard unit to beat. A host of look-alikes have tried to capitalize on its popularity, but to date none of them stack up. Vintage Air does testing of many compressor designs, both for our own uses and for other manufacturers. We recommend the Sanden because of its smooth operation, durability, bullet-proof construction, large selection of capacities, and good appearance."

It's interesting to note in these days when everything seems to come from Japan, that the Sanden compressor began as an American design. An engineer from John Mitchell Company in Dallas, Texas, designed the compressor,

The Sanden compressor is offered with different hose locations making it convenient to mount in nearly any situation. Note that the discharge and suction ports are marked.

known originally under the Abacus name. The goal was a smoother and more compact compressor than the "paint shakers" that were then on the market. Eventually Sanden obtained license rights to the design for worldwide distribution; Sanden is the US arm of Sankyo.

The Sanden/Sankyo compressor is about 5in around with a length of 8 1/2in on the 508 model (five cylinders and 8 cubic inches of displacement) and 6 3/4in on the 505 model (five cylinders, 5ci). (In these model numbers, the first number indicates the number of cylinders while the second number gives the cubic inch capacity.) More cylinders means greater smoothness and better volumetric efficiency.

To get the right compressor for a new HFC-134A system, you need merely specify that refrigerant when you order the compressor. The Sanden compressors built during the last two years are capable of running HFC-134A, even though they may be installed in a CFC-12 system. Many of these can be easily converted to HFC-134A use.

There are, of course, other axial/radial designed compressors available, so let's run through the most popular, one at a time:

Frigidaire—The time-honored A-6 is a real dinosaur. Steer clear unless you are building a limo with room for a monster under the hood. The 12+ cubic inch capacity is more than anyone needs (or wants). A somewhat better choice for many home-builders is the R-4, the fatter (7in diameter) shorter (7in) compressor used in many GM cars from the 1980s. This compressor has a capacity of 10 cubic inches per revolution and four radial cylinders. Though smaller than the A-6, this is still more compressor than many cars need.

Some 1985 and later GM cars use the Frigidaire DA-6. Remarkably like the Sanden compressor, the DA-6 is smaller, lighter, and better suited to a street rod or smaller car in its capacity. It's rated at about 9 cubic inches. The proverbial downside is the lack of aftermarket brackets and the fact that these compressors don't seem to be as durable as the Sanden compressors.

Diesel Keiki —This is a clone of the Sanden and will mount with commonly available brackets.

Nippondenso—This compressor is original equipment on new Ford and Chrysler cars, and most are sized at 9 cubic inches. Again, brackets are not available in the aftermarket and it seems a little bigger than most of us need. The other downside is the hose fittings—located in the middle of the compressor—a less than ideal aesthetic location.

York / Techumseh—These are the old "looks like a lawn mower engine" compressors, available in three capacities ranging from 6 to 10 cubic inches. The major drawback of the reciprocating style of compressor is the high peak torque loads on each stroke created by the two-cylinder design. This translates to abundant vibration, noise, and belt flop.

Hoses and Fittings

Any air conditioning installation will require

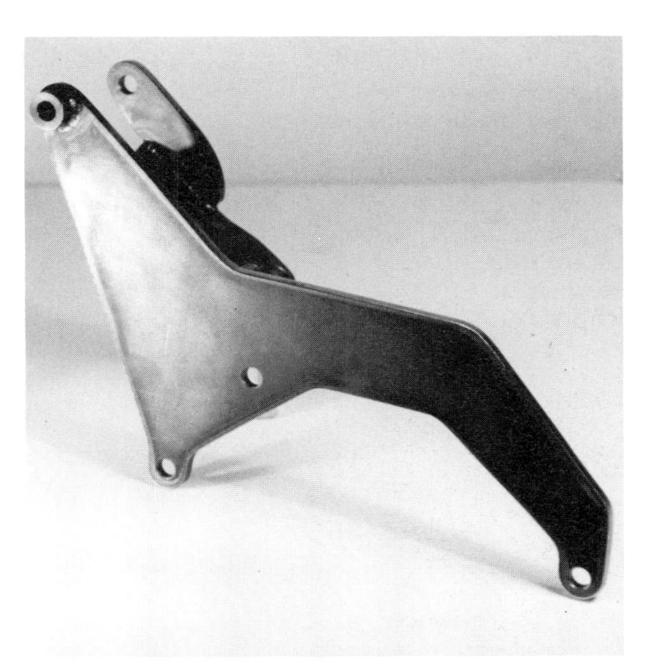

Compressor brackets can be billet and beautiful or boring and basic. This simple steel mount fits small-block Chevys and hangs the compressor on the right side of the engine. Vintage Air

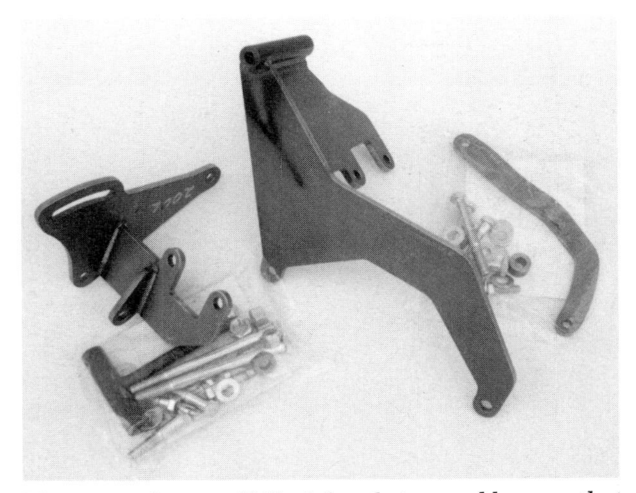

This is another small-block bracket assembly—one that mounts the compressor high for a narrow street rod engine compartment. Vintage Air

the use of hoses and fittings to attach the various components. A discussion of the fittings and lines must start with the types that are available. Because of the exacting duties that mobile fluid lines and fittings have to perform in fuel systems, brake systems, and refrigerant systems, there are different standards set by the respective industrial groups. The three that apply to this discussion are: Society of Automotive Engineers (SAE), Joint Industrial Council (JIC), and International Mobile Air Conditioning Association (IMACA).

Automotive tubing and fittings are built to SAE specifications. Within the aircraft industry, manufacturers adhere to JIC specifications. Aircraft parts would not apply to us except that someone decided that airplane parts look good on a hot rod. So a little knowledge of these parts and systems can't hurt, especially if you're trying to mix SAE and JIC parts. The IMACA standards that apply are the test standards that the A/C parts should meet.

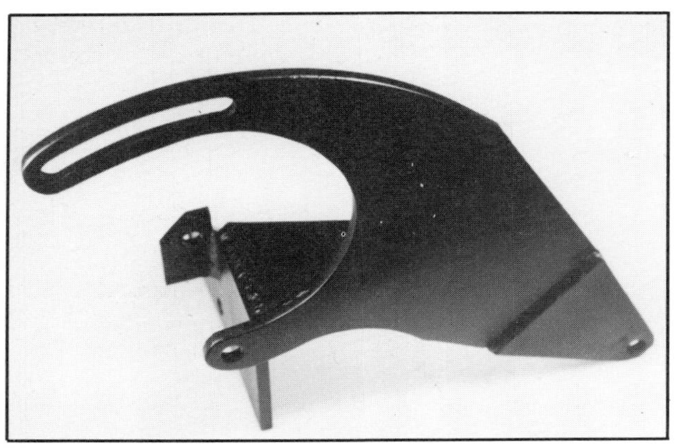

Compressor brackets don't have to be elaborate or expensive. This small-block bracket is simple in design and works very well with certain Corvette models. Vintage Air

SAE / IMACA Hoses and Fittings

Automotive fitting manufacturers make an incredible number of different fittings for practically any situation. Knowing where to fit and when to use that particular fitting is the trick. When you plumb the air conditioning system on your hot rod, truck, or classic, the easiest way to do it is with standard SAE fittings and rubber refrigerant hose (always use hose with a barrier liner).

AN / JIC Stainless Braided Lines and Fittings

This type of hose and fittings has found fairly widespread use on hot rods and street rods. These hoses are visually appealing but there are

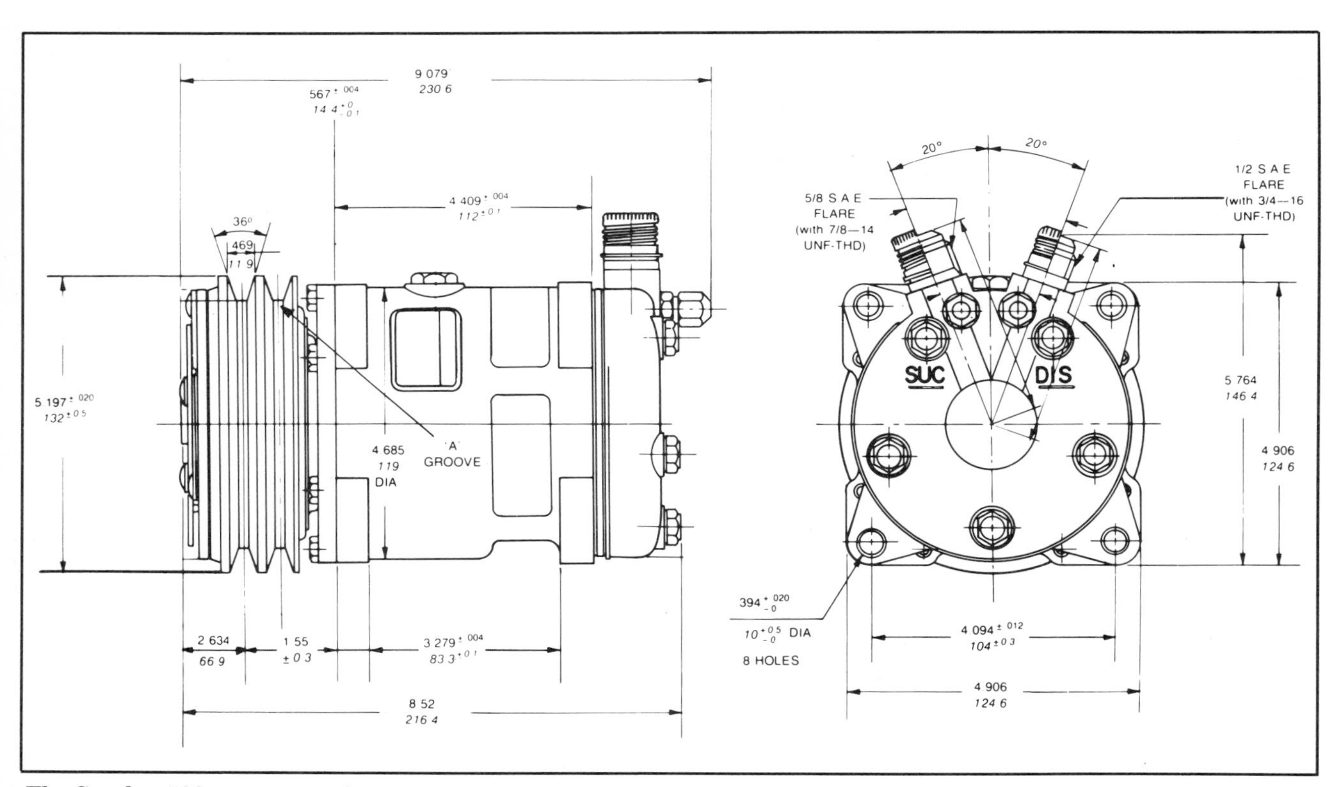

The Sanden 508 compressor is very compact—measuring slightly more than 9in from end to end. A model 505 is available with the same diameter, only 7in long.

some drawbacks. JIC flare fittings have 37-degree flares, while all the automotive air conditioning components are designed to SAE 45-degree specifications. When you place a 37-degree JIC fitting on a 45-degree seat, it cuts a ridge in it. This may seal once, or even twice, but eventually the seat will be rendered defective.

In trying to determine the right hose for your air conditioning installation, be sure the hose is designed for refrigerant (not hydraulics) and that the fittings are O-ring style fittings. Note that a new series of fittings is coming on the market for use with the new HFC-134A refrigerant.

There is another system of hoses, the Proline stainless tubing system manufactured by Vintage Air. Designed for street rods and other air conditioning applications where high performance and great aesthetics are the requirements, this system is easily installed, works with either CFC-12 or HFC-134A, and uses O-rings on all the fittings.

The Receiver-Drier

This is probably the second most misunderstood component in the air conditioning system. Because of this misunderstanding, let's review the four things the receiver-drier does:

1. Separates liquid refrigerant from vaporous refrigerant and allows only pure liquid to pass on to the condenser (when the system is properly charged).
2. Filters the refrigerant.
3. Removes moisture from the refrigerant.
4. Acts as a surge tank.

The refrigerant flows from the condenser in a

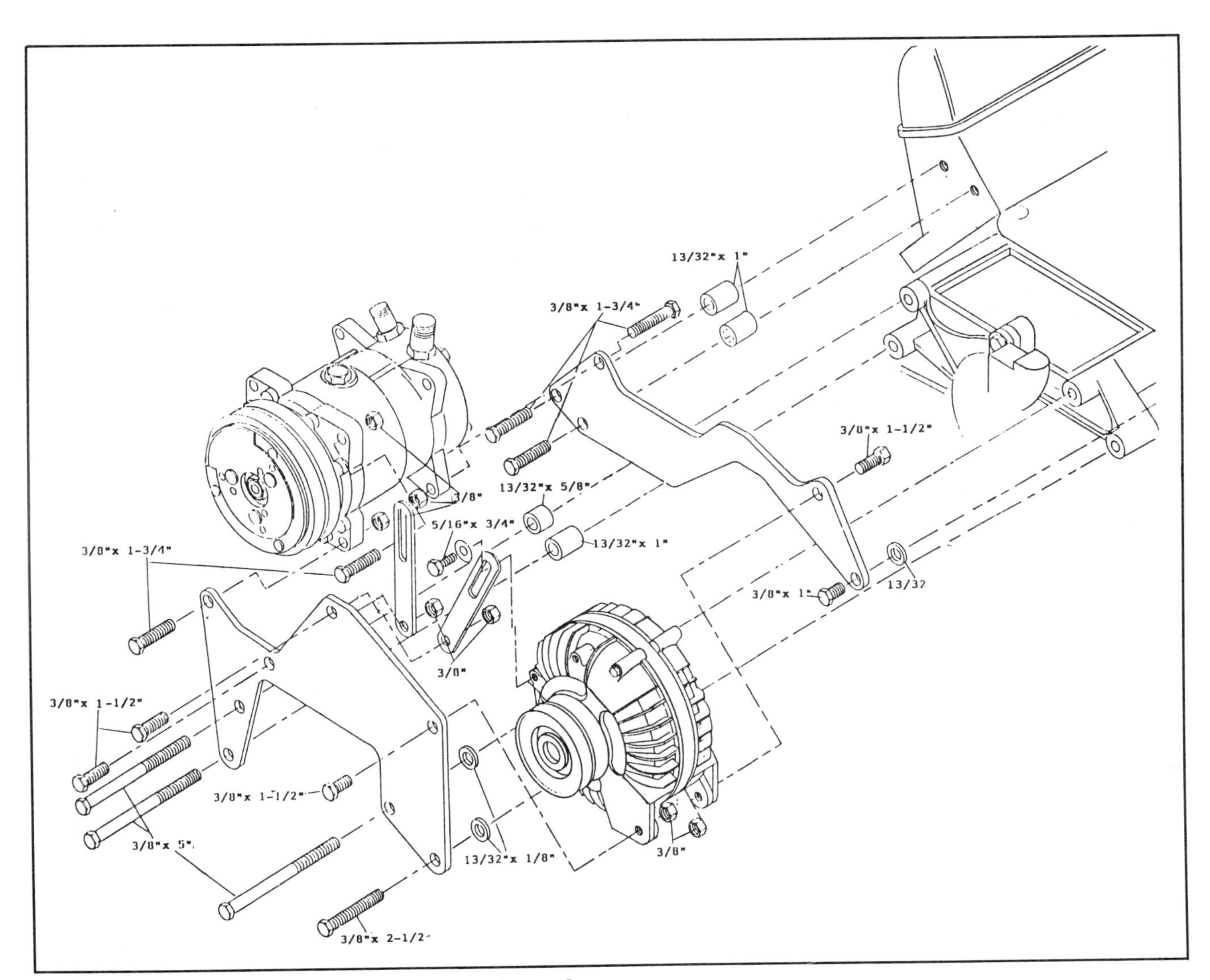

Even Mopar lovers can find a compressor bracket and alternator mount for their version of the small-block. Vintage Air

mix of roughly ninety percent liquid and ten percent gas. This mix pours into the receiver-drier, with the liquid going to the bottom of the cannister while the gas stays at the top. Because the pickup tube extends almost to the bottom of the can, it picks up only liquid refrigerant (assuming the system is correctly charged) and passes it on to the expansion valve. Passing gaseous refrigerant to the expansion valve doesn't make much sense, as the "evaporation" of the liquid is what creates the cooling effect.

Cleanliness is *essential* to the proper operation of an air conditioner, and the filtering function should never be overlooked. Commercial refrigeration systems use a replaceable, molecular sleeve/drier element rather than a simple mesh filter. Vintage Air and others make an automotive receiver-drier with just such a sophisticated filter. Before pooh-poohing the need for a more expensive receiver-drier, consider that most maintenance problems with air conditioners can be traced to moisture and contaminants in the system.

The drying function of the receiver/dryer is a simple process. The drying agent (desiccant) in some automotive driers is held inside a felt pad and placed within the receiver tank. When the refrigerant flows across and through the desiccant, moisture is captured. As in oil filters for engines, there are full-flow and bypass systems, with the full-flow type systems being preferred because they filter all the refrigerant all the time.

Note that HFC-134A systems tolerate even *less* moisture than CFC-12 systems, thus a higher quality receiver-drier with a larger capacity desiccant bag is required.

Surprisingly, most automotive original equipment driers are bypass type driers, only acting on that part of the refrigerant contacting it while it is settled in the receiver-drier tank.

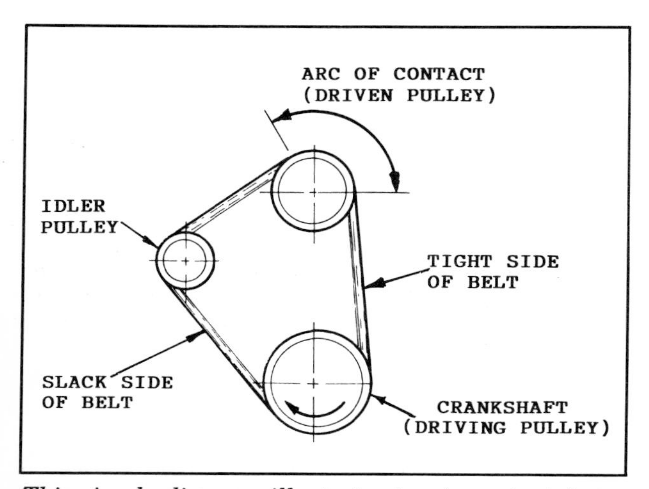

This simple diagram illustrates two important facts: Each belt needs to contact a pulley over at least one-third of the pulley's diameter, and idler pulleys should always be placed on the slack side of the belt.

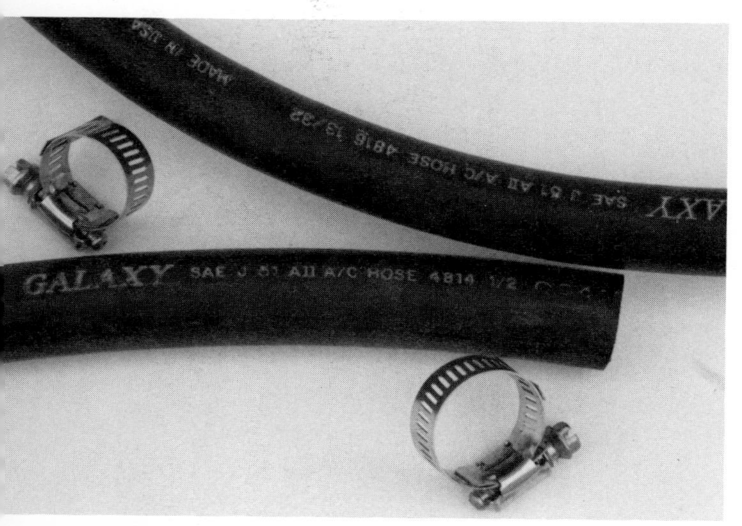

Systems using the HFC-134A refrigerant should use hoses designed for that refrigerant. Hoses used in either system should be barrier hose—with a nylon liner to stop leakage through the hose wall.

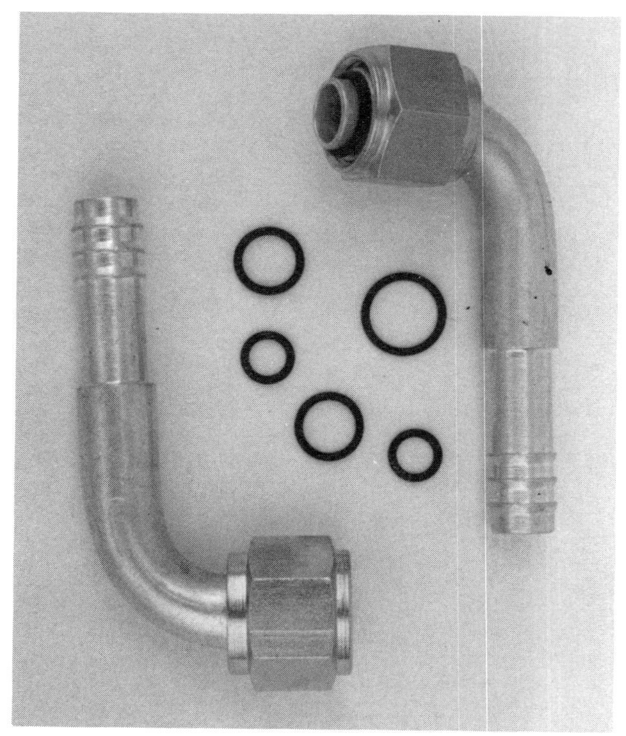

All new installations, whether CFC-12 or HFC-134A should use fittings with O-rings to minimize the minimal seepage that can occur with flare fittings.

Moisture, along with contaminants, is the greatest problem in any refrigeration system. Moisture combines with the metal in the system to produce oxides, primarily iron hydroxide and aluminum hydroxide. It also combines with the refrigerant to produce acids, notably carbonic acid, hydrochloric acid, and hydrofluoric acid. These acids further attack the base metal within the system to produce a substance like a combination of dust and sand. People sometimes wonder how the "sand" got inside their air conditioning system—it grew there.

The last thing a receiver-drier does is act as a surge tank to dampen out the surges that occur when there is a sudden burst of engine acceleration. This helps keep the pressures within the system constant.

The sight glass is just a window to the refrigerant leaving the drier. Pure liquid refrigerant is clear. When there is no liquid "seal" in the bottom of the receiver tank, the refrigerant will be a mixture of liquid and gas with bubbles visible in it. As you fill the system with refrigerant, the gas will exist only at the top of the receiver-drier and the sight glass will "see" only clean refrigerant leaving the receiver-drier.

Note: HFC-134A doesn't go from cloudy to clear in the sight glass quite the way CFC-12 does, so driers meant for HFC-134A refrigerant sometimes do not include a sight glass. In HFC-134A systems the sight glass goes from cloudy to "milky" rather than clear. Some manufacturers still advocate the use of the sight glass—the manufacturer's recommendations should be your guiding light when it comes to determining how much refrigerant to put in a system.

Most receiver-driers are similar in shape, so your choice will be governed by the style you desire and the configuration that best fits your situation. Polished receiver-driers look better for example if everything else is polished or chrome plated. For individuals who insist on the very best, full-flow, rebuildable receiver-driers are available from Vintage Air.

Evaporator

The evaporator is the heat exchanger under (or in) the dash that creates the "cool" for your ride. This is where the refrigerant changes state from a liquid to a gas and absorbs the heat of the car's interior.

A typical evaporator has a core, an expansion valve, a blower, and a set of air outlets. The expansion valve (as you know) meters refrigerant to the core where it evaporates, absorbing heat from the coils.

When selecting an evaporator, the two considerations will be: Will it fit in the car (with the kind of looks you're hoping to achieve), and will it cool the car adequately?

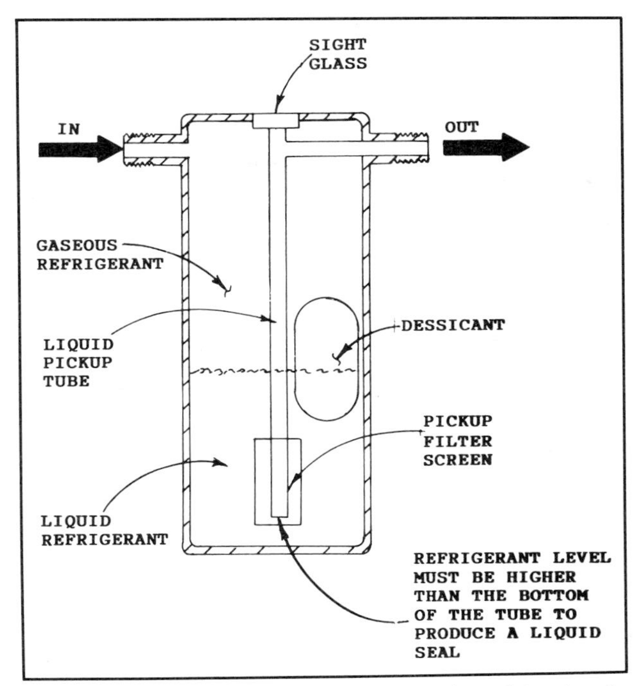

A picture is worth a thousand words—this simple drawing shows how the receiver-drier separates gas from liquid refrigerant and how it filters and dries the refrigerant.

This receiver-drier has been cut open to show the filter. Better quality receiver-driers have replaceable filters and desiccant bags.

Choosing a unit with the right look is a personal decision. Your two choices are under-dash and behind-dash units.

Under-dash units work out very well in some applications. The contemporary under-dash unit is the slim-line unit. The stylized design has a long and thin front bezel containing multiple air outlets. The direct air delivery of this type of unit is very effective and it does not interfere with glove box, radio, or other in-dash accessories.

Many of us just want the built-in look of an in-dash unit in our 1932 Ford or 1955 Chevy. With an in-dash unit the big questions are: Will it fit in the car, and what will you have to give up to get it there? In-dash units with molded ducts from the evaporator coil are found in the higher performance applications and better quality aftermarket manufacturers. The molded ducts allow direct, large-volume air delivery from a concealed in-dash unit.

When you select an evaporator, your first consideration should be the size of the interior you are trying to cool. If your car is a small coupe, then you can obviously use a smaller evaporator than the person trying to cool the interior of a '57 DeSoto station wagon.

Determining what will fit in the car is very critical—whether it's an in-dash or under-dash unit. If you buy the unit from a mail-order supplier, it's even tougher. The best place to start checking is behind your dash. Try to make a rough sketch of the area between the firewall and the dash, being sure to measure over to the kick panel. Note the location of the radio, instruments, and other accessories that are difficult to remove. When you talk to the supplier, specify the type of car you have and its body style, and tell him if the car has been altered in the firewall or dash area.

If the supplier isn't familiar with your particular car, then get any descriptive literature he or she might have. Measurements make it simpler to have a meaningful discussion about what will or won't fit. If you know the exact dimensions of

The sight glass on the top of the receiver-drier looks right down into the discharge tube and should go from cloudy to clear as a CFC-12 system is filled. The small plug is like a fuse, designed to blow out if the pressure or temperature goes too high.

Receiver-driers are available in a variety of sizes and styles for practically any application. Because the desiccant's ability to absorb moisture is limited, the caps should be left in place until you are ready to hook up all the hoses and charge the system.

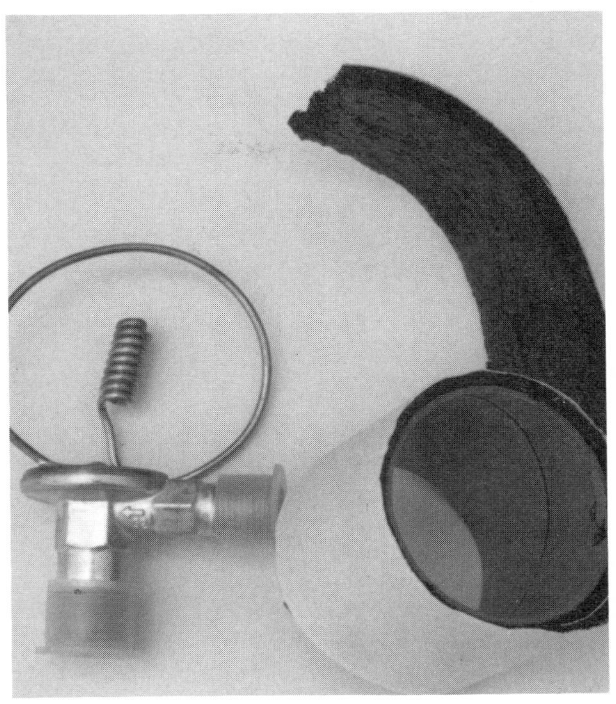

The expansion valve is really just a variable orifice, with high-pressure liquid refrigerant on one side and low-pressure liquid (evaporating to a gas) refrigerant on the other. The valve should always be wrapped from the diaphragm to the evaporator to prevent condensation from forming.

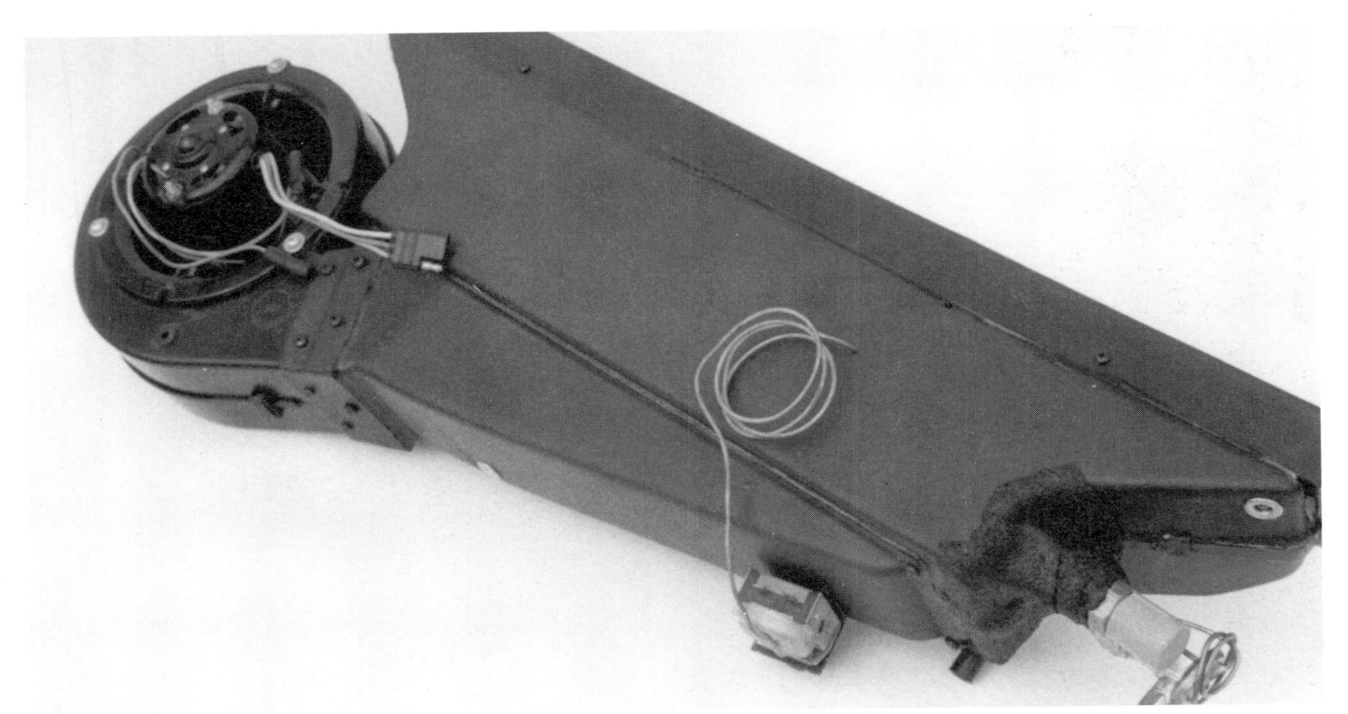

Evaporator housings come in many shapes and sizes. This is a complete under-dash evaporator well suited to street rods and other aftermarket air conditioning installations. Under-dash units are easier to install, require no duct work, and deliver good airflow.

your dash and behind-dash areas, then the manufacturer can probably recommend a unit that will fit correctly with enough capacity to properly cool the car. Buying the correct unit is mostly a matter of taking the time to measure everything and combining those measurements with a little common sense.

Don't forget to plan ahead. Rewiring a car or moving a radio can be tough and can make the job much harder than it should be. If you plan ahead, problems can be solved when they're still small. If you are building a complete car, be sure to plan the air conditioning system early in the project so it can dovetail with all the other work that you are doing.

Selecting a unit that is capable of cooling your car can be tricky. Capacity ratings are a lot like EPA gas mileage ratings—yes, your individual mileage may vary! In considering capacity ratings for an air conditioning evaporator you must be sure that the manufacturer is actually rating the output of the unit, not just giving you a theoretical coil output. Some "salesmen" will just pull a figure out of the air, based on what they would like their unit to produce. The best thing to do is ask around. Find builders and owners of cars or trucks like yours and ask them what they used and how it works.

Delivery of the Cool Air

Before leaving this discussion of evaporator design, let's delve further into the murky factors affecting the actual amount of cool air that exits the vents. Let's look at things like case design, coil capacity, and design of the ducts.

The most effective evaporator is only as good as its delivery system. As we said, the underdash units work well because of the direct air delivery from the coil. When a unit is concealed behind the dash, the air must find its way out. The simplest and most common designs route the air through flexible duct hose connected to dash mounted vents.

This is a good way to make one particular unit fit a number of cars. Unfortunately, flexible ducting limits the air delivery of any unit because the convoluted wall of the flex hose surface creates turbulence within the hose. In high-performance units, you will find a minimum of flexi-

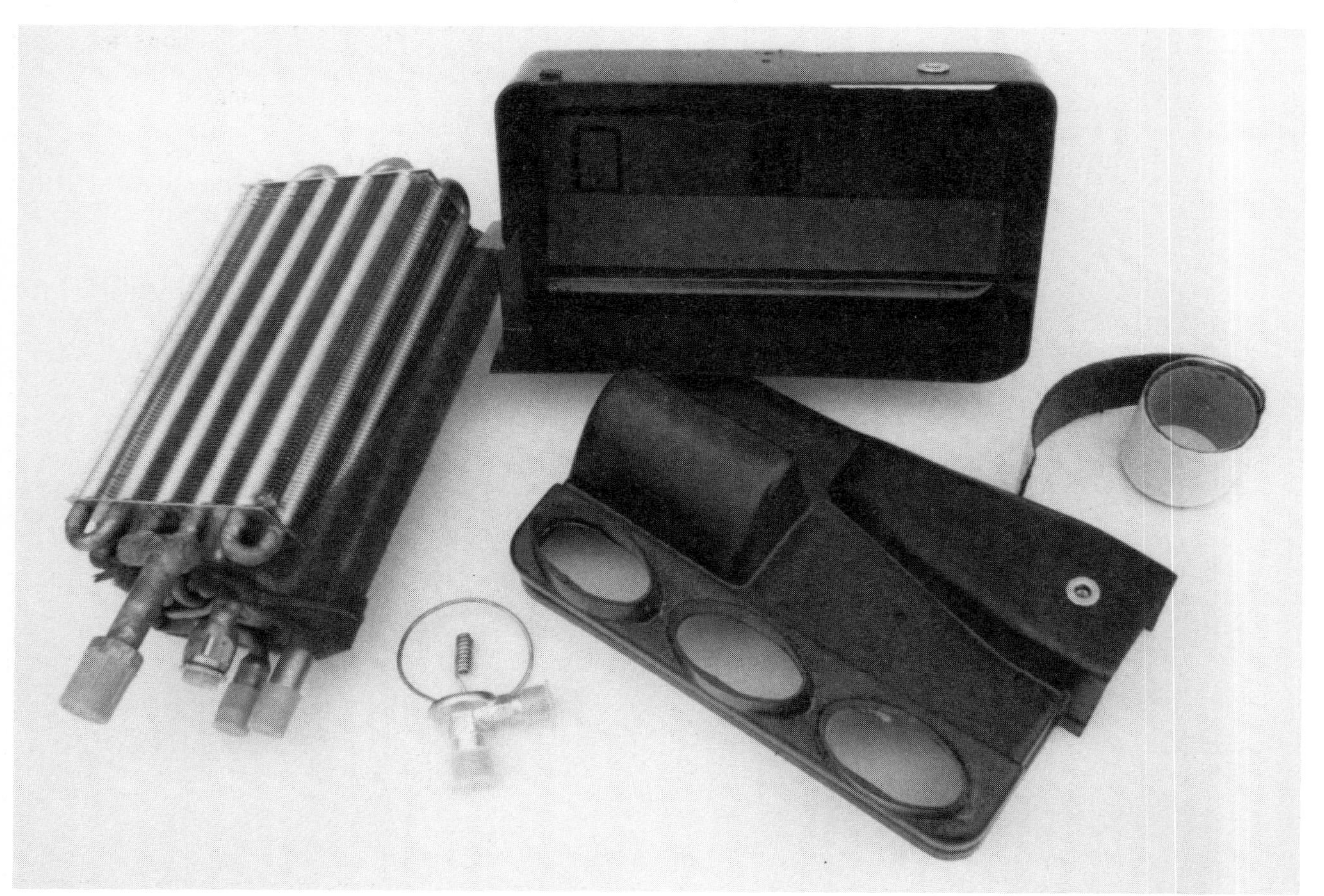

Some evaporators come with both heat and cool—note the four fittings on the evaporator coil—allowing the owner to eliminate the factory heater and create more room behind the dashboard for the evaporator housing.

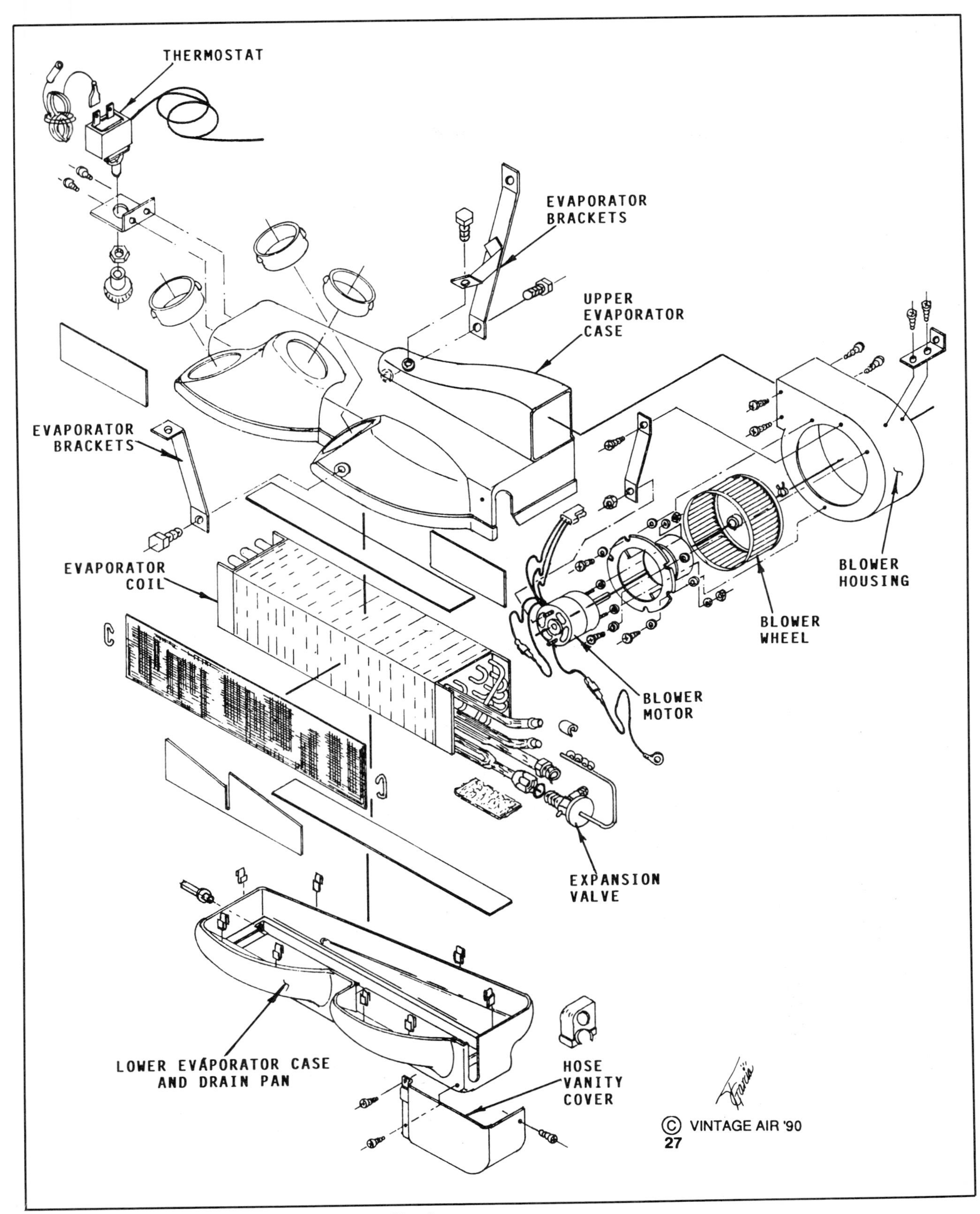

This blow-up of an in-dash evaporator assembly shows the blower , the expansion valve, and the housing itself.

The importance of a good fan and a well-designed shroud can't be overstated. The shroud allows the fan to draw air evenly over the entire surface of the radiator, improving cooling ability considerably in the process.

ble hose. Molded ducts are more effective and much quieter. Because there is less static pressure within the case there is no cavitation at the blower.

The difference really shows up as you check airflow farther back from the vent. Air delivery from a flex hose displays a rapid drop-off in airflow while a molded duct will produce greater velocity for an extended distance from the vent. In plain English—molded ducts deliver more cool air to the people in the car.

The coil capacity is determined by a number of factors, including coil mass, fins per inch, circuit design, and the number of circuit passes. Few people can see the overall size of the coil or the number of circuits of tubing. Most behind-dash evaporator coils are between 190 and 240 cubic inches and contain between twenty and sixty circuits, depending on coil design and configuration. Judging a system's efficiency solely by the number of passes in its evaporator coil is like saying your car is fast simply because it has a new Holley four-barrel carburetor.

Rated capacity of an automotive evaporator coil is based on IMACA standard 20 and is much more complicated than any one or two factors. When you buy an evaporator, buy from a well-known manufacturer, tell that manufacturer

You have plenty of options when it comes time to put a fan on your car or truck. Electric fans come in a variety of sizes and should be connected to both the air conditioning and the radiator. A clutch hub helps a belt-driven fan draw maximum air at low speeds where you need it the most.

what you have and how large an interior you intend to cool.

The blower and fan assembly are part of the evaporator—a very important part. There is no easy way to check the capacity of the blower assembly, though we can state a few generalities:

1. The larger, single-blower wheel assemblies are, by far, the most advanced in use today.
2. The larger wheels operate with higher blade tip speeds, which means they move significantly more air than smaller wheels and do it with less noise.
3. The old-style, double-shaft motors and blower don't work well in cases where the evaporator air is being ducted to vents.

The evaporator and blower are enclosed in a case or housing. The configuration and detail of the case design help make the difference between a unit that performs well and one that performs poorly. If it is well designed, the unit should flow a good volume of air, minimize turbulence, and reduce excessive pressure within the case. A good aftermarket evaporator is one with the components matched and designed to fully use the capabilities of each component within the case.

Housing design is critical. Quality manufacturers (such as Vintage Air) spend enormous amounts of time and money developing just the case and air flow through that case.

If you are ordering a system for HFC-134A

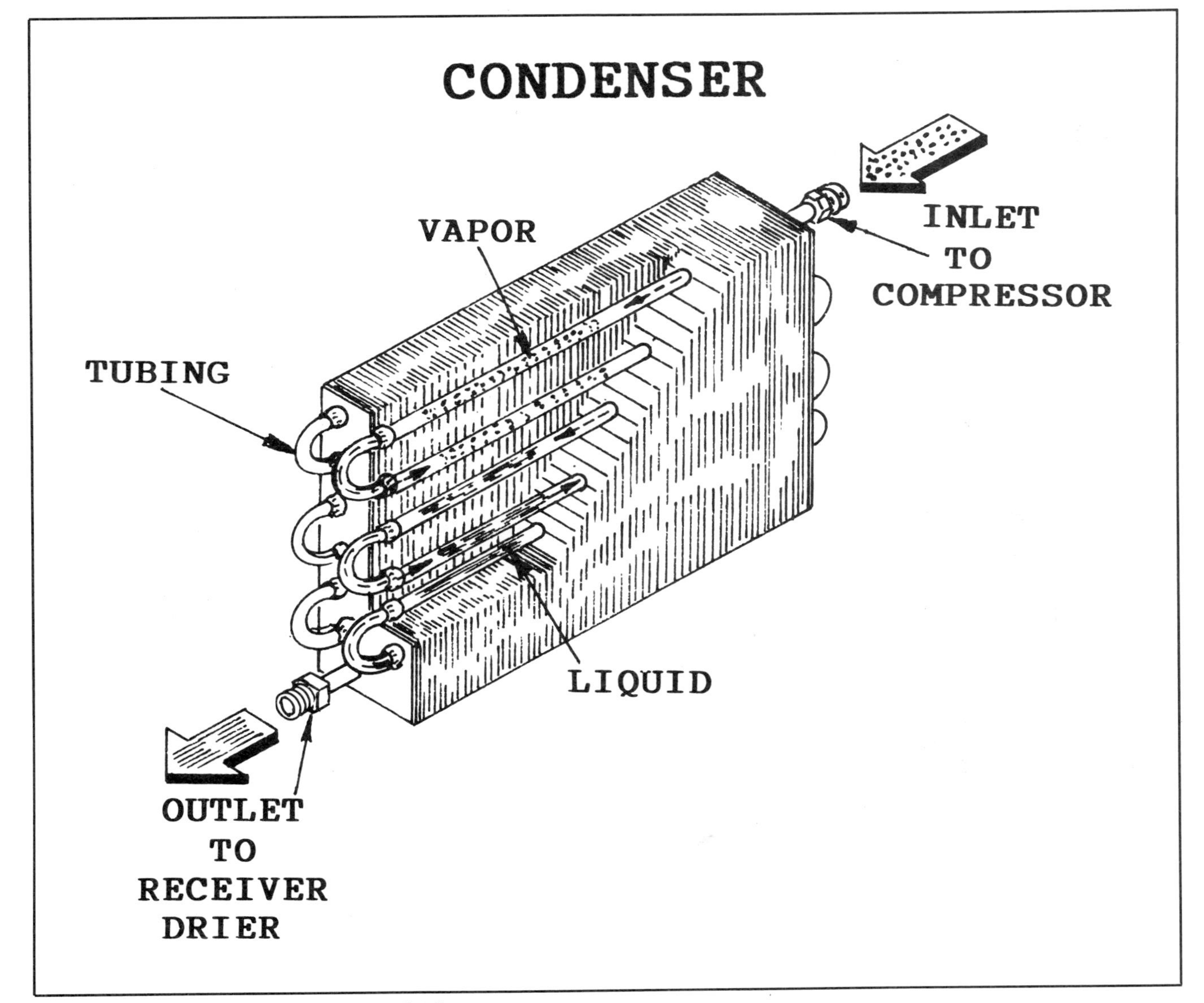

The condenser's job is to cool the hot, high-pressure refrigerant leaving the compressor so it condenses into liquid refrigerant.

use, be sure to get an expansion valve calibrated for the new refrigerant.

Controls and Fans

Before leaving this discussion of components, there are a few more things to consider. Things like pressure and safety switches, and electric cooling fans.

Most air conditioning systems use a few safety switches to control the system from damage: A high head-pressure safety switch cuts the compressor off when the internal pressure climbs too high. The high pressure fan switch turns on an electric cooling fan when the head (or high-side) pressure rises too far, and turns it off when the pressure comes back down. Finally, a low-pressure safety switch is designed to disengage the compressor clutch if the system pressure drops too low, as that probably means a loss of refrigerant and more important, a loss of refrigerant oil.

Electric cooling fans are constantly changing and are being improved rapidly. These fans have a number of advantages over the conventional, belt-driven fan. Some of those advantages are:

1. They produce maximum airflow when the engine is at an idle.
2. They don't rob power when they aren't needed; control switches sense needs and operate them on demand.
3. They fit in situations where nothing else will work.

It would be nice if we could just go ahead and recommend electric cooling fans in all situations, but things just aren't that simple. Despite the recent improvement in the design of electric cooling fans, they still do not move as much air as a good, 17 or 18in belt-driven fan operating in a good fan shroud.

A belt-driven fan has the advantage of the engine's power, meaning simply that you can use that power to move a lot of air. The use of the correct fan-clutch can make a belt-driven fan much more efficient and quieter as well.

How much air you move across the condenser and radiator has a major impact on the performance of your air conditioner. Before deciding that one type of fan is best for your situation, be sure to carefully weigh the advantages and disadvantages of each design—after checking the additional information on cooling fans in chapter 9.

The easiest way to be sure you get quality components, correctly matched to the car and to each other, is to buy a complete kit from a quality aftermarket manufacturer. If you choose to go out and source each component, one at a time, then you need to carefully consider each part and ask yourself, is it a quality component? Is it well suited to your car or truck? Will it work in harmony with the other components that make up the system?

Chapter 3

Air Conditioning in a Changing World

Older air conditioning manuals talk about CFC-12 (often known as R-12)—the refrigerant used in nearly all automotive air conditioners—as the "perfect refrigerant." CFC-12 was described as inexpensive, odorless, easily produced, and non-toxic. If all that's true, you may wonder why the changeover—at considerable cost—to a new generation of air conditioners that use HFC-134A in place of CFC-12?

The History of Refrigerants

It all started in 1928 when chemists working for General Motors (which owned Frigidaire at the time) discovered a whole new family of chemicals known as chlorofluorocarbons. The new chemicals were much better than the refrigerants being used at the time, and in 1931 the refrigerant "Freon" was first marketed by the DuPont company.

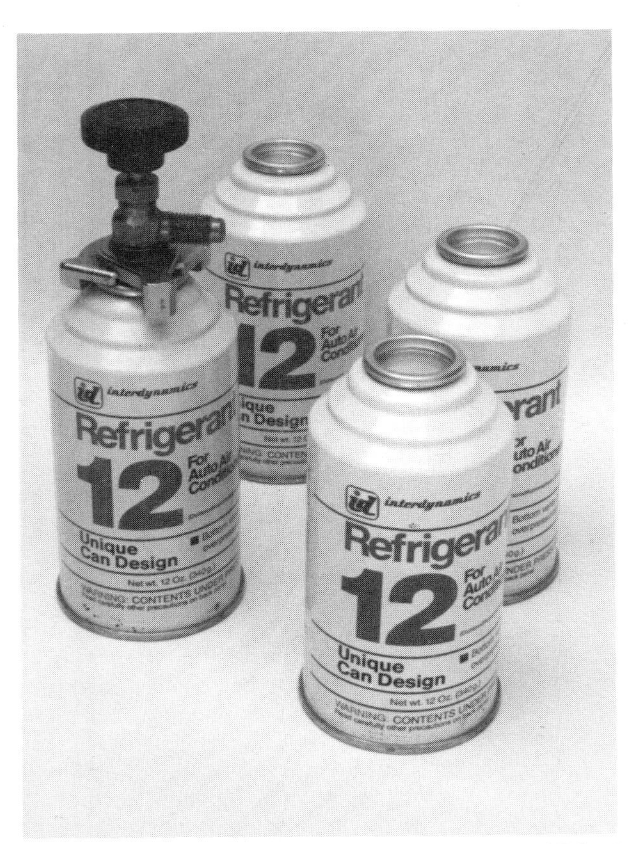

Long the mainstay of automotive refrigeration, CFC-12 is rapidly being replaced by HFC-134A. The small cans of CFC-12 can no longer be found on the shelf of the local parts store.

The new HFC-134A systems will be visually similar to the old systems, though each of the components will be changed to better utilize the new refrigerant. The new compressors will get new seals and will likely be lubricated by a new oil known as a P.A.G. oil.

This is a rebuildable receiver-drier from Vintage Air with the large replaceable filter. Any receiver-drier used with the new refrigerant will need three times more desiccant than an CFC-12 system would use—because the new P.A.G. oils are more prone to absorbing moisture.

At the rear is the old standby of the aftermarket, a tube-and-fin style of condenser. HFC-134A systems require a better condenser—thus more serpentine (as shown in the foreground) condensers will be used in aftermarket air conditioning installations.

CFCs, as the new chemicals were known, proved to be great refrigerants. In addition to being non-toxic and odorless, they were found to be extremely stable, avoiding any tendency to mix with other chemicals or break down into other compounds.

After the war, CFC use increased as more and more of our houses and cars came equipped with air conditioning. On a 100-degree day in July, with the Frigidaire keeping the drinks cold and the air conditioner keeping the drinker cool, it was hard to find fault with these cheap, plentiful refrigerants.

The trouble started in 1974 when two scientists hypothesized an ozone depletion theory. Their theory suggested that the ozone layer that protects the earth from ultraviolet radiation was being depleted by chlorine and bromine that migrate to the stratosphere (or upper atmosphere). They felt the CFCs, because of their stability, could migrate to the upper atmosphere where strong sunlight would cause a chlorine atom to break off. The chlorine atom would then be free to combine with a molecule of ozone to produce oxygen and chlorine monoxide. They further suggested that CFCs were a major contributor to the problem—providing much of the chlorine necessary for the chemical reaction.

The CFC industry considered this new theory to be " purely speculative." However, each year there was more evidence to support the theory. In 1985 scientists with the British Antarctic Survey discovered a drastic reduction in the ozone layer—the ozone hole—over Antarctica.

In 1987, NASA scientists discovered high levels of chlorine monoxide (the chemical byproduct of CFC and the prime destroyer of ozone) in the stratosphere over Antarctica. Measurements taken over the US that same year found the ozone levels to be reduced by six percent. The new data soon had alarm bells ringing all over the world. One of the first major worldwide environmental treaties, the Montreal Protocol, was signed by thirty-one countries (including the US). This agreement called for worldwide CFC production to be cut in half by 1999.

Since that agreement was signed, world and industry leaders have become even more alarmed at the accelerating levels of ozone destruction measured all over the world. Scientists feel that a reduction of only one percent in the ozone layer will increase the incidence of skin cancers by four or five percent. Because of this increasing concern, the timetable for the phaseout of CFCs has been moved up from the targets set in the Montreal Protocol.

Industry in the US is committed to the complete phaseout of all CFC production by the year 2000. In addition to the destruction of the ozone layer, CFCs are among the compounds that trap the sun's radiation, contributing to the warming of our planet.

Moving toward center stage is a new compound, known as HFC-134A. This new refrigerant contains no chlorine—thus there is no ozone depletion. Secondly, the new compound has a much lower global warming potential than does CFC-12 (by a factor of 10). So the new material is good news for all of us who share the planet, though as always, there is a price to pay for the new technology.

The differences between a CFC-12 compressor and an HFC-134A compressor are in the seals and the lubricant. Retro-fitting a CFC-12 system to run HFC-134A is possible, and the complexity of the job depends on the individual system.

When Does the New Technology Take Over, and What Can Be Done With Existing CFC-12 Systems

In order to answer questions from hot rodders, street rodders and all types of automotive enthusiasts regarding air conditioning during this period of changeover from CFC-12 to HFC - 134A, we have reproduced from here to the end of the chapter a section of the Vintage Air manual. This is the most current information available as we go to press regarding what to do with current CFC-12 systems along with the likelihood of retrofitting the old systems for the new refrigerant. You should check with your A/C component supplier for updates, recommendations, etc.

To air condition your hot rod today requires a little more knowledge and thought than just a few months ago. By the time you read this it will be just slightly over a year before the automotive world will witness the extinction of an "Old Friend." The Old Friend is a chemical affectionately known as Freon. It is known to professionals as CFC-12. The "C" portion of that designation refers to chlorine, one of the components that make up this refrigerant used so successfully over the last forty or so years in automotive air conditioners.

The reason for its demise is, by now, old news. CFC-12 has been recognized as the primary offender in the ozone depletion theory that has led legislators in this country and virtually every first-world nation globally to ban its propagation and control its existence until it is virtually nonexistent. Well, DuPont, the originator and the major manufacturer of the substance, has taken the message to heart. They have been mandated to quit producing CFC-12 by December 31, 1995. However, they have elected to actually cease production by December 31, 1994, in an effort to show support for the citizens' request to get rid of the culprit. The obvious secondary effect of this action is that this moves the "phaseout," which means gradual cutback that will end in curtailment, forward one year.

The refrigerant selected by all auto makers worldwide to replace CFC-12 is HFC-134A. The

This is a '39 Ford coupe with an existing CFC-12 system before Vintage Air converted it to an HFC-134A system. Because the car, owned by Rick Love, is driven a great deal, and the performance of the CFC-12 system was well documented, it will make a good test bed for one of the new systems.

operative letter here is the "H" in HFC. That H stands for hydro meaning that it is, loosely speaking, a refrigerant based on the relatively benign (to the atmosphere) hydrogen atom. No known atmosphere destruction, no problem!

We would like to go on record now to say that we believe anyone who will be handling the new refrigerant should act responsibly from day one and use a recycling machine to prevent loss of any refrigerant into the atmosphere. You must use a different recycling machine for each refrigerant you handle. At Vintage Air, we now have a machine to recycle HFC-134A and we no longer handle CFC-12.

So What Does All of This Mean to You?

It means CFC-12 will be scarce in 1994 and will virtually disappear by 1995. So, what if you are building a car and hope to have it running and driving in the next year or so? Well, most projects may take even longer than we expect, but let's say the best case scenario is that we get the car ready in spring 1994 as planned. CFC-12 will no doubt still be available, however, it will be in short supply during the summer. So one of a number of things could happen:

1. You will find CFC-12 readily available, service your car, pay a fair price, and hope you don't have a problem in six months.
2. You will find CFC, but in short supply, and you'll pay an inflated price. Then you will hope you don't have a problem six months down the road.
3. You can accept the inevitable and convert your components to operate with the replacement refrigerant HFC-134A. However, what if you are like most hot rodders and the project comes in about six to eight months later than expected? Some basic finger counting says that puts you in 1995, and CFC-12 is available only in very limited quantities from your buddy's stash or the smiling merchant who has been anxiously awaiting this season for his windfall sales of this treasured "commodity."

Remember the age-old laws of supply and demand. As you find yourself studying the options and searching for the wisdom to know whether to buy a system designed to operate with HFC-

These are the components used to convert the '39 Ford to HFC-134A use. A compressor designed for HFC-134A, an evaporator with a recalibrated expansion valve, a receiver-drier with more desiccant of a different type, a more efficient serpentine condenser, and hoses designed for HFC-134A.

At the bottom, the old tube-and-fin condenser. On top of it, the new serpentine style of condenser. HFC-134A requires a better condenser, so look for more serpentine and parallel-flow condensers.

134A or stick by the tried and true CFC-12, consider the previous information as well as the following up-to-date status report on the refrigerants and equipment.

The Performance System of Tomorrow is Here Today

It has been more than two years since we began this quest, and it's been a full eighteen months since my first working HFC-134A air conditioner was installed in Rick Love's 1939 Ford Coupe. We have now successfully developed, installed, and tested over fifty such systems in virtually every type of vehicle. The number of HFC-134A systems sold to customers by Vintage Air is pushing the 1,000 mark. After all this, we can say to you with confidence that these systems, if configured correctly, work at least as well as current CFC-12 systems.

Status of Refrigerant and Equipment

1. HFC-134A is now available at the same—or lower—price than CFC-12.

2. Many of the auto makers of the world now

Mounted and nearly ready to install, the new condenser is installed in front of the Ford radiator. Note that the tubes run in a horizontal direction and that the condenser is centered in front of the radiator.

The new condenser is measured to fit in front of the Ford radiator. Though no bigger than the one it replaces, the design is more efficient so more heat can be shed from a condenser of the same overall size.

use HFC-134A in their cars' air conditioners. All manufacturers will use HFC-134A by the 1995 model year. This means that the service community is now servicing HFC-134A systems. No problem!

3. If you buy your air conditioning unit today to mock-up your car for future component positioning, by the time it is running, HFC-134A will probably be the most reasonably priced and commonly available refrigerant.

4. Responsible performance air conditioning manufacturers should have HFC-134A systems available right now.

Here the new compressor—with seals designed for HFC-134A and lubricated with P.A.G. oil—is mounted and ready to connect to the rest of the system. New components usually come with caps—to keep them free of moisture and contamination. The caps should be kept in place until you are ready to connect all the hoses.

In summary, if you are buying air conditioning components today, save yourself some dollars and some grief down the road by purchasing HFC-134A type components. You will avoid the grief of updating to HFC-134A at a future date; you'll avoid having to replace several components and perform additional retrofit procedures.

If It Ain't Broke, Don't Fix it—or, What to Do With Your Current CFC-12 System

So you're saying, " OK, I'm convinced, but I have a CFC-12 system in my car now. It works fine, how does all this affect me?"

Basically, until you have a problem with your CFC-12 system, don't worry about it. You may operate that system as long as it is working properly and is not leaking CFC-12 into the atmosphere. If that CFC-12 system has a leak, you must (by Federal law) repair it before you recharge it. If a professional air conditioning technician is caught charging a leaky system, he can be fined an amount that would probably put him out of business. This legislation has teeth.

The next scenario is you have a hot rod with a CFC-12 air conditioning system that has a problem, so what should you do? Should you repair it with CFC-12 replacement parts and wait for a future date to "retrofit" the system to HFC-134A? Or should you go ahead now and upgrade the system for the new refrigerant while you're working on it? The answer depends on a number of factors, including:

Do you plan to keep the car? If you'll keep it for at least a few years, then consider updating, but not without answering the rest of the questions, which will give you an idea of the cost involved.

What kind of car is it? Is it a '32- through '39-style street rod with the standard 12in by 22in condenser in front of the radiator? Or is the condenser remote mounted under the car? These cars will probably require new-style manifold micro tube-design condensers for increased capacity without an increase in overall size. This will add a few hundred dollars to the cost of the upgrade. If your car is one that provides plenty of space for a large condenser you probably won't need to change it and you can probably upgrade for less money depending on the answers to the other questions.

What kind of air conditioning components are on the car now? You will have to follow the compressor manufacturer's guidelines for upgrading the system. If you have a recently manufactured Vintage Air system with a Sanden compressor, for example, an upgrade could be very painless.

When did you buy the system? If you bought the system in the last three years from Vintage

Air then you will have the barrier hose and a Sanden compressor that is HFC capable. (Other purchase periods may offer the same components, however you must check with Vintage Air for codes and information.) That, along with an HFC-134A capable condenser (you must check with Vintage Air for test results on your condenser), will get you a very inexpensive upgrade.

So the answer to the question—What should I do with my old air conditioner when I can't find enough CFC-12?—is not necessarily simple, but it can be answered. The answers to the question of whether you should buy HFC-134A capable components if you are buying a new system today, is probably yes, that it's a lot easier to go that route!

At this point we must add a statement regarding some new refrigerants that are neither CFC-12 or HFC-134A. In spite of what you may have heard, there are no "drop in" replacements for CFC-12. Don't use one of these new refrigerants touted as a replacement or a blend. Some of these materials are explosive, and all will contaminate your system, requiring that the system be flushed and repaired at a later date (at considerable expense). Remember that if you fill your system with an unknown refrigerant and later that refrigerant contaminates a shop's recycling equipment, you are liable for the repair to the recycling equipment.

Keep it simple and use materials recommended by the air conditioning system's manufacturer. By staying with the recommended refrigerants you are assured of maximum cool for minimum dollars.

What Makes an HFC-134A System Unique?

And now we'll explain what is different about an HFC-134A capable system. Notice we didn't say HFC-134A compatible . HFC-134A is basically compatible with any CFC-12 system; the new refrigerant itself doesn't seem to harm any components. However, some CFC-12 components are not capable of producing the desired results for a properly working HFC-134A air conditioning sys-

With the compressor and condenser in place, a technician begins to plumb the hoses for the new HFC-134A system. Hoses must be barrier hose with an inner liner and must be compatible with the new refrigerant and lubricant.

Evaporator coils won't change much, though the expansion valves will be recalibrated to match the new boiling point of HFC-134A.

tem. Let's briefly look at what is different about the components.

Refrigerant HFC-134A

The refrigerant HFC-134A must use a different oil, which is known as P.A.G. (Polyalkalineglycol) oil. The mineral oil used in a CFC-12 system is not miscible in the HFC-134A refrigerant (it won't dissolve and flow with the refrigerant). HFC-134A has a different pressure-temperature curve so that within the high-pressure side of the system there is more internal pressure at a given temperature. To keep the pressures down to acceptable levels in the high-pressure side of the system we must get rid of more heat. Well, that's the condenser's job, so we need more effective condensers.

Condensor

As we just said, the condensers will have to get rid of more heat. If they can't be larger—and they can't in many hot rods—then they need new designs that will make them more efficient. Be very careful here, folks. There are many people trying to sell condensers designed to operate with CFC-12 and fit on '32- through '39-style street rods for HFC-134A systems. Their sales pitch is that they are HFC-134A compatible. Since we designed that condenser some eighteen years ago for CFC-12 applications, we can tell

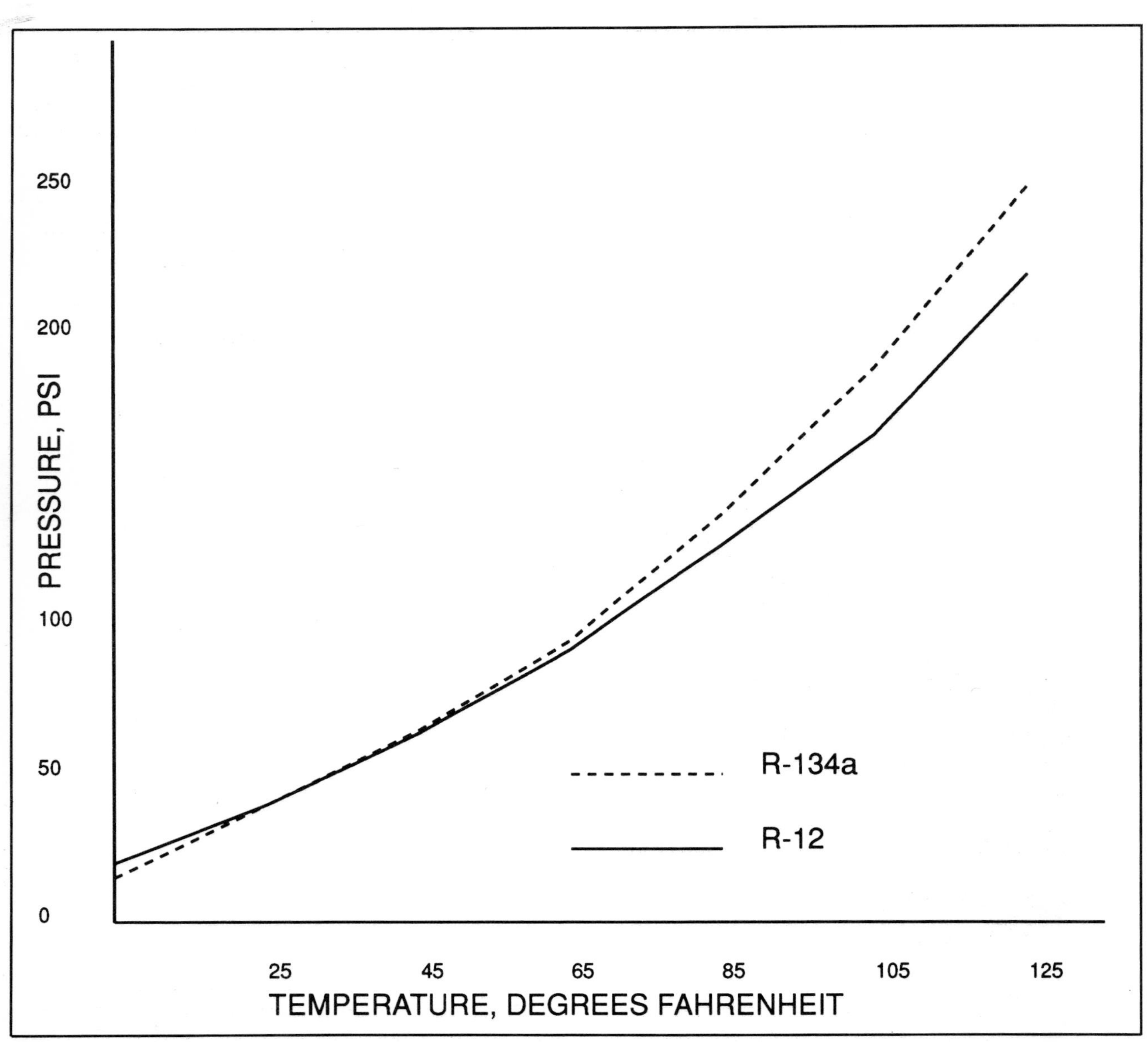

CFC-12 and HFC-134A develop similar pressures at lower temperatures—as shown by this temperature/pressure chart—but pressures differ more and more as the temperature increases.

you it isn't gonna get the job done for HFC-134A. However, there are many street rods that have larger condensers that should work fine with HFC-134A. So it is very "car specific." Just be sure you get advice from someone who has done enough testing to give you valid recommendations.

Driers

The drier desiccant for HFC-134A has changed. XH9 is now the desiccant of choice. This desiccant will work for either refrigerant. Too easy, huh? The drier will be marked or labeled for use with HFC-134A. If it's not, don't buy it!

Hose

The hose used with the HFC-134A is new and is called a "barrier hose." It has a nitrule rubber inner tube with a neoprene cover. Vintage Air has been using this hose for over two years. Call us to find out how to determine what kind of hose you have. Don't use worm-gear clamps. Use only compression collars on this type of hose.

Fittings

The current barb fittings work on HFC-134A if the proper crimp collars and crimping machine are used. New fittings are on the way. but it will take awhile for the new crimping machines to reach the field in sufficient numbers to service the new fitting with what is called "beadlock" style fittings.

Evaporator

Most evaporators seem to work fine with HFC-134A after being fitted with an expansion valve calibrated properly for the new refrigerant. They work effectively because, regardless of claims to the contrary, HFC-134A is a more efficient refrigerant. Heat transfer is better and exiting air temperature from the evaporator is often colder than CFC-12 systems.

Note: The pressure-temperature curve can bite you here if you have a pressure valve to control evaporator temperature such as OEM systems on GM, Ford, and Chrysler products of the

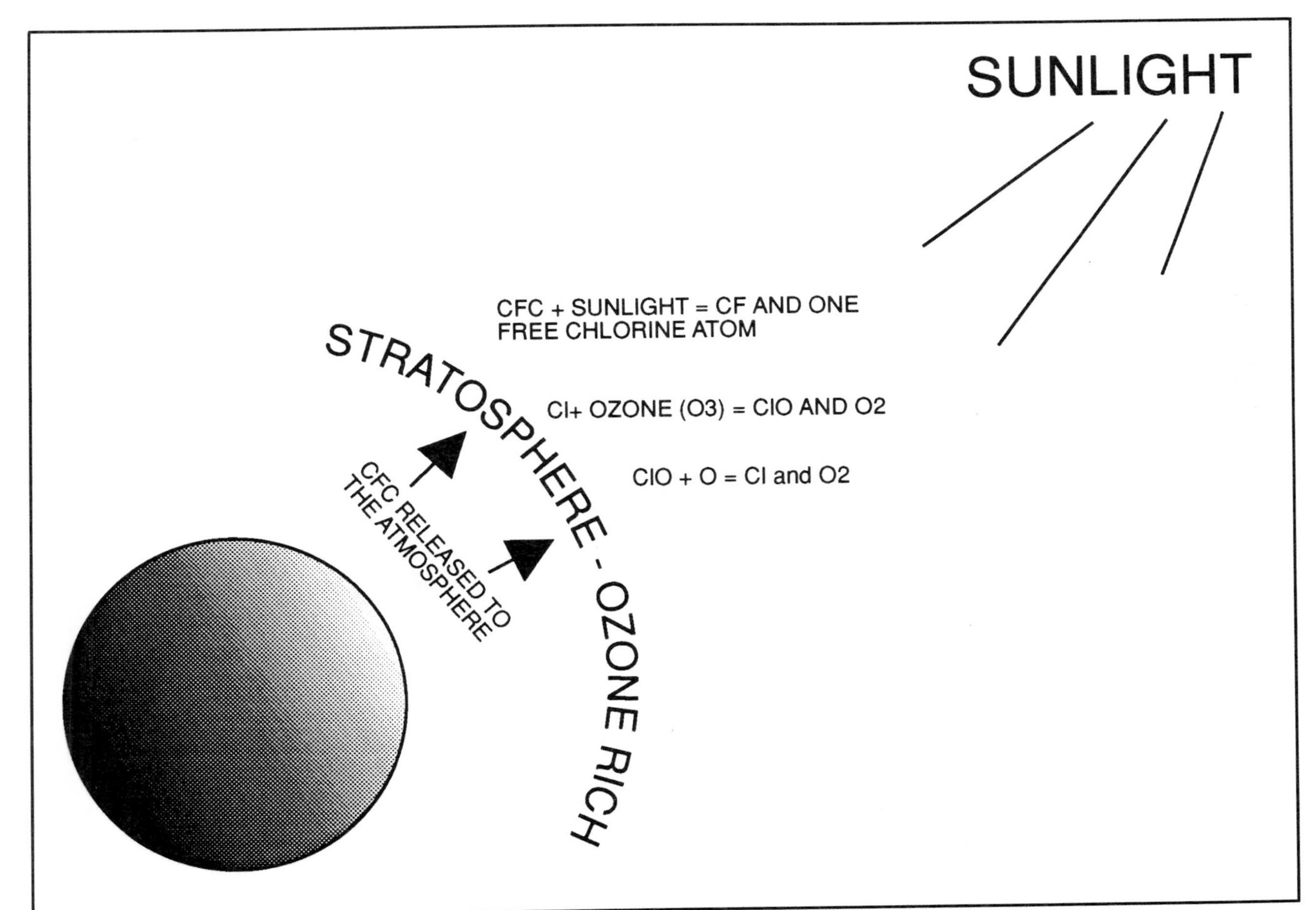

Because CFCs are so stable, they get to the upper atmosphere intact, where radiation causes the release of a chlorine atom. The chlorine atom then reacts with an ozone molecule to form chlorine monoxide and oxygen.

The chlorine monoxide later breaks down to release the chlorine atom to react once again with another molecule of ozone.

1960s and 1970s, and some late model cars. That's because, as on the high side, the low-side characteristic is different in HFC-134A than in CFC-12.

On the HFC-134A system there is less pressure of a given temperature and conversely a higher temperature for given pressure. So the CFC-12 pressure regulating valve is designed to maintain a pressure for 28 to 32psi (pounds per square inch) to maintain an evaporator refrigerant temperature of about 33 degrees Fahrenheit. This same 28-32psi will produce a 4- or 5-degree higher refrigerant temperature with HFC-134A. As a result, exiting air out of the dash vents will be considerably warmer and possibly unsatisfactory, depending on outside temperature and humidity.

Compressor

The compressor is a big variable and its suitability for HFC-134A depends on the year and make of the compressor. Vintage Air has always used Sanden compressors, and Sanden offers a superior product that is adapting very well to HFC-134A. Check with us if you have one of our systems to confirm the date code on the compressor. However, you probably will have to do no more than drain the old lubricant from the compressor, refill it with P.A.G. lubricant, replace the drier with the proper XH9 desiccant, and check the other components for HFC-134A capability. If all the other components are HFC-134A capable as described above, then you can charge the system with HFC-134A and you're cool.

When you are retrofitting a system with compressors such as the GM A-6 or R-4, or some of the Nippondenso compressors, you need to follow the manufacturer's recommendations. For those compressors that don't have specific retro-fit procedures there will certainly be people in the aftermarket experimenting and providing retrofit kits. Ester oils will probably play a major role in retrofitting of the earlier compressors. Ester oils test very well and and continue to be considered as a good alternative to the P.A.G. oils being used by all the major OEM suppliers in their HFC-134A systems. Do not, however, under any conditions assume that ester oil can be used to replace the P.A.G. oils in new HFC-134A systems.

Chapter 4

How to Properly Install Your Air Conditioning System

This chapter will discuss the best ways to mount each of the various air conditioning components. Though more specific instruction may be included in later chapters, such as the street rod or kit car chapters, the installation information presented in this chapter is useful for two reasons. First, the tips and ideas presented here will provide guidance for individuals whose cars do not fall into one of the categories covered in later chapters. Second, even if you have a street rod or kit car, the information presented here is arranged as a foundation for the more model-specific information provided in later chapters.

So don't skip this chapter in your haste to get to the "meat" of the installation information, there's a wealth of useful information here.

Compressor

The old two-cylinder compressors shook worse than a dog with fleas and required a carefully constructed and mounted bracket, one that was both strong and resistant to fatigue cracking. We recommend that you use only the later, axial style compressors. Although these new designs vibrate less than the old thumpers, you are still faced with the prospect of mounting a large piece of machinery on your engine—one that consumes 3 to 6hp, and that does still vibrate somewhat—on an already crowded and vibrating engine.

Before building or buying a compressor bracket, you need to decide what kind of material the bracket should be made from.

Most aftermarket compressor brackets are made from steel, a good choice and a good compromise between strength and weight. Steel brackets have the advantage of being strong, readily available, and easily welded if repair or modification is necessary. The only real downside is the fact that steel is harder than cast iron and will actually "cut into" the iron if there is any movement between bracket and engine block.

Machined aluminum is gaining in popularity as a material for compressor mounting brackets. Usually machined from an alloy like 6061 T6, this material is light, tough, and does a good job of absorbing vibration. Perhaps the best part is the shine that comes off a well polished aluminum compressor bracket under the hood of that very special vehicle. It may look good, but machined aluminum has its drawbacks as well as the higher cost and the difficulty most home mechanics have in welding the aluminum if the

The compressor bracket for this '39 Ford is designed to keep the compressor high to accommodate a typical street rod engine compartment. The design of the bracket is simple and effective.

need should arise.

Some aftermarket brackets are built from cast aluminum, another good choice. Though they don't have the finished look of billet, they can still be polished for a good shine. Just be sure the brackets have been heat treated or their life will be rather short.

Brackets are available for many engines in many configurations to fit the most common compressors. Before building your own brackets from scratch, you might consider using universal mounting plates as the basis.

Building your own compressor brackets will be easier if you can follow a few simple guidelines. The brackets must support both the stationary and the dynamic loads imposed by the compressor and they must do so without developing fatigue and cracking. Bracket building for air conditioning compressors follows the same principles as any other bracket design and fabrication project—the simpler it is, the better.

This type of bracket does require a few modifications, however.

You must have a way to adjust the tension of the driving belt. Sliding the compressor or using an idler pulley mounted on an adjustable eccentric are the simplest ways to adjust belt tension. Idler pulleys have the inherent problem of short service life and adding to the hardware. If you must use an idler pulley, put it on the slack side (a driving belt always has a slack and a tight side) of the belt. By doing this you will increase the bearing life by decreasing the load on the idler. You will also reduce belt flop which is always greatest on the slack side. Idler pulleys (usually spring-loaded) are often used by Detroit in the case of serpentine belts—this is an exception to the "we don't like idler pulleys" rule.

Make sure you have enough belt contacting all driving or driven pulleys. This "arc of contact" should be no less than one third of the pulley's circumference.

Speaking of belts, a single, 1/2in (measured across the back side) V-belt is adequate to power all but the largest compressors. Just because there are two pulley slots doesn't mean you need to use two belts. When installing the compressor and brackets, be sure the various pulleys are aligned properly. Though a V-belt is pretty forgiving, near-perfect alignment will insure long belt life and no problems with belt loss during rapid acceleration. If the belt on your car is a multi-grooved, serpentine style, then you don't have a choice—serpentine belt alignment must be exact.

In the days of thumping air conditioning

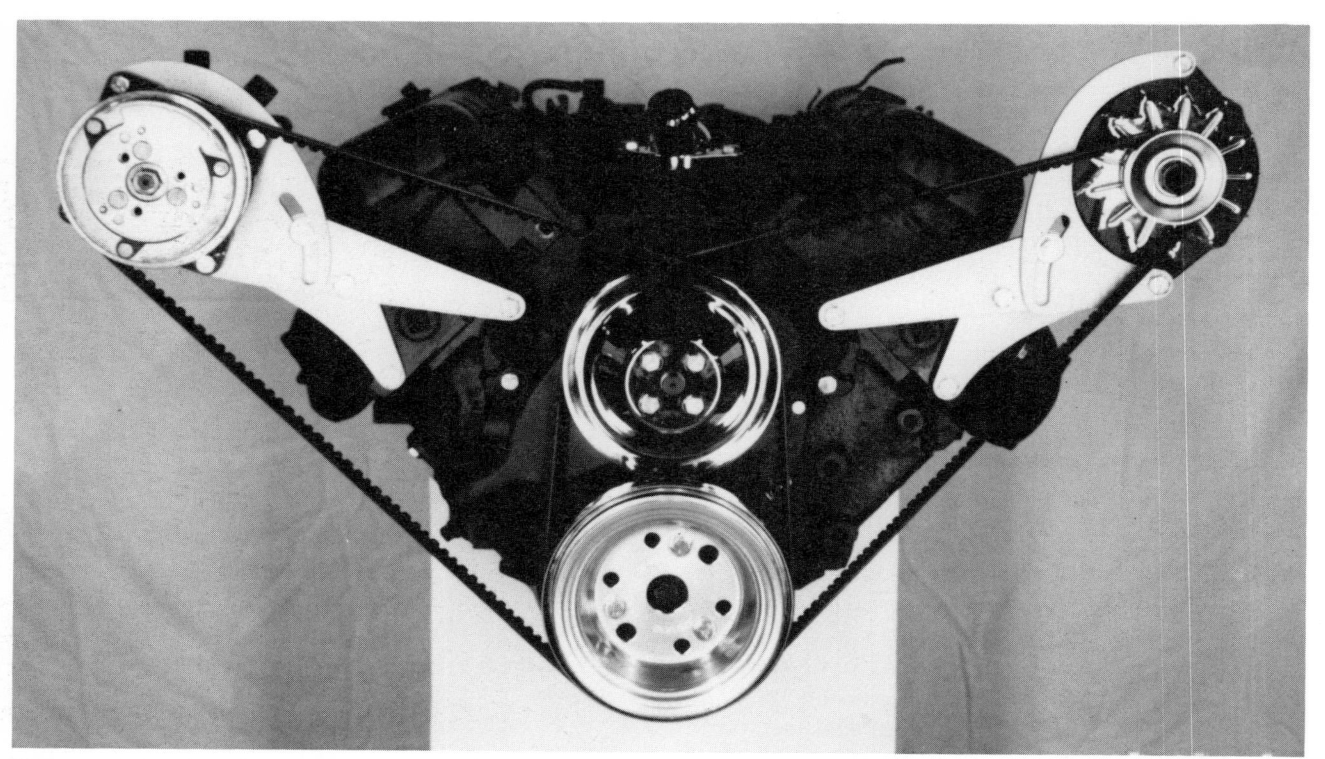

These steel brackets for compressor and alternator are from Alan Grove, designed for a big-block Chevy with a short water pump. All mounting hardware should be assembled with lock washers or self-locking nuts and at least grade 5 bolts. Alan Grove

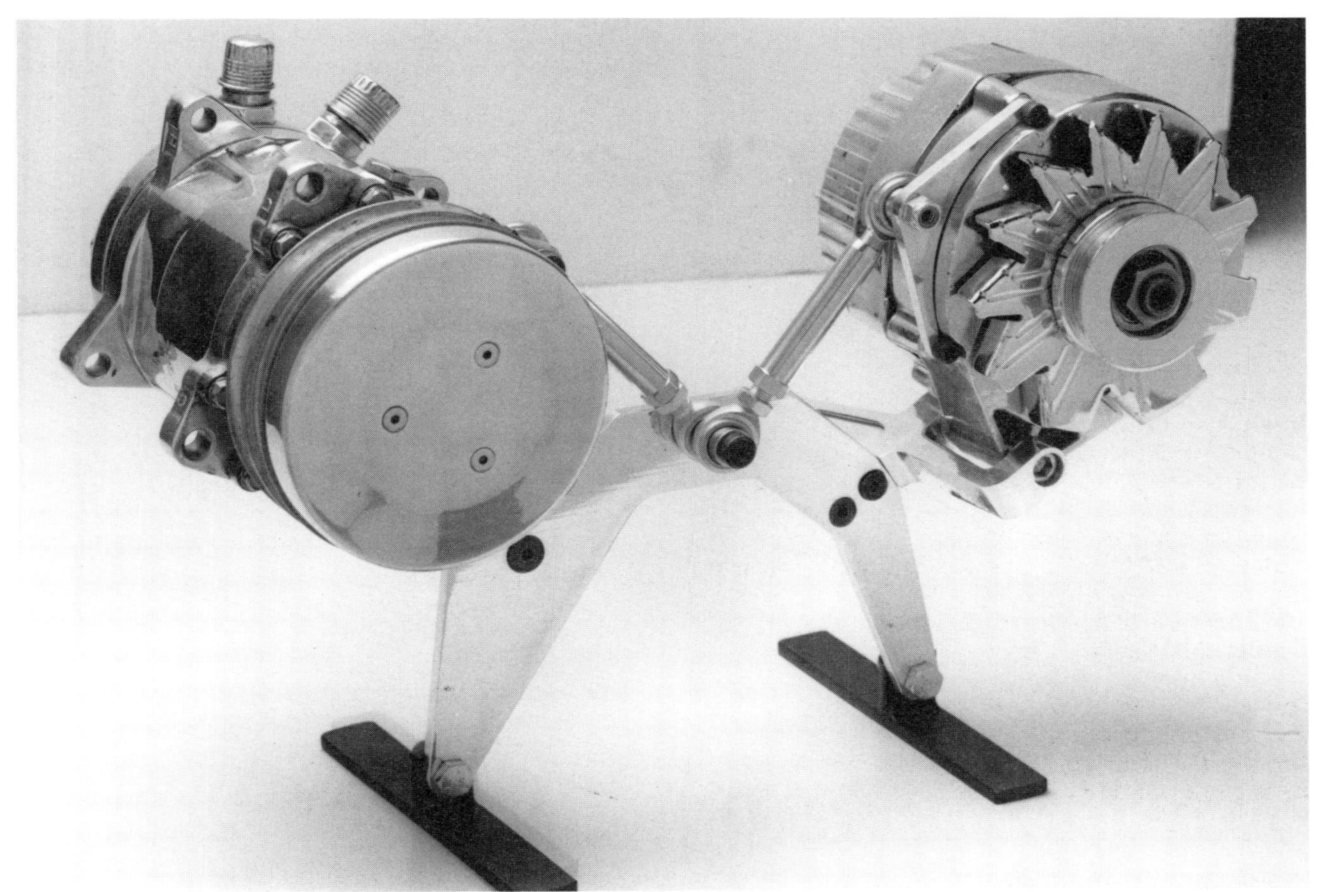

This Proline double bracket is from Vintage Air and is designed to mount air conditioning to small-block Chevys with a long water pump. Note the elegant design with heim-jointed adjuster rods. Vintage Air

compressors, mechanics often went to extreme lengths to avoid having the bracket bolts loosen up after the car left the shop. The new compressor designs have made the job of bolting the brackets together easier, though you still need to do the job right.

The bolts themselves should be at least grade five, fine thread whenever a nut is used or when threading into a fine thread female component. Use coarse threads when tapping into cast iron and aluminum. The new compressors vibrate less than the old ones, but they still vibrate so be sure to use lock washers and/or self-locking nuts.

Finally, when building the mount and mounting the compressor, remember just one thing: If the compressor mount fails, it isn't a simple failure. Secondary damage to the radiator and other accessories is often extensive and expensive. Do it right the first time.

Condenser

The condenser's job is to cool the refrigerant sufficiently so it condenses from a gas to a liquid. The condenser can't do its job if it is located in a

This is a simple, neat installation in an El Camino with a small-block Chevy engine. Brackets that adjust the belt tension without the use of an idler pulley make for simpler installations.

Here Dave Stutts at Vintage Air gets ready to mount the new serpentine condenser in front of the '39 Ford radiator. This is a conversion to HFC-134A, though the installation procedures are the same as they would be for a CFC-12 system.

dark, hot corner of the engine compartment with no fresh air flow. Most front-engine cars should have the condenser mounted out in front of the radiator. Don't put it behind the radiator, as the air there just isn't cool enough to get the job done.

You don't want any heat transfer from the radiator to the condenser, so avoid letting the radiator touch the condenser. It's a good idea to insure that there is at least 3/16in of clearance between the condenser and the radiator.

When you mount the condenser in front of the radiator, center it on the radiator and then use brackets heavy enough to mount it nice and solid. If you are installing a kit, some brackets are probably provided. Just as you did with the compressor brackets, try to keep everything simple and sturdy. If the condenser is significantly smaller than the radiator, don't use solid sheets of metal to mount the condenser as they will reduce airflow over the radiator.

By putting the condenser in front of the radiator, you provide it with a good supply of fresh air and you take advantage of the existing fan(s) to help move air across the fins and tubes. When you try "innovative" mounting locations you generally make a lot of trouble for yourself.

Unusual condenser locations, like under the car or in the trunk, seldom work as well as the preferred location at the front on the car. Prob-

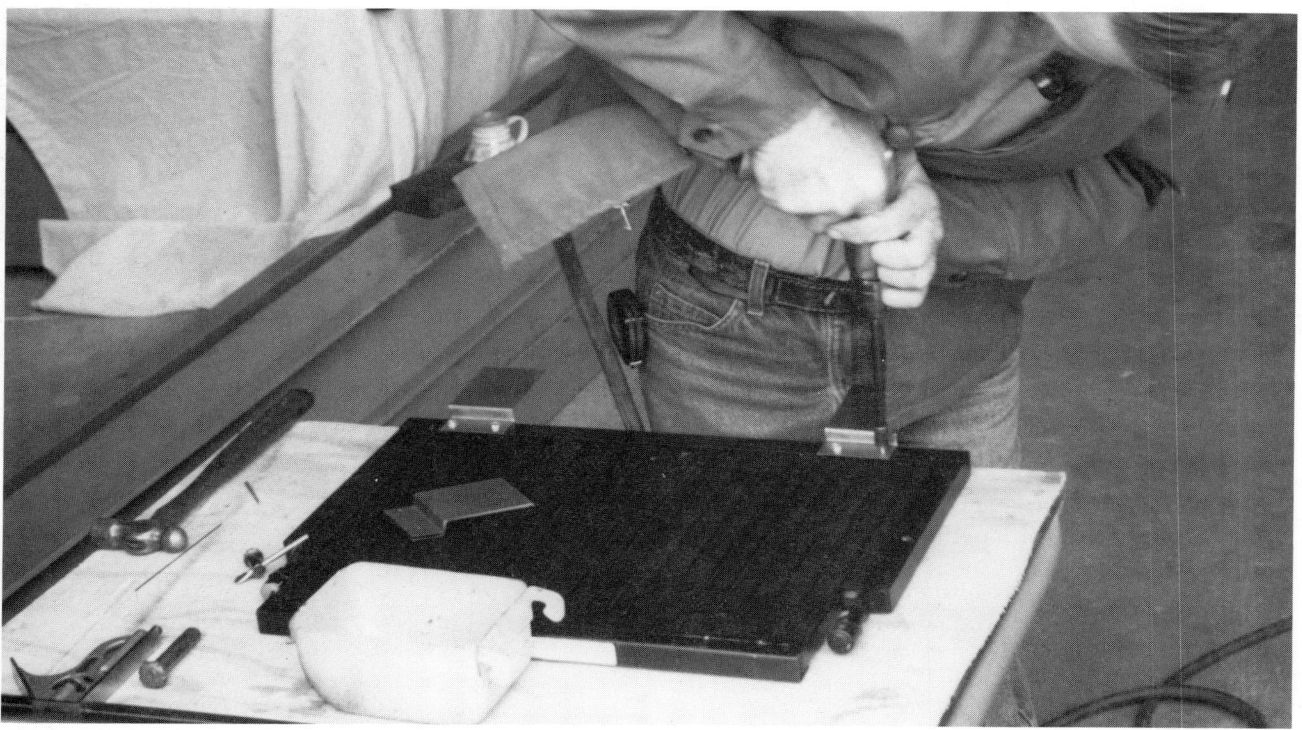

After measurements are taken, the brackets are fabricated and attached to the condenser. Note that each bracket is "stepped" so there will be an air gap between the condenser and the radiator.

lems include insufficient airflow, damage from debris, and the need for a separate fan to provide airflow in traffic situations. If yours is a conventional car (not an early VW for example), then put the condenser in a conventional location.

The oil that moves through the air conditioning system is held in suspension in the refrigerant. In certain situations however it can settle out of the refrigerant and collect inside the system. Because of this, the condenser tubes must be horizontal. Vertical tubes allow the oil to settle at the base of the tubes, restricting the flow of refrigerant. (There are exceptions to this rule for HFC-134A systems.)

Receiver-Drier

It might look like a simple little can that will mount anyplace it fits, but once again, there's a right way and a wrong way to mount the receiver-drier. The receiver-drier's job is to separate vapor from liquid refrigerant (among others). So you want it in a cool place with plenty of fresh air going by so the liquid refrigerant remains in liquid form.

The receiver-drier does its job by allowing the vapor to rise to the top of the cannister so only liquid refrigerant will be "picked up" by the tube that extends down into the bottom of the cannister. If you lay a receiver-drier on its side, the tube no longer reaches to the bottom of the cannister and the device is rendered worthless.

Receiver-driers in CFC-12 systems have the sight glass on top to determine when the system is full of refrigerant. So you need to mount the drier where you can see this sight glass. Because HFC-134A refrigerant doesn't go from "cloudy" to "perfectly clear," some HFC-134A systems do not include a sight glass. (We always recommend that the technician use the manufacturer's recommended charge as the means of determining when a system is properly charged.)

Because the receiver-drier contains a bag of desiccant and because that bag's ability to absorb moisture is limited, it's always best to keep the receiver-drier capped with the factory plugs until you are ready to install it in an otherwise finished system. For that matter, all the components should be kept capped for as long as possible to prevent their picking up a lot of unnecessary moisture from the atmosphere.

Evaporator

Before launching into a discussion of evaporator mounting, we need to back up a bit and talk about efficient air conditioner operation. The job of the air conditioner is to cool and dehumidify the air inside the car. The more heat and moisture that air contains, the harder it is for the air conditioner to do its job. Outside air that enters

Most aftermarket condensers feature perforated support tubing at the edges so sheet metal screws can be used to attach the mounting brackets.

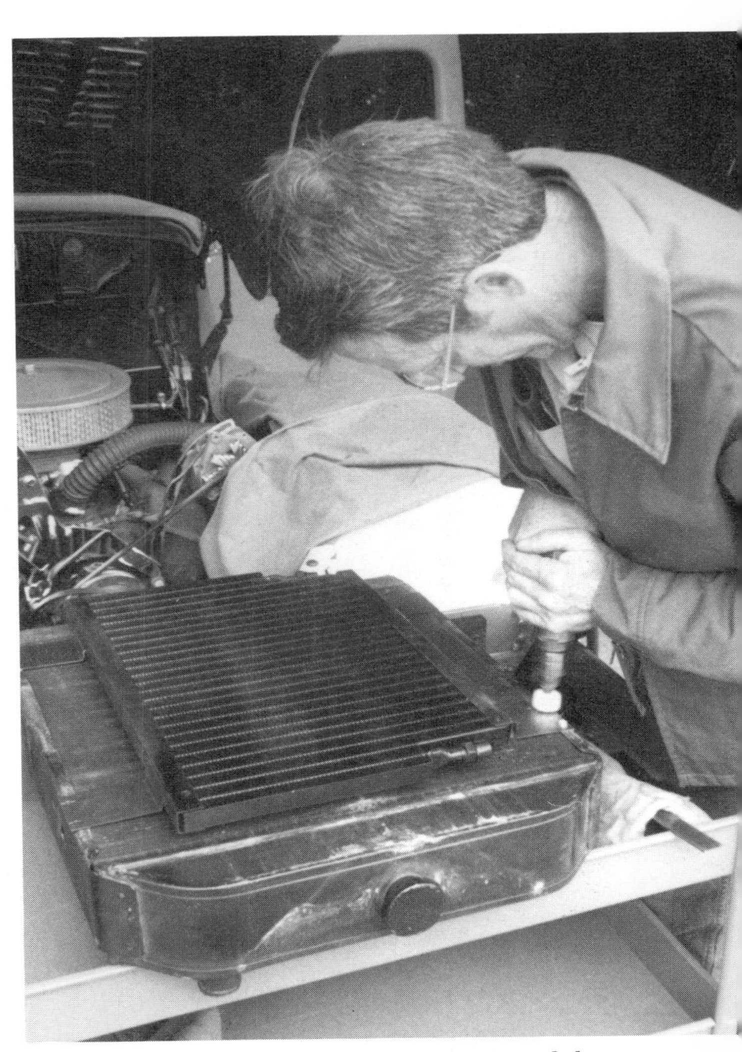

Dave has drilled through a small block of wood, leaving only about 1/8in of drill bit protruding from the end—that way he can't drill too far and puncture a tube while drilling holes in the radiator saddle.

The radiator and condenser are ready to install. Note that the condenser tubes run horizontally—if they ran vertically the oil could collect in the bends at the bottom of each tube. (Some designers feel HFC-134A systems with P.A.G. oil might be able to run vertically in the condenser tubes.) The receiver-drier has been mounted to the condenser, which puts it in an area with plenty of cool air.

Jack Chisenhall and Everist Rodriguez install the condenser and radiator. The receiver-drier mounting on the condenser provides the correct vertical mounting and makes for a neat installation.

the cabin during air conditioner operation is, by definition, hot, humid air. The greatest single thing you can do to improve the efficiency of your air conditioner is to control (read: stop) the entry of outside air into the cabin. Ideas for eliminating the entry of air are contained in the Keeping Your Cool chapter in this book.

You need to keep a few more principles in mind as you plan the location of the evaporator. First, the air leaving the evaporator needs to blow on the people in the car. You aren't just cooling the air in the car's cabin, you are blowing cool, dry air past and onto the individuals in the car. The difference as felt by the car's occupants is profound. Remember too that cool air is heavier than hot air, so it falls to the floor. What all this means is that cleverly installed and invisible evaporator vents located below the front seats don't work very well—because the cool air doesn't blow on the driver and it doesn't circulate.

The best location for the evaporator is under or behind the dash with vents located to blow air directly on the driver and passenger. In-dash units are much neater, though they are also more difficult to install. If you are building a car from scratch or doing a major renovation, careful planning can eliminate much of the hassle of putting the evaporator behind the dash.

Under-dash locations allow for much easier installation and in some cars and trucks look perfectly "normal" and neat. The hardest part of under-dash installation is the plumbing, which is more visible. Therefore, it's important that your hose routing be as neat as possible.

Whether the evaporator housing is mounted behind the dash or under the dash, there are a few things to keep in mind. First, remember to allow for a water drain so the condensation that collects in the evaporator will find its way out.

Second, never plug any of the evaporator air outlets. Most units that go up behind the dash have three or four large air outlets. Installers sometimes hook up only the two, outer outlets, and tape the center outlet(s) shut. Logic would suggest that when you tape off one outlet of the three that leave the evaporator housing, you reduce the air output by one-third. In reality, the reduction in airflow is much greater than that. The limited airflow in the evaporator case will cause the blower fan to cavitate—resulting in a further reduction in total air output.

When you install the evaporator behind the dash, use all the outlets the evaporator case provides. The outer ones are usually run to vents located at the corners of the dashboard. If you want to keep the installation as neat as possible, use vents designed for the car or the aftermarket aluminum vents.

The outer vents at the corners of the dash are the most visible. Your options include aftermarket under-dash or in-dash aluminum vents. A neat effect can be created in a car like a '55 Chevy by using factory outlets (used in factory A/C installations) at the outer edges of the dash and a simple aftermarket vent in the center hanging from the lip of the dash. If you want, the center vent can be painted flat black and set back from the edge of the dash to make it nearly invisible.

Hoses and Fittings

Hoses and duct work should be given as much thought as the rest of the installation. Not just for the sake of neatness, but for the sake of good airflow. In particular, the old twin 3in blower fans (usually used on older under-dash units) should never be used when a duct-hose delivery system is used. Though the duct might look like a path of no resistance, there is considerable resistance within the duct to the passage of air, resistance that the small-diameter fans are unable to overcome.

The duct work supplied with most A/C kits is of the accordion style. This works fine and has the advantage of being easily bent around various obstructions under the dash. The problem is the negative effect of the ripples along the inside surface on airflow. Vintage Air's Jack Chisenhall suggests that if you are going to use flexible ductwork supplied with the kit, stretch it between the evaporator and the dash vent and then cut the duct to that stretched length. By stretching the duct work you tend to smooth out the ribs and ripples on the inside surface.

For individuals who want to go one step further, Jack suggests using plastic pipe or smooth-molded vinyl tubing with a diameter of at least 2 1/2in. By using smooth-walled plastic pipe and avoiding any sharp bends, you can increase the airflow leaving the evaporator and likewise reduce the noise level. Jack recommends against using metal duct work as it collects water and creates condensation problems.

Most flexible ductwork is 2 1/2in in diameter.

This is the new under-dash evaporator for the '39 Ford. Installation is not quite finished—the drain hose can be seen hanging below. The drain hose must run to the outside of the vehicle so condensation that drips off the cool evaporator does not collect in the car.

Always use the largest diamater ducts and dash vents (within reason) to assure maximum airflow.

Routing the Hoses

A certain amount of plumbing is involved in any air conditioning installation and there are some guidelines to follow when installing the hoses and pipes.

As mentioned earlier, the flexible hose, whether yours is a CFC-12 or HFC-134A system, should be "barrier" hose, or hose with a liner to reduce the porosity of the flexible lines.

The routing of each individual hose should go like this: The high-side hose leaving the compressor and running to the condenser should be kept cool, as you want this refrigerant to condense back into a liquid. The liquid line leaving the condenser and running to the receiver-drier and then onto the evaporator should also be kept cool, for the same reason. If you route it along frame rails or inner fender panels, try to keep it away from engine heat.

You can tie the liquid line to the suction line (the one leaving the evaporator and running to the compressor). Do not, however, tie the liquid

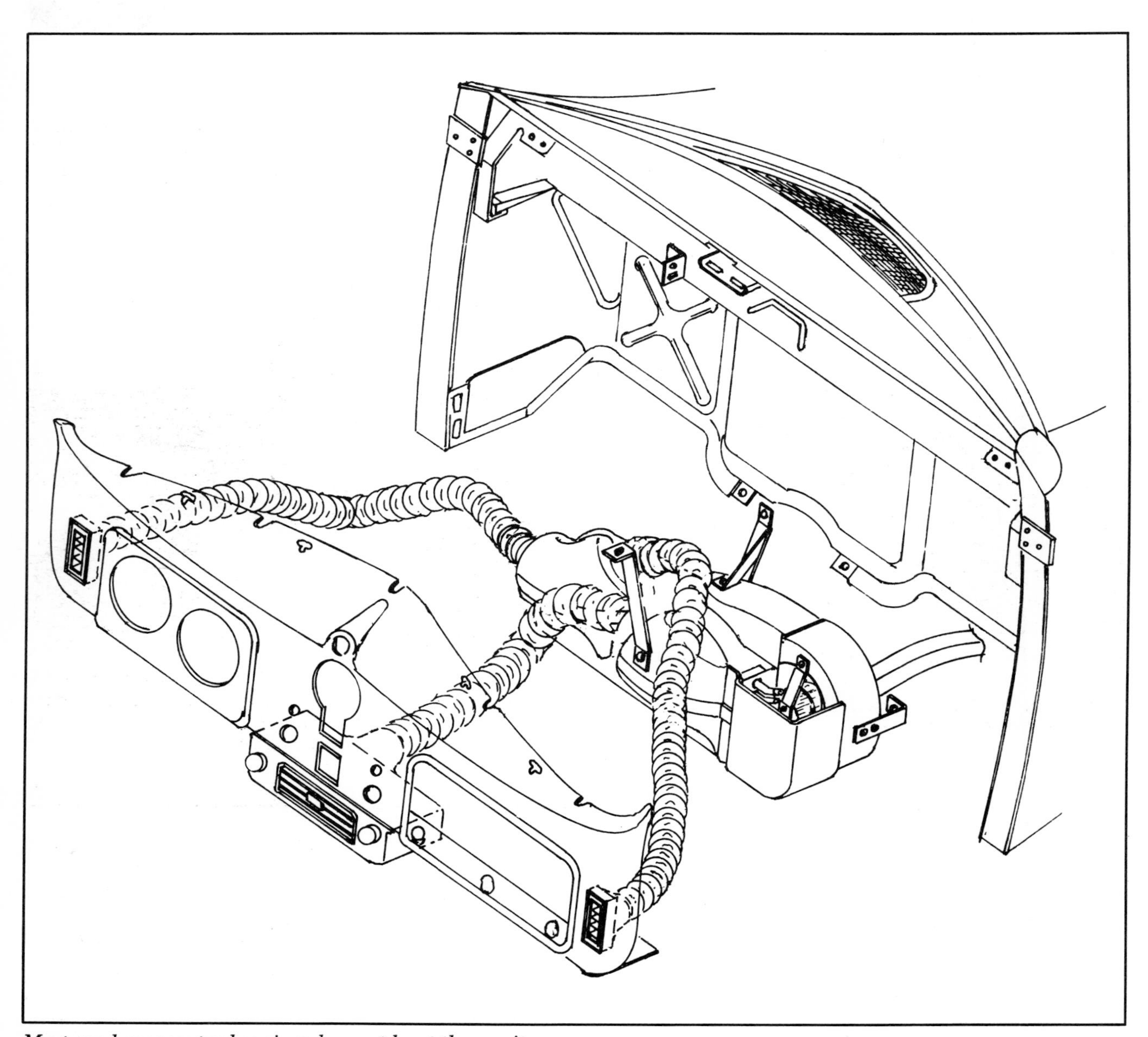

Most good evaporator housings have at least three exits for airflow. Duct work should be kept as short as possible to limit resistance to the air and minimize noise.

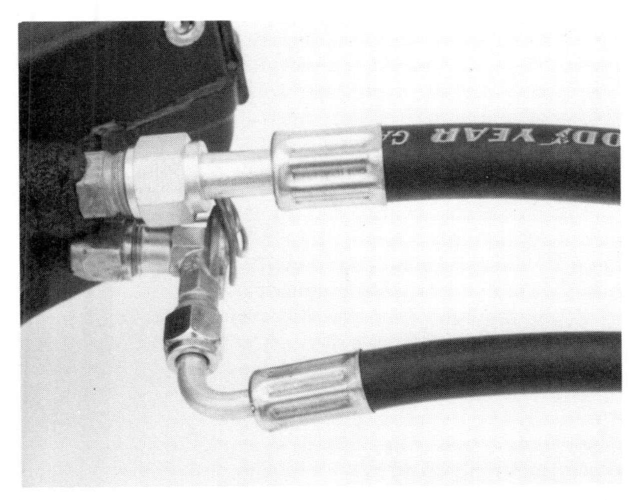

This picture shows the back of the evaporator with the liquid line coming into the expansion valve and the suction line (on top) leaving to return to the compressor. These metal fittings get cold during operation, condensation forms, and drips onto the carpet.

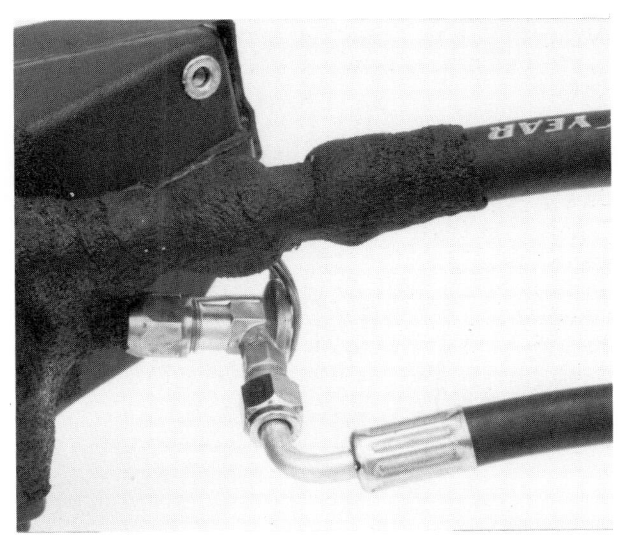

All metal parts of the suction line have been wrapped. The pipes must be very clean or the tape won't stick. A neat job is accomplished by pulling the tape tight around each fitting.

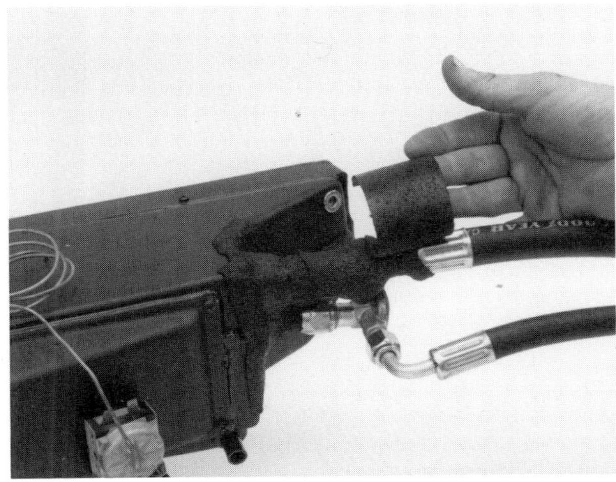

The answer to exterior condensation is black cork tape. This is an insulator and will prevent condensation from forming and dripping onto the carpet. Here we begin wrapping the two pipes. Note that these fittings have been crimped.

The expansion valve should be wrapped too, from the diaphragm housing to the evaporator case. The other half of the expansion valve is hot—not cold—during operation of the air conditioning.

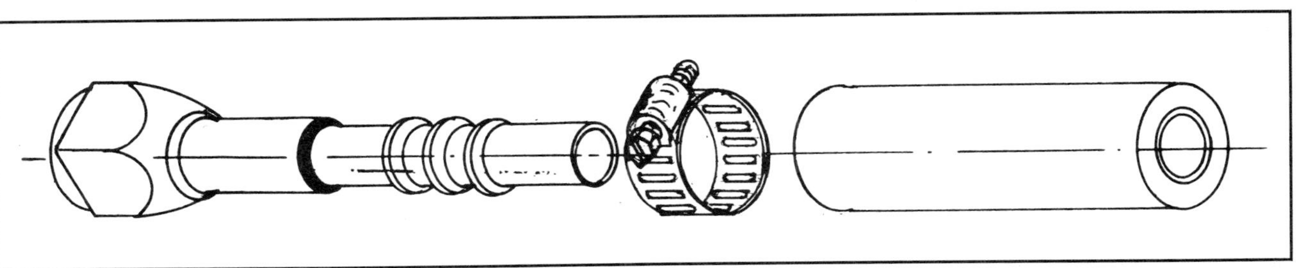

When hoses are pushed on the barbed fittings, it's important that the hoses go all the way onto the fitting. Wormgear clamps should no longer be used with barrier hose. Instead, use a compression style or crimped clamp instead.

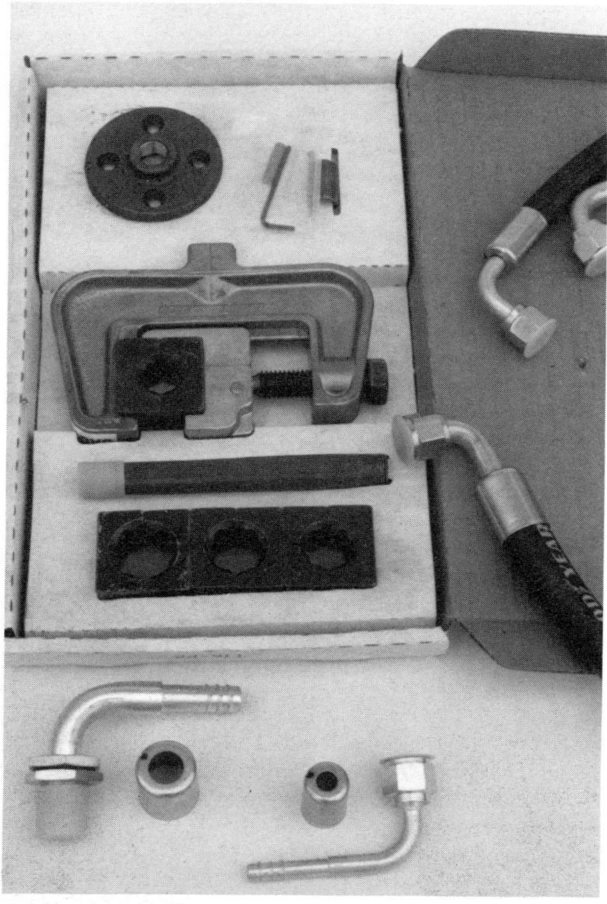

This small crimping tool will allow you to crimp air conditioning hoses for a factory-finished look. The small size allows crimping on the car. These tools are available from Vintage Air or a good air conditioning supply house.

Vintage Air makes a stainless line kit for street rodders who insist on a very neat engine compartment. Here a tubing bender is used to bend the stainless tubing. Vintage Air

Hoses should always be well clamped to keep them out of the way and to stop vibration.

line to the discharge line from the high-side of the compressor.

The suction line can be routed close to the engine, where it will gain heat. This hose contains vaporous refrigerant and you want it to stay a vapor—you don't want to feed liquid refrigerant to the suction side of the compressor.

At the firewall, you need to either run the hoses through the metal, using a grommet to protect the hose, or run the hoses up to the firewall and then use a bulkhead fitting designed for air conditioners to neatly get the hoses inside the car.

Don't use hydraulic hose and don't use braided steel line with JIC flare fittings on the end. Remember that flare fittings are no longer considered good enough, even for a CFC-12 system, so use O-ring fittings throughout the system. If you are installing a new HFC-134A system, use the new fittings and clamps designed for that type of system—don't use worm gear clamps on the new barrier hose.

Once you've got the hoses inside the car, remember that anything cold will condense water and drip it on the floor. Always wrap most of the expansion valve (see pictures for more detail) and the suction line, with black cork tape. The tape acts as an insulator and helps stop moisture from condensing on the cold lines and fittings. The suction line is, by the way, the larger of the two hoses inside the car. Because it is larger, the suction line isn't very flexible and is thus hard to route neatly. This is a case where it pays to take your time and plan out the exact location of the evaporator housing and the routing of the suction line so everything ends up looking as neat as possible.

Cooling Fans

We would be remiss if we neglected to talk about cooling fans at this point. As a rule of thumb, the typical V-8 radiator and air conditioning condenser need a minimum of 2300cfm of airflow for adequate cooling.

At the very least (assuming this is a conventional engine layout), you probably want to add a fan with more blades when you install the air conditioning to insure an adequate amount of airflow. The flexible fans work well, in metal or fiberglass (metal seems more durable). They are intended to draw the maximum volume of air through the radiator at slow speeds, and less air (with less draw on the engine) at higher engine speeds.

Clutch hub fans are meant to work the same way. Providing maximum flow at low speeds with less draw and less load on the engine at higher speeds. Fan hubs come in two styles, hydraulic and the more sophisticated thermostatically controlled hubs. If you buy one in the aftermarket, buy a simple hydraulic clutch known as a viscous drive. The thermostatically controlled fan hubs require a shroud and must be matched with the fan and radiator—as in a factory installation. The results of a mismatch might be a fan that doesn't engage until the engine is already too hot.

Many new cars are equipped with electric fans, powered through a relay and controlled by a temperature probe or sensor usually located near the outlet of the radiator. If the coolant

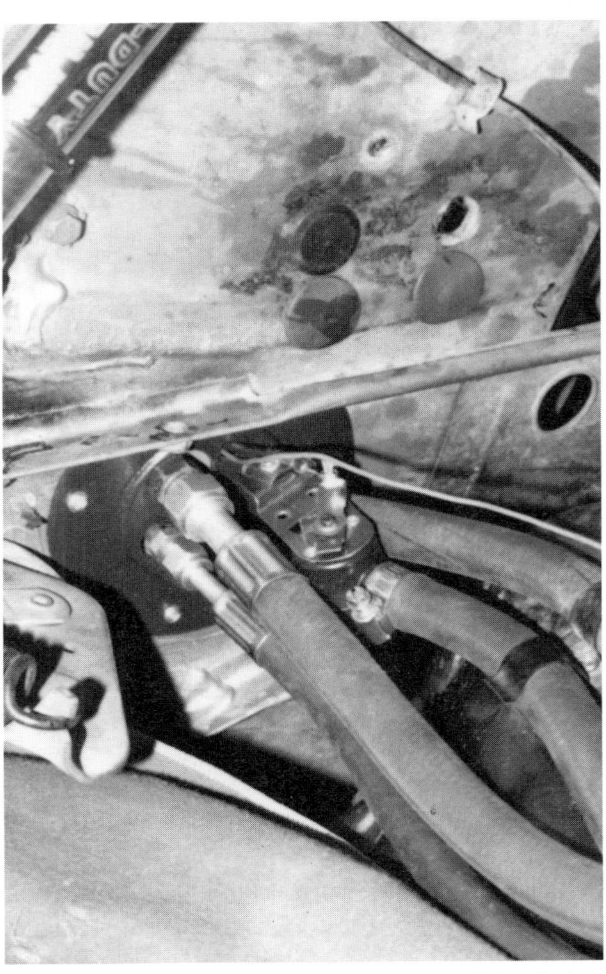

Many of the aftermarket kits include a bulkhead plate so hoses can be neatly run through the firewall. Most plates bolt into existing holes—like the hole where the factory heater fan would normally protrude.

This is the finished installation in the '39 Ford coupe. Note that all the hoses are neatly clamped and that the liquid and suction lines are clamped together.

A good shroud is critical if you want to avoid overheating problems. This shroud is from Vintage Air, and similar models are available from Walker.

You need to make the shroud fit the radiator. Here, Jack Chisenhall marks where the shroud will have to be trimmed to clear the upper radiator hose.

passing through the radiator hasn't cooled sufficiently by the time it hits the sensor, then the fan is turned on. These fans have the advantage of running only when needed. On a cool day or when you're going down the highway, there is no need for the fan and no draw on the engine.

Aftermarket electric cooling fans are available, though the problem is getting one big enough to move enough air past the radiator. When you combine a powerful V-8 engine and air conditioning, you've created a situation where a lot of airflow is needed. In the past, electric fans couldn't always meet that demand for air. As we go to press, Vintage Air and others have some new fan designs intended to solve the problem.

A good fan can't operate efficiently without a shroud of some kind. A well-designed shroud allows the fan to draw a maximum amount of air over the entire surface of the radiator. Ideally, you want a full shroud so the fan can draw air over the radiator surface, being careful to keep the shroud far enough back from the edge of the radiator surface and keep air moving through.

To cut the hole in the shroud, you need to temporarily install it on the radiator and in the car to locate the fan-center, then mark the circumference of the hole.

Once you know the location of the fan's center and the diameter of the fan, a simple tool like this can be used to mark the hole.

Here's the shroud ready to install on the radiator. Large diameter tubing was used to make the cutout for the upper radiator hose. A recess was created from sheet metal at the bottom to clear the lower hose.

Ready to cool, the finished shroud has been attached to the radiator saddle with sheet metal screws.

(Shrouds are available from firms such as Vintage Air and Walker Radiator.)

A shroud can easily make the difference between a car that overheats and one that doesn't. If it seems impossible to find a full shroud for your car, at least use a simple ring shroud to improve the fan's ability to draw air over the radiator. A simple ring shroud can be fabricated in the home shop and has been shown to provide roughly half the advantage of a full shroud.

While we're discussing this issue of fans, keep yours between 3/4in and 1in from the radiator—when using no shroud or a fan ring. When using a shroud, the fan blades should go at least one third of the way into the shroud opening but not more than one half of the way in.

When you add air conditioning to an existing car, the addition of a shroud and a fan with more blades will usually compensate for the increased heat load the air conditioning creates. If you are designing a car from scratch, you might want to use a table like the one provided to help determine how much radiator you need.

The key to doing a good air conditioning installation is mounting each component in a neat, sturdy fashion. In addition, you need to mount it so the component can do its job with maximum efficiency.

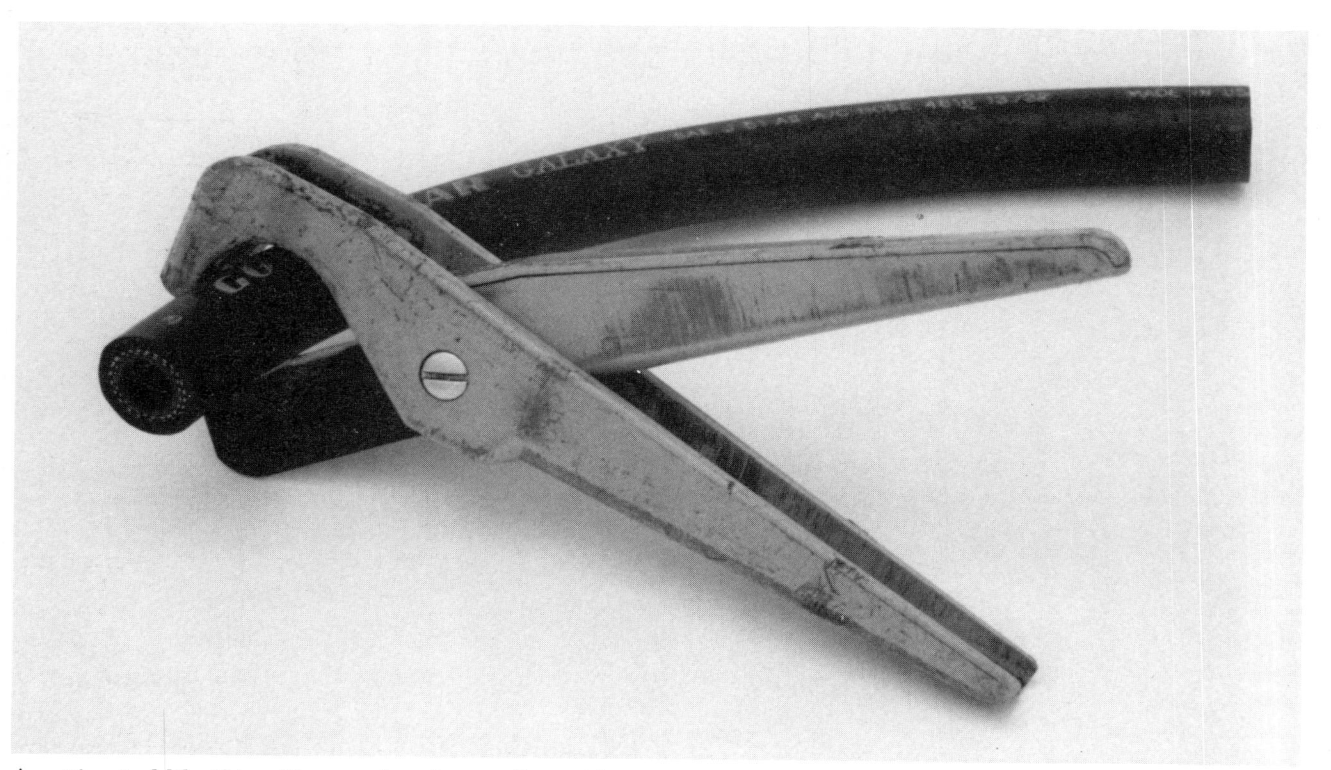

A cutting tool like this will save a lot of struggling with your pocket knife and give you nice, neat cuts of refrigeration hose.

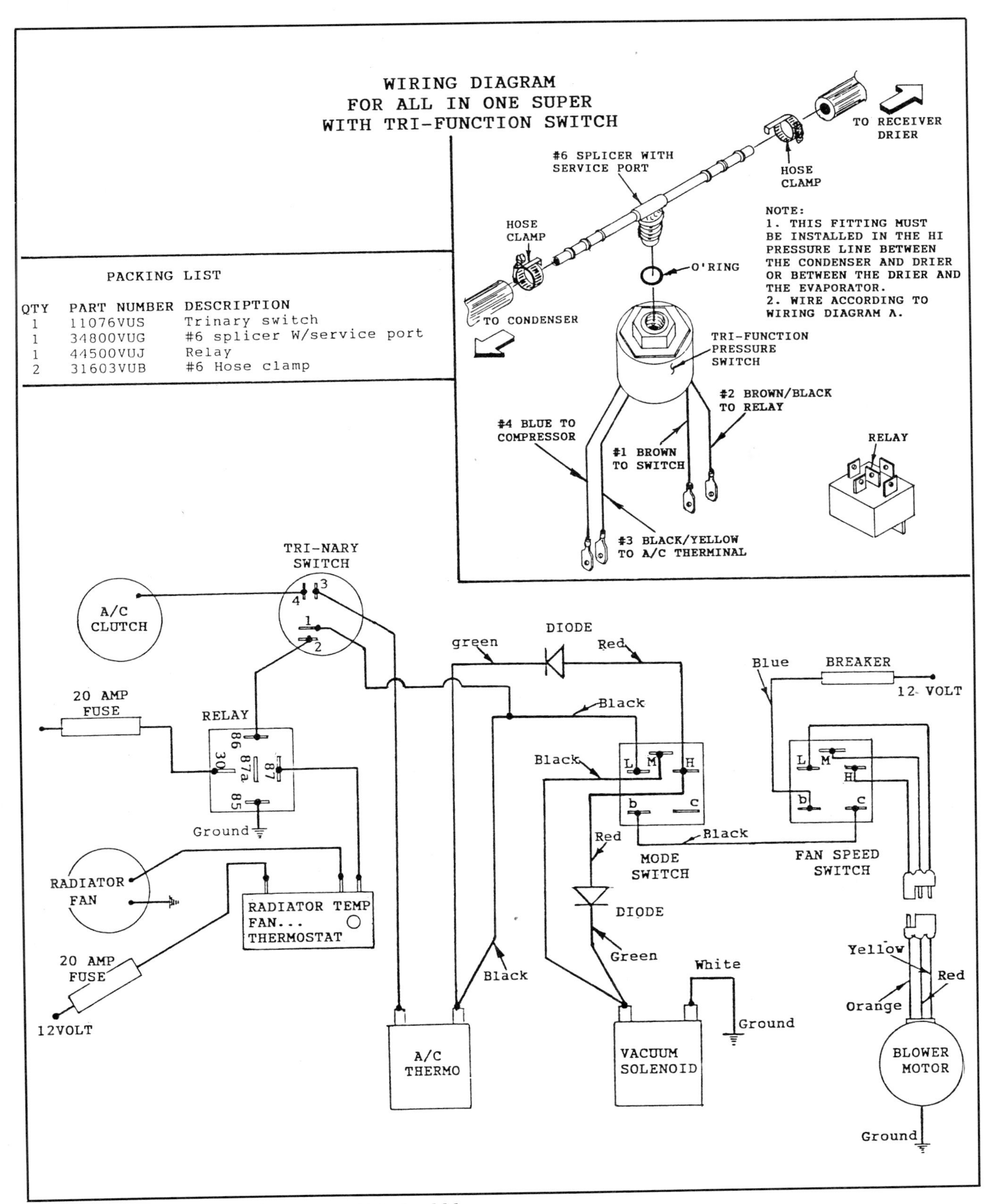

This diagram shows how a three-way switch should be wired to control the cooling fan and the power to the compressor clutch.

Chapter 5

Installing A/C in a Street Rod

Street rods have their own peculiar shapes and their own unique problems when it comes to installing air conditioning. Typical street rods, especially early cars, have small underhood areas and small dashboards. What you have is a group of cars without much room for the air conditioning components, owned by a group of people who not only insist on air conditioning, but insist on a very neat installation as well.

Buying and Installing the Right Components in Your Car

Buying the right components for your car involves more than just choosing quality parts. You

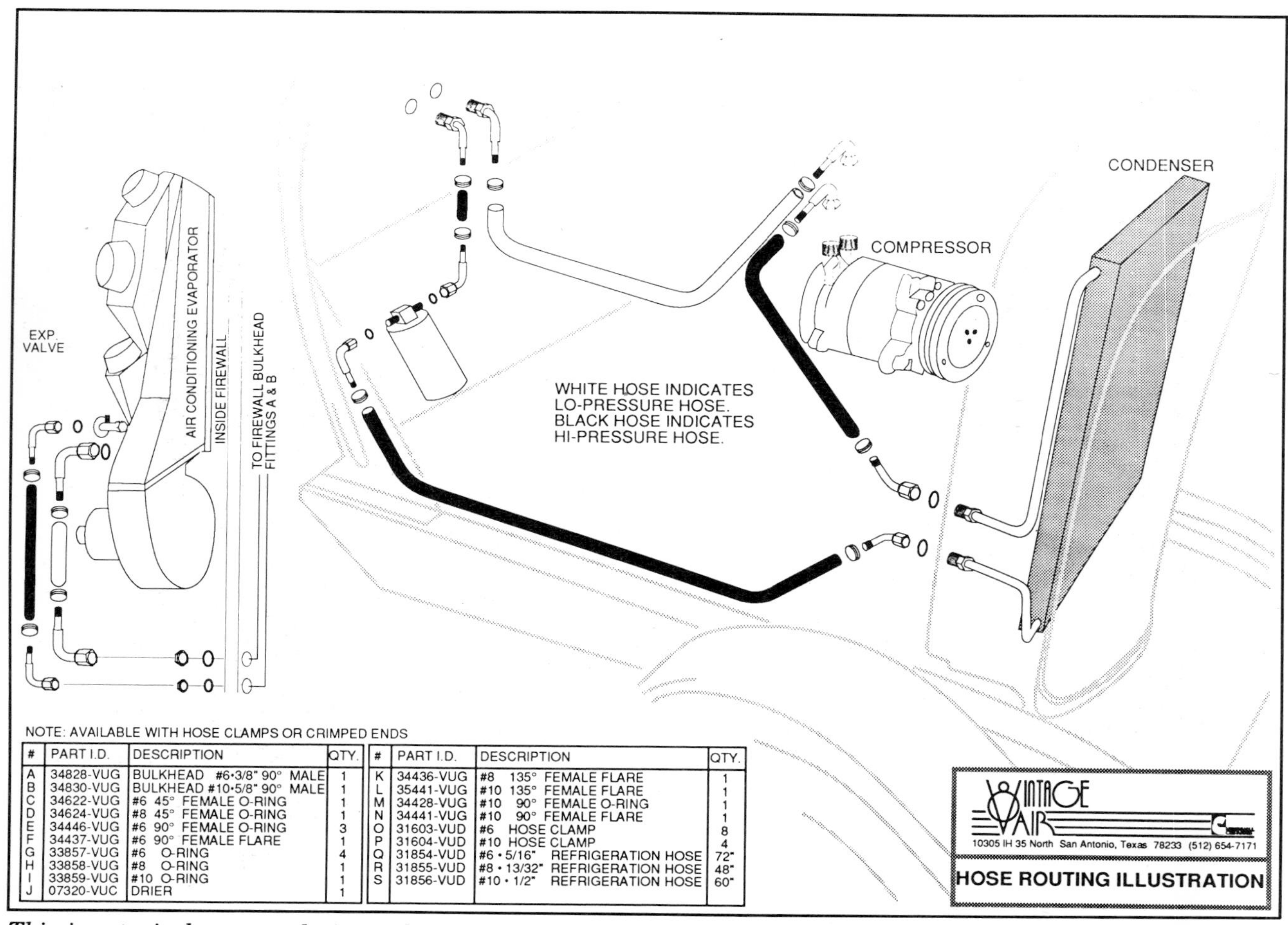

NOTE: AVAILABLE WITH HOSE CLAMPS OR CRIMPED ENDS

#	PART I.D.	DESCRIPTION	QTY.
A	34828-VUG	BULKHEAD #6•3/8" 90° MALE	1
B	34830-VUG	BULKHEAD #10•5/8" 90° MALE	1
C	34622-VUG	#6 45° FEMALE O-RING	1
D	34624-VUG	#8 45° FEMALE O-RING	1
E	34446-VUG	#6 90° FEMALE O-RING	3
F	34437-VUG	#6 90° FEMALE FLARE	1
G	33857-VUG	#6 O-RING	4
H	33858-VUG	#8 O-RING	1
I	33859-VUG	#10 O-RING	1
J	07320-VUC	DRIER	1

#	PART I.D.	DESCRIPTION	QTY.
K	34436-VUG	#8 135° FEMALE FLARE	1
L	35441-VUG	#10 135° FEMALE FLARE	1
M	34428-VUG	#10 90° FEMALE O-RING	1
N	34441-VUG	#10 90° FEMALE FLARE	1
O	31603-VUD	#6 HOSE CLAMP	8
P	31604-VUD	#10 HOSE CLAMP	4
Q	31854-VUD	#6 • 5/16" REFRIGERATION HOSE	72"
R	31855-VUD	#8 • 13/32" REFRIGERATION HOSE	48"
S	31856-VUD	#10 • 1/2" REFRIGERATION HOSE	60"

This is a typical street rod air conditioning installation. Street rods need special components and mountings due to the tall, narrow engine compartments and the small interiors.

also need components that are sized correctly to the car and to one other. The easiest way to do this is to purchase a kit from a well-known aftermarket manufacturer of air conditioning kits and components.

A kit made by a quality manufacturer will contain a condenser, compressor, and evaporator that are selected to work together. By asking the manufacturer intelligent questions regarding the right system for your car, you can be assured of buying a kit that fits and has enough capacity for your particular application.

A detailed discussion of the various components and the problems of mounting them on a street rod should start with the compressor.

Compressor

Jack Chisenhall feels there is really only one compressor for a street rod, and that is the Sanden/Sankyo axial-style compressor (as discussed in chapter 2). These compressors have the advantage of minimal vibration, compact size, and neat appearance. Most coupes and smaller sedans need only the model 508, (five cylinders and 8ci of displacement). Very small coupes or applications where underhood space is very limited might get by with the model 505 (five cylinders, 5ci), though performance at low speeds could suffer. The model 510 or 709 would be a good choice for very large cars like Packards or Cadillacs with a large evaporator (or two evaporators) and a lot of interior to cool.

When you put an engine in your street rod, you probably figured that something "a little too big would be just about right." Choosing a compressor is one of those places where bigger may not be better and could easily be worse. A compressor that's too big for the rest of the system creates too much head pressure—which translates into more vibration at the compressor and higher power requirements. When in doubt, use the smaller compressor.

When it comes time to mount the compressor, your options are somewhat limited. Most

Air conditioning needn't clutter the engine compartment of your street rod. The polished compressor looks right at home here.

street rods, especially early cars, have tall, narrow engine compartments. The hood sides nearly touch the exhaust manifolds, leaving no room on the side of the engine for accessories like the compressor or the alternator.

The small engine compartment means you only have two basic options for the compressor location. You can mount the compressor high or low, on top of the engine or under the engine. Many street rodders like to hang the compressor low—out of sight for a very neat installation. Logic, however, dictates that the compressor be mounted high rather than low.

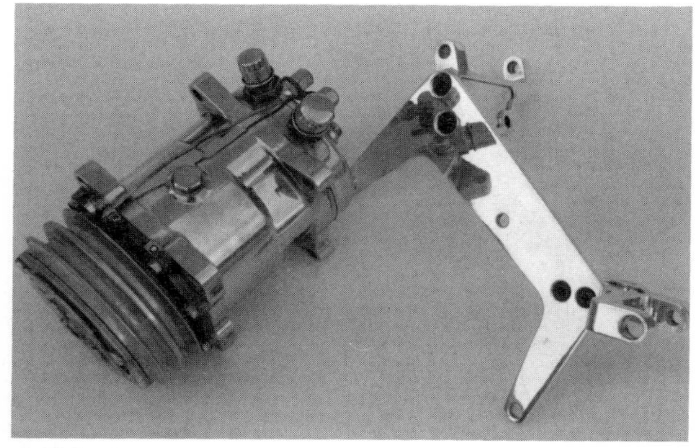

Sanden compressors are available in polished form to match the brackets. These components are from Vintage Air.

By putting the compressor on top of the engine you avoid a host of clearance problems. Hanging it low usually creates clearance problems from the cross-member, straight axle, fuel pump, and motor mounts. Compressors mounted on the lower side of the engine are also subject to more heat, road dirt, and water. With a top mount you only have to keep clear of the upper radiator hose. It becomes relatively easy to mount the compressor on one side of the radiator hose (usually the right side) and the alternator on the other side. If the engine is a small-block Ford or Chevy V-8, a large variety of compressor brackets are available from the aftermarket for mounting both the compressor and the alternator.

Each year there are more brackets available on the market, and not just for small-block Chevy and Ford V-8s, but also for less-popular street rod engines like wedge and small-block

This '33/'34 Ford carries the compressor high on the right side so it clears the hood sides. Vents in hood-sides are a good way to increase airflow through the engine compartment.

Mopars, Hemis, Ford Y-blocks, and many six-cylinder engines. If you're running a flathead or some other engine and simply can't find a compressor bracket, then universal brackets can be purchased to make the job of fabricating a strong, neat bracket much easier. If you decide to build your own brackets, be sure to check the ideas listed in chapters 2 and 4.

Finally, remember that even with the newer compressors, the brackets still take a beating. Use at least grade five bolts and always use lock washers or lock nuts. Use fine thread bolts unless you're cutting threads into cast iron or aluminum, in which case coarse threads actually hold better.

Condenser

Getting a condenser of the right size is again made easier if you buy a good kit. Vintage Air recommends that the condenser be twenty-five percent larger in mass than the evaporator. Thus a 200ci evaporator needs a 250ci condenser. (These rules of thumb apply to CFC-12 systems using tube-and-fin style of condensers.) Because the condenser is the unit that actually sheds the heat to the outside air, you do not want it too small. As a place to start, a basic coupe or small sedan with a 508 compressor needs a minimum of 210 square inches of two row, copper tube-and-fin style condenser. By adding another row to the condenser, you gain cooling ability, yet there is a slight trade-off because the thicker core offers more restriction to the airflow.

As time goes on, new types of condensers are reaching the aftermarket. The serpentine condenser and the parallel flow condenser offer greater efficiencies, or a greater cooling capacity in a given size, as compared to the old tube-and-fin style of condenser. While the parallel flow condenser offers the greatest cooling in a given package, the costs for new tooling are considerable. HFC-134A systems will often use these newer types of condensers as this refrigerant requires roughly twenty percent more condenser capacity than would a similar CFC-12 system.

Just as important (maybe more important) as the size and style of the condenser is the amount of airflow that reaches the condenser surface. As a rule of thumb, the condenser and radiator of a typical V-8 street rod must see at

You don't need the big A-6 Frigidaire compressor unless your street rod seats eight like this one.

least 2300cfm of the coolest air possible. The condenser *must* be right out there in the airflow.

In an effort to hide the air conditioning, street rodders have tried innovative condenser locations, like under the car or in the trunk. Don't. Put it right out there in the airstream where everyone can see it and the maximum amount of air is made available for cooling. Insufficient airflow means more internal pressure, a compressor that works too hard, and a car that probably isn't as cool as it should be. Don't work so hard at being cool that you actually give up your "cool."

Most street rods—except fat-fendered models—present problems for the person trying to install a condenser. Cars like Model T's and Model A's really have no provision and no room for a condenser in front of the radiator. The logical answer is a combination radiator/condenser like one of the units from Walker Radiator. By combining the two units, there is considerable space savings and a radiator and condenser can be fit into a grille designed for only a radiator. You also have the satisfaction of knowing that both units were designed to handle the considerable loads placed on modern street rods with V-8 engines, automatic transmissions, air conditioning, and plenty of low-speed cruising.

When building a car, the problem of allowing adequate space for the condenser should be considered. That way you don't have to jerry-rig a condenser into a space that was never meant to accommodate one. If you know the car is going to carry air conditioning, be sure to mock up the radiator and condenser before deciding on the final location for the motor mounts. By moving the engine back just a few inches you can create

This is a small-block Ford with the compressor mounted on top of the alternator using an idler pulley for belt tension. Idlers add complexity though they are sometimes necessary. Vintage Air

Condensers should be mounted right up in front of the radiator where they receive the maximum amount of the coolest air. Mounting the receiver-drier on the condenser is a good idea if there's enough space behind the grille.

enough room to correctly and neatly mount the condenser. (See chapter 9 for more tips on engine location.)

Remember that when you add air conditioning you need room for more than just a condenser. You probably will need to run a radiator shroud (if you don't have one already), and possibly a large fan. You also need to allow enough room under the hood so the air will move through the radiator and have someplace to go.

Speaking of hot air, consider that Henry and Louis vented their hood-sides for a reason. Smooth-sided hoods may look great but they make it tough to move a lot of air through the radiator. The bottom of the engine compartment is the only place left for the air to exit.

Modern cars use small air-dams to create low-pressure areas and thus keep air moving through the radiator and through the engine compartment. The front splash pan on a '32 Ford acts in a similar fashion. Later Fords use the low-pressure area in the fender well to help pull air through the radiator and engine compartment. This line of thinking can be pursued by the innovative street rodder for increased airflow and better cooling.

The person building a street rod or adding air conditioning to his or her street rod needs to think about airflow to and through the radiator. Good airflow will do more than prevent overheating; it will ensure good air conditioning operation and long component life.

Walker Radiator builds radiators with integral condensers—a great space-saving measure. In the case of a car like a Model A, it's almost the only way to neatly mount a condenser.

Receiver-Drier

Street rodders tend to buy polished aluminum receiver-driers. That's fine, but as long as you're paying extra money, you should try to get a top-quality unit. Don't just buy a polished OEM-type unit. Get a full-flow, rebuildable unit so the desiccant and filter can be replaced if necessary.

Mount the receiver-drier following guidelines established earlier. Keep it vertical and keep it cool so the condensed liquid refrigerant stays in liquid form. If there's room behind the grille, bolt it to the front of the condenser. Otherwise a firewall location is adequate. You can even mount it inside the car.

Polished aluminum brackets to match the polished housing are available if you're mounting the receiver-drier in a good location and want it to look as trick as possible. Finally, remember to leave the receiver-drier capped until you are ready to install it in a nearly finished system in order to preserve the capacity of the desiccant.

Evaporator

When it's time to buy the evaporator or the

A variety of polished receiver-driers are available to dress up the air conditioning installation in your street rod. The best units feature filters and desiccant bags that can be replaced. Vintage Air

When you connect the hoses to the back of the evaporator be sure to hold the fitting on the evaporator with one wrench while you tighten the fitting with another wrench.

Who says that air conditioning installations add clutter to a street rod dashboard? This is a good example of what happens when an in-dash evaporator is well installed.

A variety of through-dash vents are available for your dash. This simple design works well with the rest of the dash and interior.

air conditioning kit for your street rod, you may have a hard time determining how large an evaporator to install. The evaporator or kit manufacturer is a good source of information. Read the brochures and don't be afraid to call and ask questions.

Most of the evaporators designed for street rods have three outlets and will do a good job of cooling a coupe or small sedan. If your street rod is bigger than most, however, then you might want to buy the largest evaporator available, probably a unit with four hose outlets to move more air. If in doubt, ask a well-known air conditioning manufacturer and follow that advice. Choose carefully because you can't easily change your mind once the car is finished.

Like the condenser, a neat evaporator installation is far easier if you can plan ahead. Though the dashboards of most street rods are pretty small, there's usually more room behind those dashboards than people think.

You have two options: an under-dash or in-dash evaporator. The under-dash unit has the advantage of being easy to mount in nearly any car and provides good air delivery direct from the air plenum to the driver and passenger. Some of the new under-dash units are really a clever combination of the two types. The Super Cooler from Vintage Air, for example, tucks most of the evaporator housing up behind the dash with a central vent that blows directly from the air plenum while the side vents are connected to the plenum by duct hoses. This system provides massive air flow from the central plenum and gives good air delivery to the back seat area of large cars

True in-dash units are, of course, much neater though more complex to install. In-dash

Here the center vent is integrated into the dashboard and the side vents are tucked up under the lip of the dash.

This is the driver's compartment of a Chevy street rod limousine. The center vent (you almost always need at least three) is hidden up under the dashboard, and side vents are mounted to the bottom lip of the dashboard.

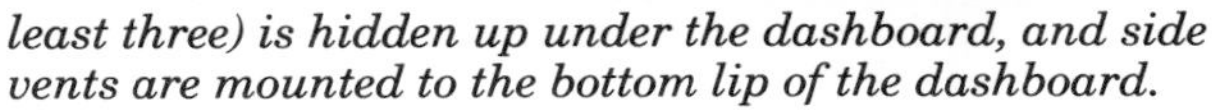

The rear evaporator for the limousine—with its own temperature controls—is hidden in this cabinet in the passenger compartment.

evaporators put the evaporator housing behind the dashboard and tend to encounter interference problems from the glove box, instruments, radio, and cowl vent. If you are building the car, most of these interference problems can be easily overcome. If you are installing air conditioning in an existing car and don't want to tear the dashboard apart, then an in-dash unit becomes much tougher to install.

The glove box can often be saved, though a new, smaller liner may be necessary. Some aftermarket air conditioning kits include just such a smaller inside box as part of their kits. Street rodders who aren't too attached to the glove box can simply eliminate it altogether.

Clearance problems with the instruments cluster around the speedometer (no pun intended). If the speedo cable is the problem, you can either go to an electric speedometer or install a right-angle drive to move the cable over and out of the way. The rest of the gauges should be kept clustered on the driver's side to avoid interference with the evaporator housing.

The fuse panel should also be mounted on the driver's side to keep it clear of the evapora-

Another very neat evaporator installation is in Jamie Musselman's Ford. The evaporator housing is tucked up behind the dash until it's nearly invisible.

The driver's side of Jamie's dash. The narrow vent set vertically works well on the left side of the gauges. The center vent is same design, turned ninety degrees.

tor. This will also keep most of the major wiring junctions on the driver's side and easier to get at if trouble develops.

The cowl vent problem is really a problem of interference with the linkage. Your options include sealing the vent or redesigning the linkage to work around the evaporator housing. Some enterprising street rodders have converted the cowl vent to cable operation and others have electrified the vent's operation with a screw motor.

If the unit you purchase is an in-dash evaporator, you need to decide if the vents should be mounted in the dash or under the dash. Through-dash installations are neat and look more finished, though in most cases it means cutting holes in that jennie sheet metal. Some innovative solutions have been found to this dilemma—like the ashtray-vents available for '40 Fords.

Some very clean-looking aluminum vents are available for through-dash vent installations. You probably need one on each end of the dash and one central vent. If you want to hide the central vent (don't block it off at the evaporator case) just paint it flat black and tuck it up under the lip of the dash. The result is a very neat and unobtrusive air conditioning installation. The ducts and round dash vents should be at least 2in in diameter, and 2 1/2in would be better. (Remember that a small increase in the diameter of a opening results in a large increase in the area.)

Many of the new evaporator assemblies offer both heating and cooling. Anyone installing an in-dash evaporator should consider eliminating the factory heater as a means of opening up some space behind the dash. The heater built into the heat/cool evaporator assembly probably works better than the factory unit anyway, and most of

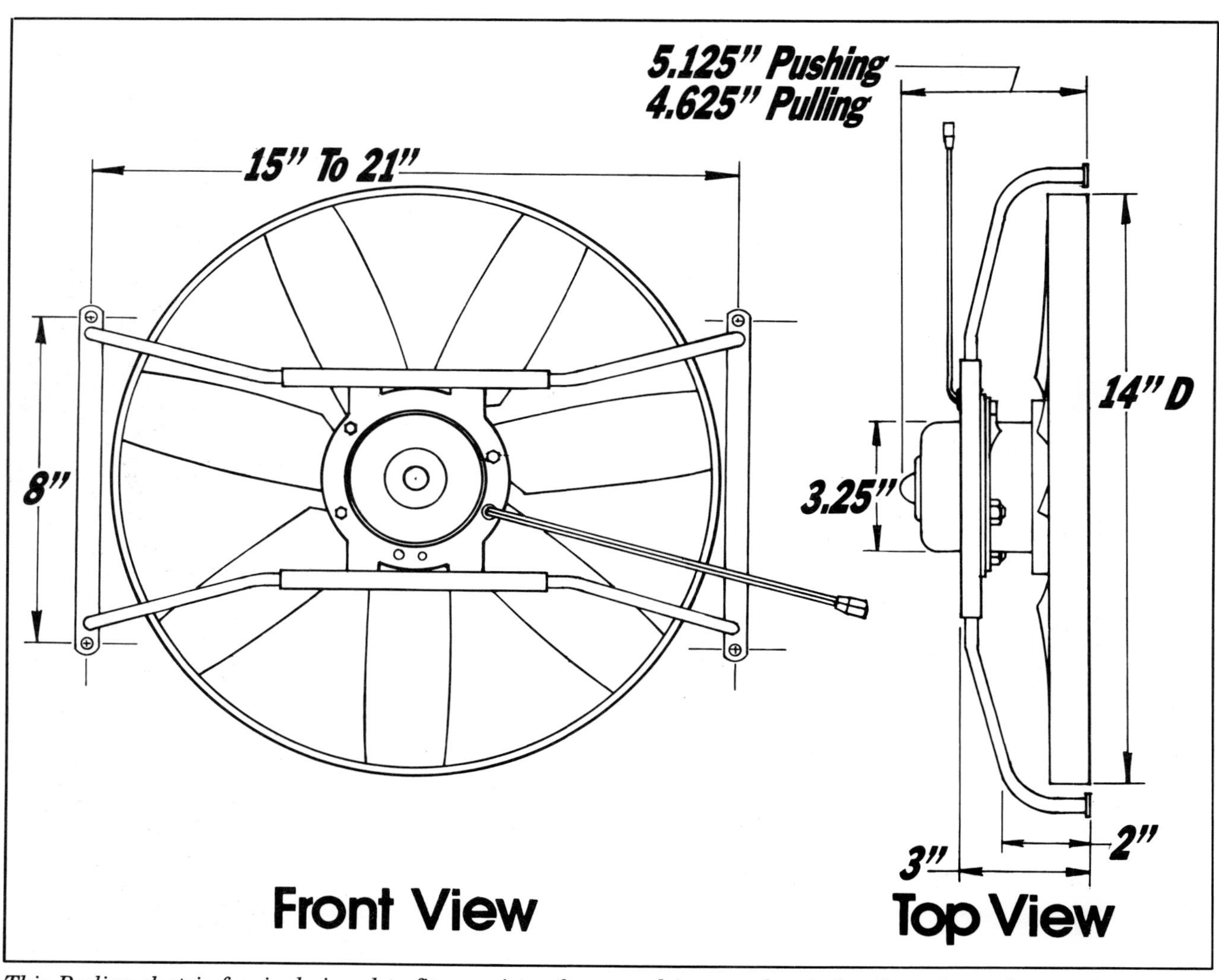

This Proline electric fan is designed to fit a variety of radiators and move a lot of air. Whether you use a belt-driven or electric fan depends on the car, the installation, and your personal preferences. Vintage Air

these units offer optional defrosters.

When you install the evaporator, it must be set in the car with the drain pan and tubes pointing down so the condensation will drain out of the car. The air outlets should be positioned so they blow directly on the driver and passengers. Other locations usually produce disappointing results. The evaporator housing should be as close to the outlets as possible—keep the ducts as short as you can. The thermostat tube should be inserted at least 2in into the evaporator coil and the blower should always recirculate the cabin air. (The manufacturer will probably provide for the correct location of the thermostat tube).

Note: the thermostat tube is charged with refrigerant, so don't bend the tube so sharply that it cracks or you will lose the refrigerant and need a new thermostat.

Before actually hanging the evaporator housing, be sure to plug up any holes or cracks in the firewall to limit the entry of hot, humid air from outside the car. Insulate the floor and firewall—before doing the final mounting of the evaporator housing. It's best to take some time and mock-up the evaporator housing in what seems like the best location and then check the routing of the ducts and hoses before drilling holes and making brackets.

Once the unit's installed and operating, remember to limit the entry into the cabin of outside air (via windows, open doors, etc.) and thus limit the entry of hot, humid air.

Hoses and Fittings

Most aftermarket kits are supplied with enough hoses and fittings to completely plumb the air conditioner. Due to the special needs of each street rodder, sometimes something other

The '39 Ford showing the way the hoses are routed and clamped. Note the crimped fittings and the way the hoses to and from the evaporator are clamped together so the hot liquid line can warm the cool suction line, and the suction line can help to cool the liquid line.

The use of crimped fittings and neat bulkhead fittings at the firewall make for a super-neat installation.

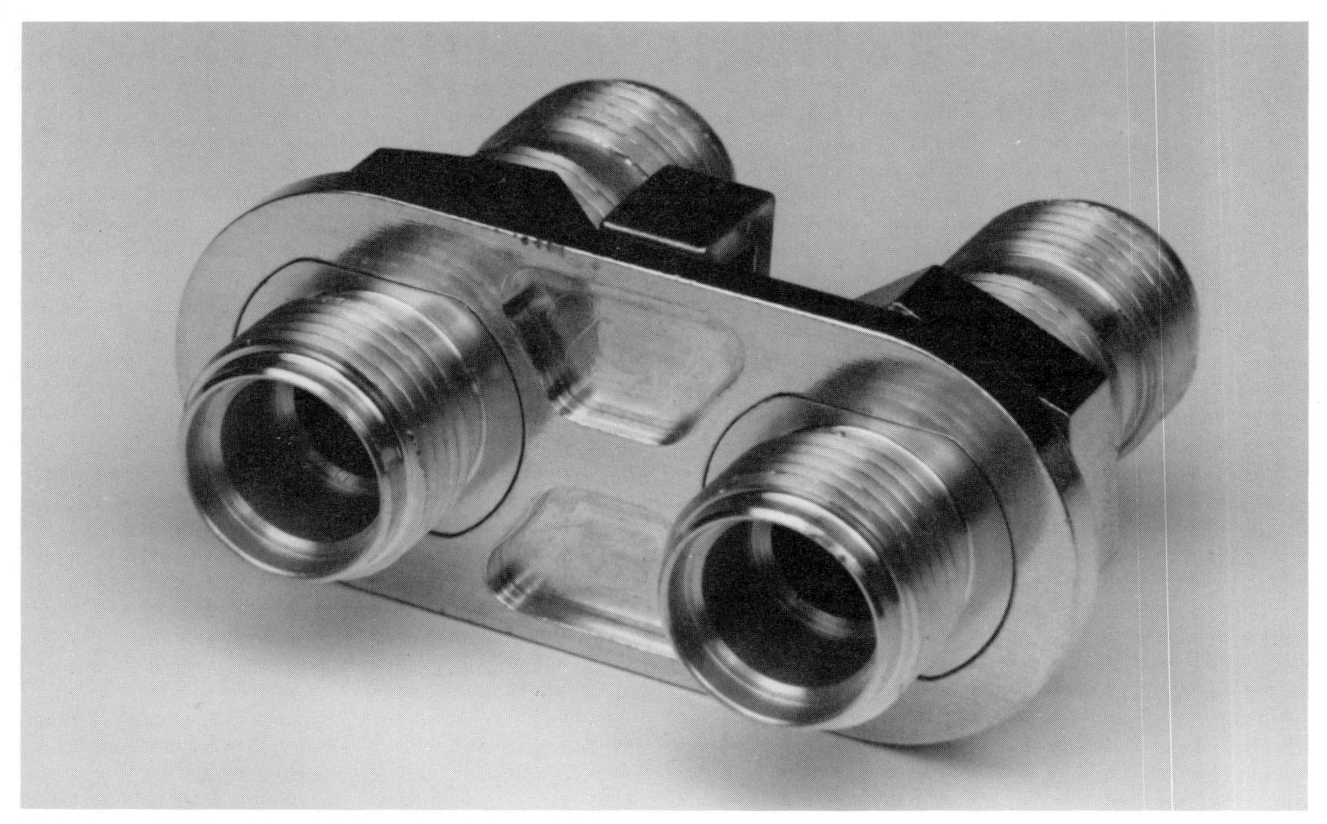

This clever, billet bulkhead fitting plate is intended for the street rod market though it would ensure a neat installation in nearly any car. Vintage Air

This high-rise water pump housing is designed to raise the water pump—and the fan hub—on street rods where the engine sits very low in the frame. The housing accepts a six-cylinder Chevy pump. Not all of these housings have the same mounting points for alternators and other accessories.

than the standard hose kits may be needed. In particular, stainless steel tubing kits (which are available from suppliers such as Vintage Air) help create a very clean installation. If you choose to stick with conventional hoses, be sure they have a nylon liner (whether yours is a CFC-12 or HFC-134A system). Where the rubber hose meets the metal fittings, you can use either the new compression-style clamps (no worm gear clamps on barrier hoses) or a crimped fitting. Compact crimping tools are available, so crimps can be made in your shop—even on the car. Or you can pre-cut the hoses and determine which fittings are needed for the end of each hose, and take it all in to the local air conditioning shop and let them crimp the ends.

The fittings themselves should be O-ring style, as flare fittings just don't seal well enough anymore. If you are installing an HFC-134A system, be sure all the hoses, fittings, and O-rings are compatible with the new refrigerant and lubricants.

The evaporator is supplied with at least two refrigerant hoses (heat/cool units need four hoses, of course). The larger hose (often 1/2in in diameter) is hard to bend around obstacles under

INSTALLATION INSTRUCTIONS
CONTROL PANEL
(49120-VUQ)

1. Cut out template on outer doted line.
2. Tape template to dash with masking tape.
3. Mark dash with marker or scribe.
4. Snip opening for panel.
5. Wire panel according to wiring diagram.
6. Insert panel from front of dash.
7. Install switch mounting plate to panel with two screws. This will secure panel in place.
8. Test controls.
   - A. Top left lever is fan speed.
     - •LO,MEDIUM AND HIGH.
     - •This will also engage the A/C Compressor clutch in any position other than OFF.
   - B. Top right lever is unit Thermostat.
   - C. Bottom right lever is mode switch.
     - •ECONOMY
     - •A/C
     - •HEATER
     - •DEF.

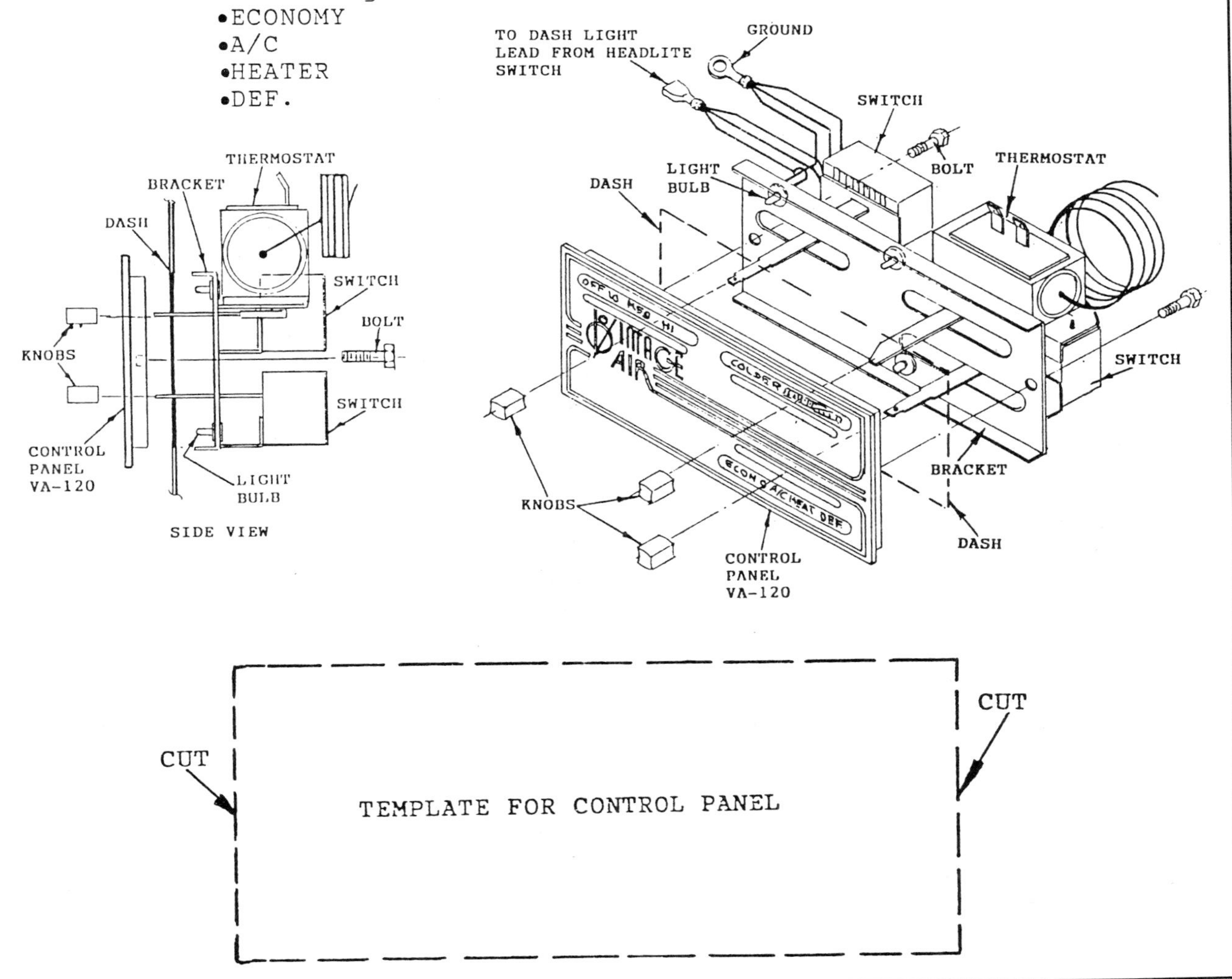

This instruction sheet shows the installation of a typical aftermarket air conditioning control panel. Most aftermarket units feature three controls—the air conditioning thermostat, the fan switch, and the mode switch. Vintage Air

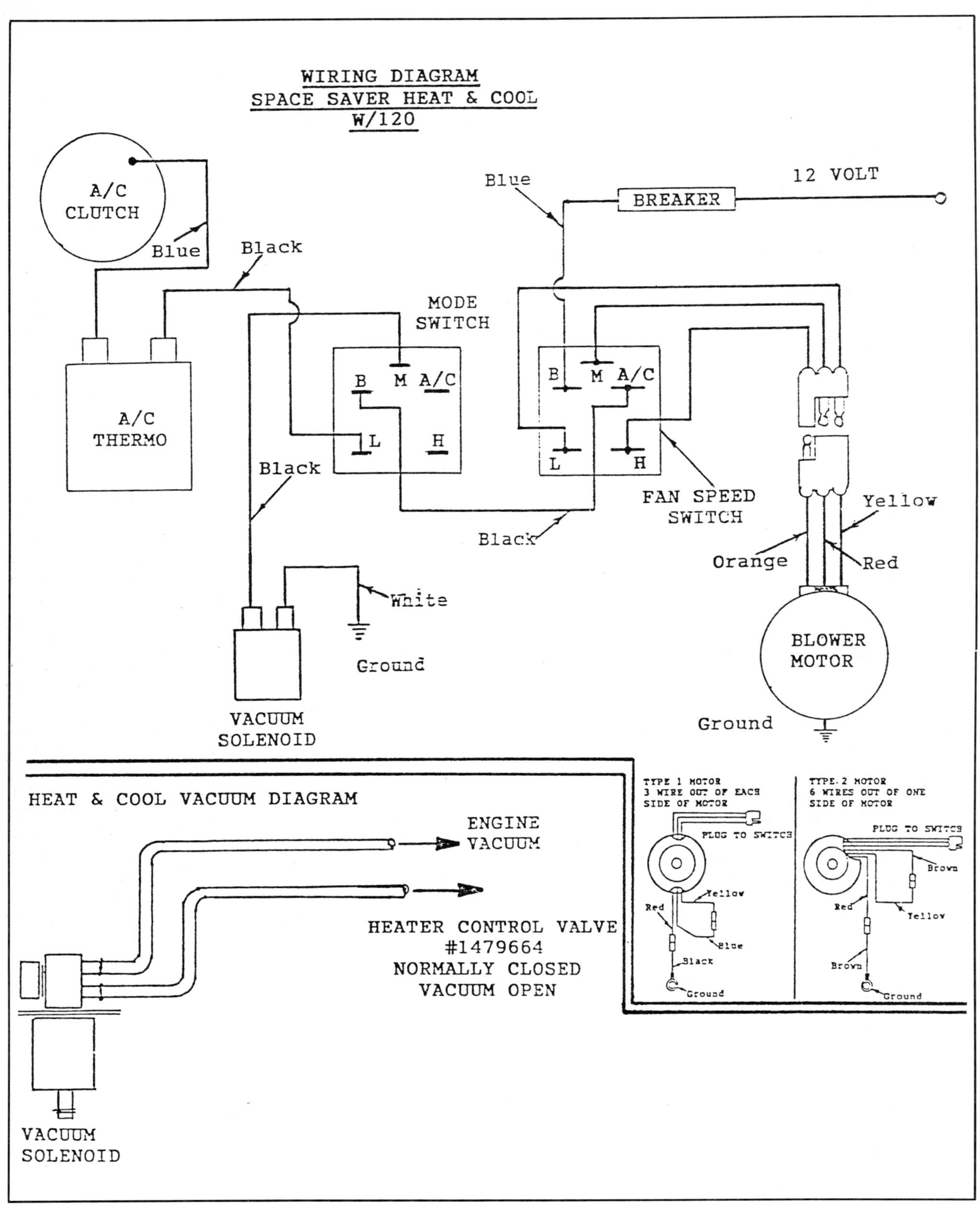

Wiring an aftermarket air conditioner is pretty simple, as illustrated by these instructions. You should make all wiring as neat as possible, solder all connections and wrap any loose wires into a small harness. Vintage Air

the dash. That's why it's best to mock-up the evaporator and then give considerable thought to the routing of the hoses.

On some later cars, like a '48 Chevy, the hoses can run from the evaporator to the kick panel, and pass through the kick panel instead of the firewall. This makes a neater installation and keeps the firewall nice and clean. From the kick panel the hoses can run along the frame rail to the compressor and condenser.

Cars like a Deuce or Model A will have to run the hoses through the firewall. You should use a grommet at the firewall to protect the hoses where they pass through the metal firewall. A variety of two and four hose bulkhead fittings are available in aluminum to help make the hose routing as neat as possible.

Once you have determined the correct routing for the evaporator hoses, the evaporator will have to be pulled out of the car one more time so the fittings can be tightened. Be sure to use two wrenches, one on the fitting and one on the evaporator. You also need to be sure to wrap the fittings with press-tape to avoid condensation dripping off the fittings onto the carpet.

The routing you choose for the hoses as they run from the firewall to the compressor and condenser will depend on the car, the location of those other components, and your personal taste. Remember that the high-pressure hose coming into the evaporator (smaller diameter) should be kept cool and that the suction line that runs from the evaporator to the inlet of the compressor (larger diameter) can run close to the engine where it will gain some heat. These two hoses can even be clamped together.

When Detroit designs an air conditioning system, they leave enough flex in the hoses so the compressor can be pulled off the engine—without opening the system—if the engine must be removed from the car. Considering the expense of recharging the air conditioner, that seems like a very sound idea.

When the system is completely installed, it's a good idea to have it evacuated and leak tested by a professional before you put all the shielding and the interior back together. That way, if there's a leak, it's easier to find and repair.

Cooling Fans and Switches

Every car with air conditioning needs a good fan to draw air over the condenser and the radiator. With street rods this is especially true and especially tough to do. Street rod engines often end up rather low in the frame relative to the radiator position. There are a number of possible solutions to this dilemma, and two of them in particular seem most logical.

First, you might want to raise the level of the water pump and thus the fan. Yes, a "high-rise" water pump housing is available for the small-block Chevy that will aid in putting the fan up where it ought to be. (There is also a solution for the other extreme—where the engine ends up too high—as is the case on some '39 and '40 Fords. For these situations, a kit is available to mount the fan to the lower crankshaft pulley.)

The other solution is to install one or two electric fans controlled by a radiator thermostat and a high-side pressure switch. The final decision is yours and will depend on your car, the available room, the cooling needs of your engine, and your personal preferences. If you do install electric fans, be sure to buy fans that are big enough to move enough air, and be sure to put them on the inside—in a pulling position—rather than the outside. By putting them on the inside of the radiator, they won't obstruct airflow trying to move through the radiator when you're going down the highway. (Auxiliary fans can be put on the outside of the radiator if necessary.)

Installing air conditioning in a street rod is tougher than in some other cars. There's sometimes no place to put it and the rest of the car is so perfect, that nothing less than perfection in the air conditioning installation will do. To solve this apparent dilemma requires above-average mechanical ability, above-average parts, and more than enough time to carry out the project. It all begins with some careful planning.

Installing A/C in an American Classic Car

When it comes to installing air conditioning, each type of car has advantages and disadvantages . The classic American car from the 1950s and 1960s is a different animal than a street rod, an old classic, or a kit car. Buying and installing air conditioning in one of these fine old vehicles provides a unique set of challenges.

Because these 1950s and 1960s classics are essentially modern cars, with hydraulic brakes, good suspension, and powerful engines, they cry out for more use. "Drive me," they cry from the garage stall. And in order to more fully utilize these cars they need just a bit of modernizing in the comfort department. The addition of air conditioning means that instead of taking the daily driver to the picnic on a warm Sunday afternoon, the owner can take the '55 Chevy or the '60 Pontiac, because it has air conditioning just like the new daily driver. Air conditioning is the one thing lacking in most of these cars. It's the one

An American classic with a straight eight—and an alternator with enough power to run all the accessories and the air conditioning. Note the receiver-drier mounted low in the firewall.

Another classic, this Packard has been updated and equipped with a better-than-average air conditioner. The owner had air conditioning installed so he could get more use from the car.

The dashboard of the Packard. The evaporator hangs in a custom under-dash unit that leaves the original dashboard intact and eliminates the necessity for ducts. On large cars like this, under-dash units work well and leave plenty of foot room.

thing that can transform the car from "garage queen" to a "real car," one that can be used on a regular basis.

What is an American Classic?

For our purposes, an American classic is an American car built between the years 1949 and about 1975. 1949 makes a good starting point, as that was the year that started the great post-war automotive revolution, and most street rodders consider 1948 to be the last year for a true street rod. The upper end is harder to define. 1975 seems about right, as the cars built after that date took on a new, smaller, look. Not only were the later cars less like their classic predecessors, by the mid-1970s many cars carried air conditioning as standard equipment.

This group of American Classics breaks down into two groups: The early cars manufactured from 1949 to about 1952 or 1953, and the later cars manufactured after 1953. Though manufactured after the war, the early cars aren't nearly as "modern" as the later models. Cars from the late 1940s and very early 1950s tend to carry older style engines, small fans, 6volt electrical systems, and wide, old-style fan belts. There are complete kits available for some of the more popular cars from this period. However, if your classic ride is a '53 Dodge rather than a '52 Chevy, installing air conditioning is going to be a little more difficult.

The Problems Unique to Early Classics

The problems of installing air conditioning in one of these early classics are many, so it will help to discuss each problem, one at a time.

One of the biggest drawbacks is the 6volt electrical system. All the aftermarket air conditioners are designed to run on 12volts. Yes, you can convert the pulley clutch, the fan, and the controls to 6volts, but the effort may not justify the results. In particular, 6volt fans (or a 12volt fan converted to 6volts) tend to be rather anemic in air delivery when compared to 12volt fans.

A better solution is to bite the bullet and convert your electrical system to 12volts. Go just one step further while you're at it and replace the generator with an alternator. An alternator with a minimum of 65amps will ensure that you have

The trunk of the Packard—two more evaporators. Multiple evaporators can be controlled by in-line solenoids that control refrigerant flow.

enough power to handle the lights, accessories, and your new air conditioning system as well.

The subject of converting an electrical system from 6volts to 12volts could be a book in itself. For guidance we turned to Steve Stutts, from Texas Industrial Electric in San Antonio, Texas.

Steve feels that each conversion is different, that the job depends on the car and the car's owner. The owner of a '49 Ford with stock running gear and no air conditioning will need a different electrical system than the owner of a '49 Merc custom. The owner of the Mercury needs to power the air conditioner, the killer stereo with its own separate amplifier, the halogen headlights, and the electric windshield wipers.

For this book we assume that everyone needs 12volts and enough amperage to run all the standard accessories *and* the air conditioner. Converting to 12volts means converting everything, all the bulbs, the ignition, and all the accessories.

Before getting too far along with this discussion, we need to back up and review Ohm's law. Mr. Ohm figured out that the amount of current

In this Corvette air conditioning installation the Frigidaire compressor was used to give the installation a factory look.

(amperage) moving down a wire is dependent on the voltage pushing it divided by the resistance of the wire. Written as a formula, it looks like: $C=V/R$. From looking at the formula, you can see that if you double the voltage on a circuit you cut the amperage in half. So, in going from 6volts to 12volts you cut the amperage in the circuit by half.

Amperage is the primary factor affecting the size of wire needed in a circuit. Going from 6volts to 12volts means that the standard 6volt wiring is now more than heavy enough because each circuit is carrying roughly half the amperage it was originally designed to carry.

The wiring we're dealing with is obviously heavy enough and can often be left intact for the conversion. Steve Stutts likes to examine the original harness to check its condition and to see if it's been affected by "tinker-itis." If the harness has been "repaired" in a dozen places and the insulation is in poor condition, then he recommends a new harness. If, however, the harness has been left alone and the insulation is in good condition, Steve uses the stock wiring as the basis for the conversion.

Changing the bulbs is really just a matter of taking the bulbs down to the local parts store and buying a 12volt replacement for each 6volt bulb. Steve reports that most 6volt starters will run just fine on 12volts, without any converting.

The generator should be replaced with an alternator. Steve feels that 65amps of output is the minimum necessary for a car with air conditioning. If the car carries other electrical accessories, then 65amps probably isn't enough. He recommends that you add up the total of all your accessories and consider that figure as eighty percent of the total alternator output. If your total draw was 80amps, then you should mount an alternator with a capacity of 100amps.

Some people want to keep their generators, thinking that a heavy duty generator with 45 or 50amps is enough. The problem here isn't just total output. That generator might put out 50amps, but only when the engine is at 3000rpm or more. At idle, the generator is only going to

A Sanden 508 on a simple steel bracket was used on this El Camino installation. The belt must contact the pulley over at least one-third of its circumference.

Another 508 compressor, this time on a '57 Chevy. Belt alignment must be good or there will be problems with belt loss and short belt life.

put out 5-10amps, and the air conditioning (drawing 20amps by itself) will create a major discharge on the battery. An alternator with the same 50amps output will put out nearly half that output at idle. The advantage of converting to an alternator isn't just total output, it's the output available for low-speed operation, like idling and slow-speed cruising.

When Steve puts an alternator on a car with old, wide belts, he often changes the alternator pulley to match the old belt size. His source of pulleys is an alternator shop that specializes in agricultural and heavy duty equipment where pulleys of the right width, diameter, and shaft diameter can usually be found.

Street rodders and owners of old cars converted to 12volts like the idea of the one-wire GM alternators because of their simplicity. The modification (as Steve does it) is to the regulator inside the alternator. He also recommends that you buy your alternator from a good, quality rebuilder—avoid the sale special at the local discount store.

Steve has learned a number of tricks in his years of converting old cars to modern 12volt systems: "Those old cars don't have any protection for the circuits. They didn't have any fuses, just a few in-line fuse holders stuck up in the wiring someplace. If we don't put in a whole harness with a new fuse block, I like to add a fusible link to the main feed wire. If the feed wire is a ten gauge for example, then I add a fourteen gauge fusible link in that ten gauge wire. That way an electrical short won't melt the whole wiring harness."

The other problem area in most 12volt conversions is the gauges. You can convert the whole affair to 12volt aftermarket gauges, or your can convert the 6volt gauges to run on 12volts. The two gauges that must commonly be converted are the gas gauge and the water temperature gauge.

The correct way to convert the gauges is to measure the amperage draw of each gauge while they operate on 6volts. Next, plug that amperage draw into Ohm's law to determine the resistor

This is a '55 Chevy with stock running gear and a Sanden 508 compressor. The Chevy was already a 12volt car so no electrical conversion was necessary.

you need to keep the gauge at that current draw when it runs on 12volts. For example, a 6volt gas gauge with a draw of one amp has a resistance of 6ohms (1 amp = 6volts/6ohms) When the voltage increases to 12volts, the resistance must increase to 12 also, to keep the amperage through the gauge the same.

Steve often uses a resistor from Niehoff that is rated at 1 1/2 ohms (#UN 135A), running more than one in a series to get the correct amount of resistance. (Don't put them in parallel unless you know what you're doing.) Be sure any resistors you use are heavy duty, ceramic resistors in a housing of some kind, and remember that these get hot, so mount them accordingly. For those who don't want to figure out Ohm's law, there are conversion boxes available from some of the big automotive stores and warehouses that will convert your gauges to run on 12volts. However, the easier route of course costs more.

Steve's final words of advice are: "Don't skimp on the electrical part of the job. People think nothing of spending a thousand dollars on a paint job, but they argue over nickels and dimes when they come in here to have the car

Here is a two-row tube-and-fin condenser, mounted in front of the radiator on this '57 Chevy. Sturdy installation brackets are part of the installation kit for this car.

Condenser size should correlate to evaporator size, so ask the manufacturer if you're in doubt about which condenser to purchase.

converted to 12volts. I know it's hard to spend the money on things they can't see but with electrical work you get just what you pay for. Cheap work means a cheap job with inferior products, work and products that are likely to fail someplace down the road. Electrical work is the one thing most owners won't do themselves—so they should spend the money and have it done right—that way they won't ever have to fool with it."

Though Steve often leaves the alternator running on wide belts, you need to choose the best belt to drive the compressor. Compressors can be ordered with wide pulleys, or you can convert all or part of the drive belts on the car to modern belt sizes. If the alternator (or another pulley) will run on the same belt as the compressor, then the choice of alternator and the drive-belt selections are tied together.

Some owners like to convert all the pulleys to modern sizes. A double groove, 1/2in pulley takes up only about as much room as a single 3/4in pulley. Often you can find a pulley that will bolt on at the crankshaft. If not, a new pulley can be welded to the old pulley base with the correct

This Vintage Air kit is made for Corvettes. The condenser fits neatly with the kit's brackets. All parts are designed to look neat and eliminate the need to drill holes and fabricate brackets.

bolt pattern. Perform this operation carefully, as a failure can be expensive as well as annoying. Be sure the shop that does the welding does a good job, and that the new pulley is concentric and spaced correctly so the belts run true.

Your actual solution to the belt problem will depend on the car, the number of belt-driven accessories, and how you plan to route (and tension) the drive belt for the compressor. This is a situation where planning pays big dividends. More ideas are available in chapter 4, from Vintage Air, or by checking at a car show to see how other individuals with cars similar to yours have solved the riddle of the drive belts.

Some of these cars, especially the Chevrolets with their six-cylinder engines, don't have much room between the radiator and the water pump. With the addition of air conditioning you're going to want a bigger fan, no doubt driven by a modern fan belt. Jack reports that Chevrolets from the early 1950s with stock engines have enough room for a bigger, thicker fan and a shroud—but just barely. The central peg on the water pump is bigger (nearly 1in) on these old cars, so the fan will have to be drilled larger to slip over the water pump. The fan hole must stay perfectly centered—or the new fan won't run true and might take the radiator out with it.

By listing the problems of installing air conditioning in an early classic, we may have made the job seem tougher than it really is. There is a silver lining here. Complete air conditioning kits are available for some cars, early Chevrolets for example. If your car is an Oldsmobile, creative research might prove that many of the Chevrolet components will adapt to the Oldsmobile, or Pontiac. Even if complete kits are not available, compressor brackets often are. Brackets are available for six-cylinder Chevrolets, and Flathead and Y-block Ford engines.

Installing air conditioning in an early American classic isn't impossible, just a little more challenging than for some other cars.

American Classics Built After 1953 or 1954

Compressor

Putting a compressor on an American Classic is a reasonably simple operation, especially with the later cars. Most of these engines have ade-

The condenser in this El Camino mounts with brackets supplied with the air conditioning kit. This too is a tube-and-fin style of condenser—though that will change as the industry changes over to HFC-134A systems.

quate power to run the compressor and feature modern-sized drive belts. You first need to know how big a compressor to mount, then choose the best way to mount it to the engine.

Once again, the 508 model Sanden/Sankyo compressor is the overwhelming favorite. This compressor has enough capacity to cool anything but a limousine or an application with two evaporators. Because these classic cars are bigger than street rods (which often use the 508 compressor), it might seem you need a bigger compressor for a bigger car. Once again, you must avoid the bigger is better mentality. The compressor needs to be matched to the evaporator and these American Classics cool off just fine with evaporators that are about the same size as those used in the smaller street rods. Too much compressor means more internal pressure, more vibration, and the need for more horsepower to operate the unit.

Owners of very large sedans, with very large or double evaporators, can use the larger 510 compressor. A better choice might be the model 709, with seven cylinders and 9ci of displacement.

Mounting the compressor is relatively easy for most of these classics as there is abundant room under the hood. The location for the compressor will often be dictated by the available bracket rather than by underhood restrictions. In general, these cars have more room to the sides of the engine than do street rods. When laying out the bracket and drive belt, remember that you need an alternator to ensure enough amperage for air conditioning operation. Many of the brackets are designed as an assembly, to mount both the compressor and the alternator. This makes the job of laying out brackets and belts much easier.

Mounting the brackets requires common sense. Remember to use lock washers or lock nuts and bolts of high quality on all brackets and hardware. Belt alignment needs to be very good if you're running V-belts, and nearly perfect if you use a serpentine belt. More hints for a clean compressor installation can be found in chapter 4.

Condenser

Getting a condenser of the right size is again made easier if you buy a good kit. Jack's recommendation is that the condenser be twenty-five

Large American cars like this '55 Chevy generally have plenty of room to mount big condensers—it's always better to have it too big than too small—and the receiver-drier in front of the radiator. The generator on this car is scheduled to be replaced with an alternator.

percent larger in mass than the evaporator. Thus a 200ci evaporator needs a 250ci condenser. (Note, these rules of thumb apply only to CFC-12 systems using tube-and-fin style condensers.) Because the condenser is the unit that actually sheds the heat to the outside air, bigger tends to be better.

If these big American cars have an advantage when it comes to air conditioning installations, it is the abundant room under the hood. If the condenser you're installing is a tube-and -in design, a size of 14x23in or maybe 14x20in is a good starting point (in CFC-12 systems).

Because of the abundant room, you probably won't have to use a serpentine or parallel flow style of condenser with their greater efficiencies. Remember, though, that the condenser cannot touch the radiator and that the tubes must be horizontal rather than vertical (on CFC-12 systems).

Individuals who make their own condenser brackets should remember that there must be an air gap of at least 3/16in between the condenser and the radiator and that the condenser should never touch the radiator. Jack recommends that you center the evaporator over the radiator and use mounting brackets that don't block off too much of the airflow over the radiator. (The condenser should be centered over the engine fan if you don't have a shroud.)

The brackets should attach to the radiator saddle or flange, or the radiator support brackets. By using a small brake (or just the edge of the bench) you can create a nice, neat stepped bracket that will securely mount the condenser and leave an air gap between the condenser and the radiator.

Receiver-Drier

The receiver-drier you buy depends on your car and the rest of your system. If everything else is chrome plated and polished, you may want a polished receiver-drier and bracket as

By placing the receiver-drier in front, it gets plenty of fresh air so the liquid refrigerant remains a liquid. It also puts the sight glass right up there where you can see it during charging.

This '57 Chevy kit puts the receiver-drier up front, mounted directly to the condenser. With the use of tubing instead of hose, the installation becomes very neat and very effective.

This in-dash installation in a '55 Chevy shows how an aftermarket kit can be designed and installed to look like a factory installation. The evaporator housing mounts behind the dash, and factory outlets are used at the outside of the dash.

A similar factory-look installation in a '57 Chevy. Outer vents are from Chevrolet. The center vent could be tucked up under the dash to hide it from view.

The use of factory vents, like these '57 Chevy units gives an in-dash unit a very nice "finished" look.

well. If you're installing an HFC-134A system, then the receiver-drier will have to be designed to operate with that new refrigerant. If all you're doing is installing air conditioning without regard to how show-worthy the underhood area is, then any of the standard receiver-driers will work. For the best in quality, buy a full-flow receiver-drier, one with a replaceable filter and desiccant bag.

The large space between the grille and the radiator on most of these cars means that the logical place to mount the receiver-drier is in front of the condenser. Mount the receiver-drier to the condenser with the right bracket and mount them in front of the radiator as a unit.

The abundant fresh air will help keep the liquid refrigerant in liquid form. The high visibility of the behind-grille location makes it easy to see the sight glass and easy to service the receiver-drier when necessary.

A custom panel with vents was manufactured for this classic—making for a neat installation yet leaving the stock dashboard alone.

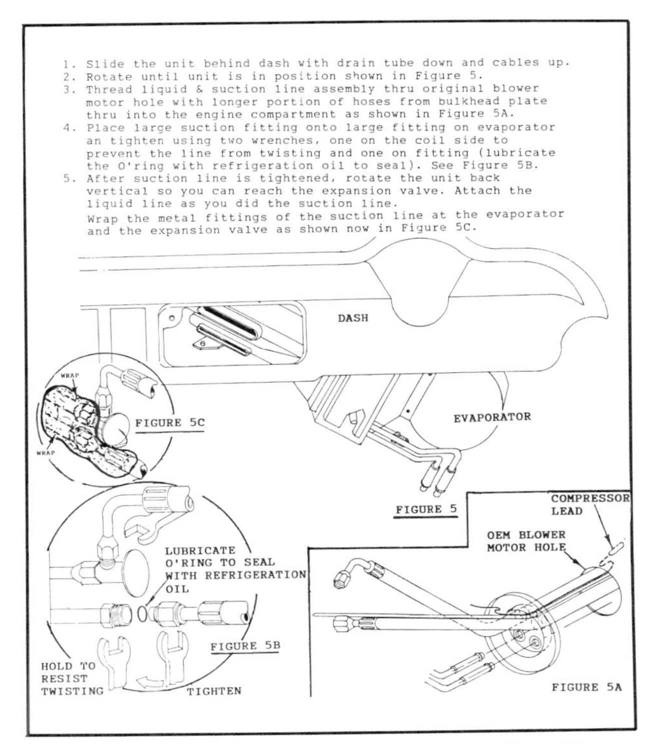
1. Slide the unit behind dash with drain tube down and cables up.
2. Rotate until unit is in position shown in Figure 5.
3. Thread liquid & suction line assembly thru original blower motor hole with longer portion of hoses from bulkhead plate thru into the engine compartment as shown in Figure 5A.
4. Place large suction fitting onto large fitting on evaporator an tighten using two wrenches, one on the coil side to prevent the line from twisting and one on fitting (lubricate the O'ring with refrigeration oil to seal). See Figure 5B.
5. After suction line is tightened, rotate the unit back vertical so you can reach the expansion valve. Attach the liquid line as you did the suction line.
Wrap the metal fittings of the suction line at the evaporator and the expansion valve as shown now in Figure 5C.

These instructions are intended for a '55/'56 Chevy, but they give a good overview of the work involved in installing air conditioning in a vehicle of this sort.

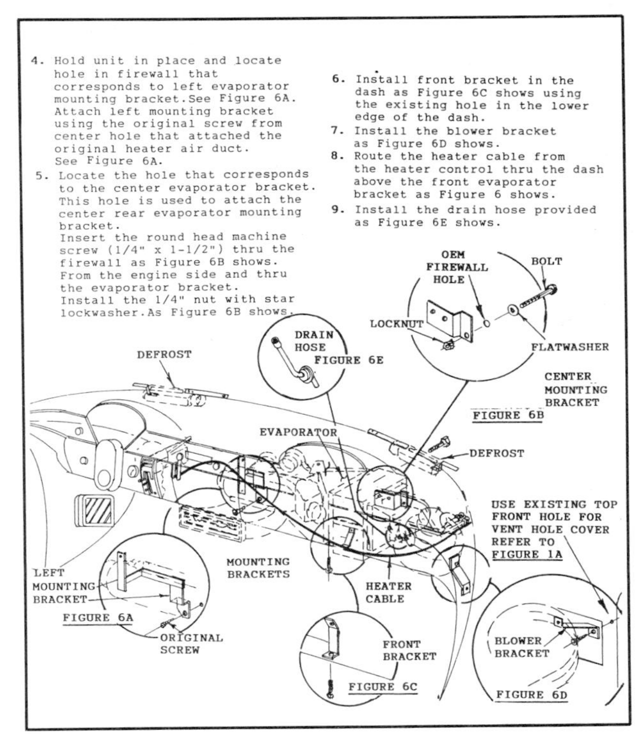
4. Hold unit in place and locate hole in firewall that corresponds to left evaporator mounting bracket. See Figure 6A. Attach left mounting bracket using the original screw from center hole that attached the original heater air duct. See Figure 6A.
5. Locate the hole that corresponds to the center evaporator bracket. This hole is used to attach the center rear evaporator mounting bracket.
Insert the round head machine screw (1/4" x 1-1/2") thru the firewall as Figure 6B shows. From the engine side and thru the evaporator bracket. Install the 1/4" nut with star lockwasher. As Figure 6B shows.
6. Install front bracket in the dash as Figure 6C shows using the existing hole in the lower edge of the dash.
7. Install the blower bracket as Figure 6D shows.
8. Route the heater cable from the heater control thru the dash above the front evaporator bracket as Figure 6 shows.
9. Install the drain hose provided as Figure 6E shows.

When you buy a kit, look for quality parts—and quality instructions. Vintage Air

Very few factory big-block Camaros of this vintage came with air conditioning as the engine left darned little room for the necessary components. This one has been air conditioned with an aftermarket kit.

The interior of the same Camaro. A Vintage Air in-dash evaporator and kit was used for an incredibly clean installation. This kit eliminates the factory heater to create room for the evaporator (which includes a heat option).

This Camaro installation even leaves the glove box (at least part of it) intact and usable.

Evaporator

If your Classic American cruiser is a true classic, like a '57 Chevy, then this part is easy. Evaporator assemblies designed to fit many popular Chevrolet and Ford products are available. Suppliers such as Vintage Air make evaporators to fit everything from a '49 Chevy to a '64 Mustang. Custom evaporators are available for '65 Corvettes, restored Thunderbirds, and Camaros and Firebirds, to name just a few.

Owners of less popular cars still have plenty of evaporator assemblies to choose from. The first decision is again, in-dash or under-dash. These large cars take an under-dash unit with ease, leaving plenty of room for passengers' feet. Aftermarket manufacturers make a variety of under-dash evaporators, nearly all with ample capacity to cool the interior in all but the most enormous sedans.

Many of these under-dash evaporators are available as heat/cool units, allowing you to replace the old factory heater or install a heater in a car that didn't come with one. Not only are these evaporators easy to install, they deliver good airflow—direct from the plenum without any restriction caused by hoses and vents.

Doing a nice job of mounting an under-dash unit means taking the time to mock-up the installation and then carefully considering the routing of the hoses. Bulkhead fittings are available for many of these cars that run the hoses into the car through the firewall where the heater fan would normally protrude. Obviously, this is not an option if you decide to leave the old heater intact.

The underhood view of the big-block Camaro. Note how the hoses run neatly, enter the interior through what was the hole for the factory heater fan.

Mounting an in-dash evaporator is of course more work, yet the good news is that the final result will likely appear to be factory installed air conditioning. Because many of these cars came with some kind of factory air you can often purchase the factory dash vents and connect them to the aftermarket evaporator for a true factory installed look. If this is the route you want to take,

Aftermarket air conditioning kits often include controls that closely resemble factory controls. This unit for a '55 Chevy is hard to tell from a Chevrolet part.

spend some time calling the aftermarket air conditioning manufacturers. Tell them which car you have, give them the behind-dash dimensions, and they can probably match up an evaporator that fits.

Factory style control assemblies are available for some of these cars—so your '56 Chevy's air conditioning and heater are both controlled by the very original looking, cable-operated controls on the dashboard.

Cars from the 1950s and 1960s have plenty of room between the firewall and the dashboard, though as they got more modern, they also became more crowded under the dash. One of the biggest obstacles to the easy installation of an in-dash unit in many of these cars is the factory heater. The answer? Throw out the heater and buy an evaporator with heat/cool and defrost. This also opens up the hole in the firewall where the heater fan/housing protruded so you can run the liquid and suction lines through the existing hole (with the use of a bulkhead assembly from one of the aftermarket companies). The result is a neat installation, done without cutting any holes in the firewall.

The fittings for the liquid and suction line running to and from the evaporator will need to be tightened with the evaporator on the bench, using two wrenches to avoid damaging the evaporator or expansion valve.

Hoses and Fittings

Again, a wide variety of hoses and fittings are available. If you buy a complete kit, then all (or at least most) of the hoses and fittings will be provided. Stainless steel tubing kits (designed for the street rod industry) are available from suppliers such as Vintage Air, to produce the ultimate in a clean installation. If you choose to stay with conventional hoses, be sure they have a nylon liner (regardless of whether yours is an CFC-12 or HFC-134A system). Hoses for a HFC-134A system should be marked with the new SAE specification: "J51AII."

Where the rubber hose meets the metal fittings, you can use either a compression-style clamp (no worm-gear clamps on barrier hose), a crimped fitting, or the new fittings designed for HFC-134A. Small crimping tools are available, so the fittings can be crimped in your shop—or on the car. Or you can let the local air conditioning shop crimp the hose ends for you.

The fittings should be O-ring style, as flare

This Corvette kit features four vents and requires a minimum of drilling.

fittings just don't seal well enough. For HFC-134A systems, make certain that all the hoses, fittings, and O-rings are compatible with the new refrigerant and lubricants.

The evaporator is connected to two refrigerant hoses. The larger hose (or suction hose, often 1/2in diameter) is hard to route past obstacles under the dash. That's why it's best to mock-up the evaporator and then carefully consider exactly how you intend to route the hoses. Don't forget to carefully wrap the suction line fitting and part of the expansion valve with cork tape.

The routing you choose for the hoses as they run from the firewall to the compressor and condenser will depend on the car, the location of those other components, and your personal taste. Remember that the high-pressure hose coming into the evaporator (smaller diameter) should be kept cool, and the suction line that runs from the evaporator to the inlet of the compressor (larger diameter) can run close to the engine, where it will gain some heat. These two hoses can be clamped together.

Leave enough flex in the hoses near the compressor so the compressor can be pulled off the engine with the hoses intact if the engine must be removed from the car. That way you don't have to open the system (and later recharge it) every time the engine comes out of the car.

When the system is completely installed, it's a good idea to have it evacuated and leak tested by a professional before you put all the shielding and the interior back together. That way if there's a leak, it's easier to find and repair.

Cooling Fans and Other Details

Most of these American cars came with shrouds on the radiator. If your car did not, you will probably have to buy one or adapt one. A larger fan is probably a necessity as well (often available from the junk-yard or dealer) and maybe a catch-can for the radiator.

It goes without saying, but the air conditioning will put additional loads on the cooling system. If you're in doubt about the condition of the radiator or any other cooling system components, repair or replace them now—not after the car overheats fifty miles from home.

By installing air conditioning in your American cruiser, you've increased the "usability" of the car. It might not have more horsepower and it might not handle better than it did before the installation. Yet, by increasing the comfort, you've increased the performance—as measured from the driver's seat.

The evaporator for this Corvette hangs below the glove box on the right side yet leaves good legroom for the passenger.

Chapter 7

Installing A/C in a Pickup Truck

So you got yourself a good old all-American truck, and you've had it repainted and lowered. You put in a stereo system and a new interior, and now there's only one thing missing.

What's missing is air conditioning.

Because what Uncle Bob expected from his F100 in 1953 is a heck of a lot different from what you expect from the same vehicle forty-some years later.

Like cars from the same period, pickup trucks are modern in many ways and can easily be used as regular transportation. Trucks built after World War II feature good brakes, reasonable suspension, and modern (mostly) power plants. What's often missing is the comfort factor and thus the need for air conditioning.

The trucks covered in this chapter are those built after the war, trucks that are modern in

The compressor of choice for most aftermarket truck installations is the 508 Sanden. Brackets and complete kits are available for most popular Chevrolet and Ford trucks. This Ford bracket mounts the compressor on the left side and leaves the alternator on the right.

most of their characteristics.

The problems and advantages of these old trucks parallel those of the American classic cars. These trucks break down into two smaller groups, determined by the year of manufacture. The trucks built up through 1953 or 1954 belong to one era, and are harder to fit with air conditioning. Those built after 1954 are more thoroughly modern and can more easily be equipped with air conditioning.

Pickup Trucks Built Before 1953 or 1954

Trucks built immediately after the war lack much of the equipment that we take for granted today—equipment that makes installation of aftermarket air conditioning much easier. When you lift the hood on one of these old stockers, you will see no alternators, no 12volt batteries, and no modern 1/2in drive belts. On the positive side, however, you will see a cavernous engine compartment with plenty of extra space for mounting the components.

Planning the installation of air conditioning must include a way to overcome these obstacles.

The 6volt electrical system is probably the toughest problem. Again, it seems best to jump in with both feet and convert the entire vehicle to a 12volt electrical system. All aftermarket air conditioning systems are designed to run on 12volts. Yes, you can convert the pulley clutch, the fan, and the controls to 6volts, but the effort may not be justified by the results. In particular, 6volt fans tend to be rather anemic in their air delivery when compared to 12volt fans. A better solution is to take the plunge and convert your electrical system to 12volts.

Chapter 6 contains good information on the conversion of 6volt systems to 12volts, and owners of 6volt trucks are encouraged to read that section.

When you convert the electrical system you can add an alternator at the same time. That way you are sure to have the 65amps necessary to run a vehicle equipped with air conditioning.

The alternator decision can be part of the larger decision concerning the drive for the compressor and any other accessories. Since you are going to install an alternator, you might choose

Trucks with small-block Chevy power can run these steel compressor and alternator brackets designed for use with the short water pump. Alan Grove

If your truck isn't a Chevy or a Ford you can fabricate compressor brackets easily by starting with these universal brackets.

to convert the truck to modern belts. The crank-pulley can be replaced with an aftermarket pulley, or a hybrid pulley can be fabricated by combining the old pulley base with a new 1/2in pulley.

If you decide to run a bigger fan with more blades, you'll need to install new pulleys. As trucks have plenty of room under the hood, you don't need to worry so much about how much room a new fan will take up. Buy a fan with at least five or six blades, 18in in diameter and 2in "thick."

Your solution to the belt problem will depend on the truck, the number of belt-driven accessories, and how you plan to route (and tension) the drive belt for the compressor. This is another case where planning ahead is rewarded with big dividends. Most of the decisions made to modernize an early truck are interrelated. The 12volt electrical conversion is part of the alternator conversion, which is often part of the belt-drive conversion—which is affected by and affects the new fan you intend to run. Look to chapter 4 for some guiding light or ask suppliers such as Vintage Air.

Individuals who have their hearts set on retaining the early belts can order a compressor with a special pulley to match the 3/4in belts. As

Big-block Chevys with the long water pump can use these brackets made of steel, designed to get the components up nice and high. Alan Grove

mentioned earlier, alternators can also be converted to wide belts with the addition of the right pulley (see chapter 6).

Many of these trucks, even the early ones, ran a shroud from the factory. If your truck lacks one, you'll have to add a shroud to insure good airflow over the condenser and the radiator. With abundant room under the hoods of most of these old workhorses, there is plenty of room for a shroud and a bigger fan.

As these old trucks get more and more popular it becomes easier and easier to find air conditioning kits and components. Complete kits are available for Ford trucks as far back as 1953 and for Chevrolets as far back as 1949.

Pickup Trucks Built After 1953 or 1954

Compressor

Putting a compressor on a pickup truck is a straight-forward operation, especially with the vehicles built after 1953 or 1954. Most of these engines have adequate power to run the compressor and have modern-sized drive belts. To select and install air conditioning, you must determine how big a compressor you need and how to mount it to the engine.

Once again, the 508 model Sanden/Sankyo is the overwhelming favorite. This compressor has enough capacity to cool nearly any pickup truck, even a crew cab dually. The compressor size needs to be matched to the evaporator. Trucks cool off well with evaporators of about the same size as those used in street rods and American sedans. Too much compressor just translates to more internal pressure, the need for more horses to operate it, and increased vibration.

It's usually easier to mount the compressor on trucks than on cars because of the room available. The compressor's final resting spot will be the result of the bracket you use. When laying out the bracket and drive belts, remember that you need an alternator so there's enough juice for all the electrical accessories, the air conditioning clutch, and the fan. Many of the brackets are designed to mount both the compressor and the alternator, making the job of laying out brackets and belts much easier.

Mounting the brackets requires common sense. Remember to use lock washers or lock nuts and bolts of high quality on all brackets and hardware. Belt alignment needs to be precise if you're running V-belts, and nearly perfect if you're going to use a serpentine belt. More tips

Trucks tend to have plenty of room for a condenser and receiver-drier mounted in front of the radiator.

for a clean compressor installation can be found in chapter4.

Condenser

Getting a condenser of the right size is easier if you buy a good kit. Jack Chisenhall's rule of thumb suggests using a condenser that is twenty-five percent larger in mass than the evaporator. Thus a 200ci evaporator needs a 250ci condenser. (Note, these rules of thumb apply to CFC-12 systems using tube-and-fin style of condensers.) Because the condenser is the unit that actually sheds the heat to the outside air, it would be hard to have one too big. A basic pickup truck probably needs a two-row, tube-and-fin condenser measuring at least 14x20in. You can add a three-row condenser for more heat transfer, though there is a slight decrease in the amount of air passing through the condensor—at a given speed—when compared to a thinner, two-row condensor.

In situations where space for the condenser is tight, a serpentine or parallel flow condenser might be used. On most trucks however, there's plenty of room for a large condenser right in front of the radiator.

When you mount the condenser, be sure to leave an air gap of 3/16in between the condenser and the radiator so there is no heat gain in the condenser caused by the radiator. Jack recommends that you center the evaporator over the radiator. In most cases, though, you can center the condenser over the fan just as well. When the evaporator is smaller than the radiator, try not to block off too much of the airflow over the radiator with the evaporator brackets.

The brackets should attach to the radiator saddle or flange, or the radiator support brackets. By using a small brake (or just the edge of the bench) you can create a nice, neat stepped bracket that will mount the condenser securely and leave an air gap between condenser and radiator.

Receiver-Drier

The receiver-drier you buy depends on your truck and the rest of your system. If everything else is chrome plated and polished, you may want a polished receiver-drier and bracket. If you're installing an HFC-134A system, then the receiver-drier will have to be compatible with that new refrigerant. If all you're doing is installing air conditioning, period, then any of the standard receiver-driers will work. For the best re-

This condenser and receiver-drier combo is intended to mount to F-100 Ford trucks without drilling or fabricating brackets. Receiver-driers should be kept capped until you are ready to hook up all the hoses. Vintage Air

sults, buy one of the full-flow, rebuildable receiver-driers with a replaceable filter and desiccant bag.

The large space between the grille and the radiator on most trucks will make it possible to mount the receiver-drier right on the condenser. The condenser and receiver-drier become a unit, easy to mount in front of the radiator. The "up front" location makes it easy to see the sight glass when it comes time for charging or servicing the air conditioning, and the fresh air will help the receiver-drier do its job.

Evaporator

Like the American classic cars, most of these trucks have abundant room under and behind the dashboard. Evaporator kits are available to fit most popular Chevrolet and Ford trucks. Many don't even require that you drill holes for the mounting brackets. If you're driving a Mopar or an old Binder, then you're going to be looking at the universal mount evaporators, though again it's a lot easier with all that room behind the dashboard.

You must first decide whether to mount the evaporator in-dash or under-dash. These trucks accept an under-dash unit with ease, leaving plenty of room for passengers' feet. A variety of under-dash evaporators are available on the aftermarket, and nearly all have plenty of capacity to cool an average pickup truck.

Some of the custom units are actually hybrid designs, with features from both in-dash and under-dash evaporators. Trucks are so big inside that the plenum box can actually hang down under the dash and still leave lots of legroom under the dash. By ducting at least some of the cold air right out of the plenum , the amount of air delivered is better than with many in-dash units that rely on ducts for their air delivery.

While installing a custom or in-dash evaporator in a car often means giving up the glove box, there's no such sacrifice with many trucks. Though there is more room behind the dash of most trucks than there is on most cars, it may still be advisable to take out the factory heater—to create more room—and rely on the heat/cool ability of the new evaporator.

Doing a nice job of mounting an under-dash unit means taking the time to mock-up the installation and then carefully considering the routing of the hoses. Bulkhead fittings are available for many of these trucks that use existing

If you are adding a compressor or converting the belts to modern sizes, pulleys like these might make the job go easier. Try to get pulley ratios about the same as those used by the factory. Vintage Air

holes in the firewall.

It's generally assumed that mounting an in-dash evaporator will be more work. That's not necessarily the case with some pickup trucks. In some cases, the custom evaporator is so well adapted to a particular truck that it's easier to install than an under-dash unit.

Hoses and Fittings

A vast array of hoses and fittings are available on the aftermarket. If you buy a complete kit, all (or at least most) of the hoses and fittings will be provided. The hoses you choose should have a nylon liner (whether yours is a CFC-12 or HFC-134A system). New compression-style clamps are recommended for the barrier hose, rather than the old worm-gear clamps. Small crimping tools are available to create factory-style crimp fittings in your shop. Large commercial shops have crimping tools and will often crimp the hoses you bring into their shop. A trick

This evaporator assembly is designed to hang below the dash on Ford F-100 pickup trucks. This unit leaves the glove box and dashboard alone and requires the installer to drill no holes. Vintage Air

This GMC truck uses an in-dash evaporator and ducts to three vents below the dashboard. Factory-style controls are used to give it a factory-installed look. Vintage Air

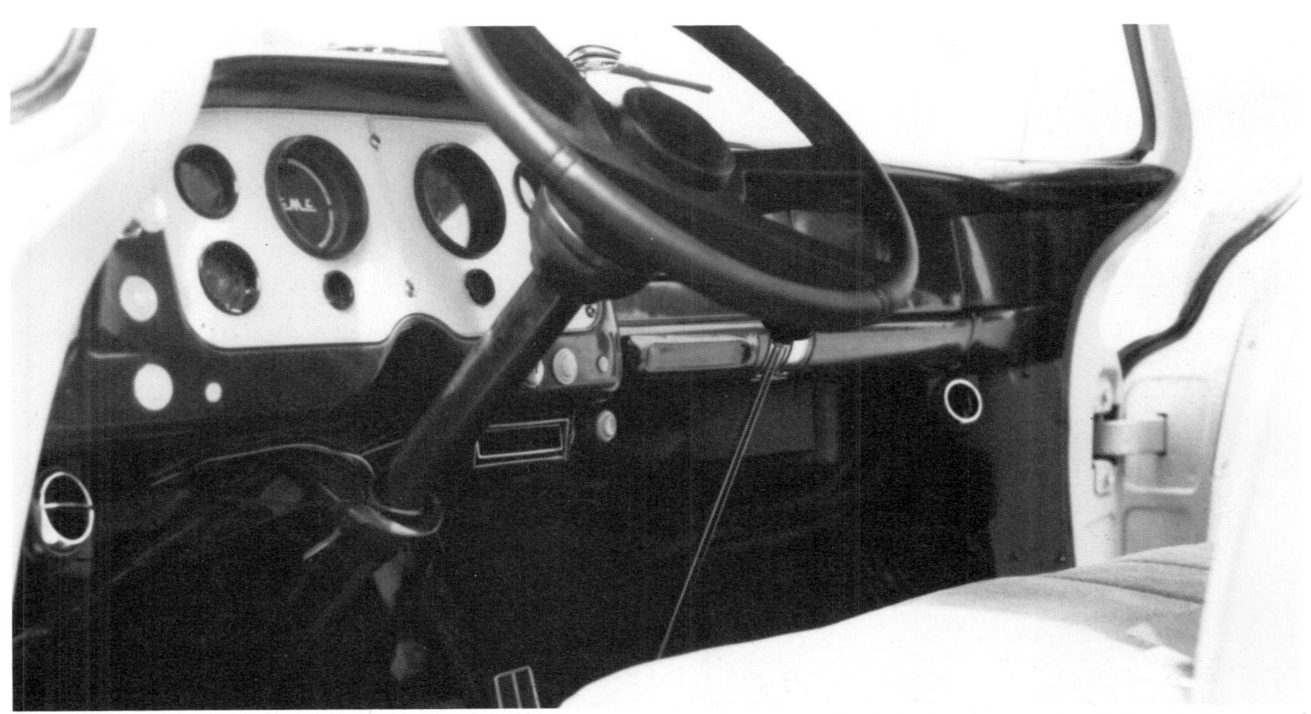

Duct work that runs to vents like these should always be kept as short as possible. By stretching out the wrinkles in the flexible duct work the airflow is increased while the noise is decreased. Vintage Air

In-dash and under-dash vents are available to fit nearly any truck. Duct work or solid plastic tubing (more 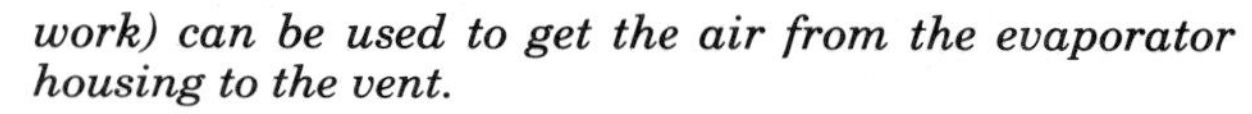 *work) can be used to get the air from the evaporator housing to the vent.*

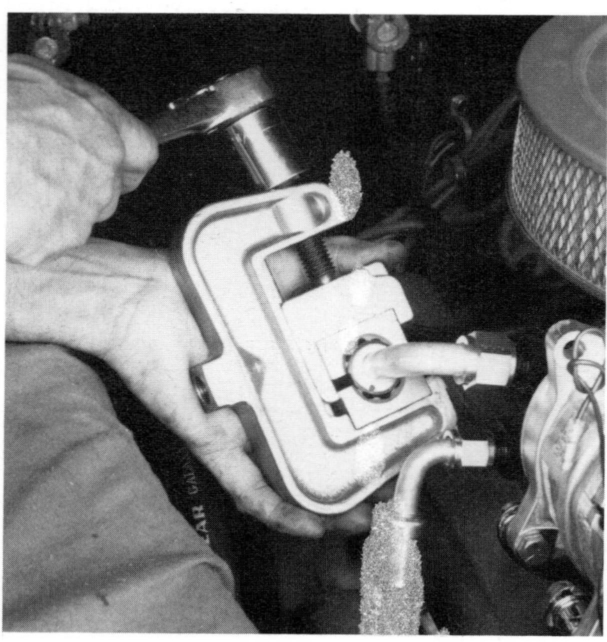

A small crimping tool like this can be used on the truck for neat crimps that make your hoses look like they came from the factory.

trucker might want to run the Proline seamless stainless tubing from a supplier such as Vintage Air for an ultra-clean installation.

The fittings should be O-ring style, as flare fittings are no longer up to the task. For HFC-134A systems, make certain that all the hoses, fittings, and O-rings are compatible with the new refrigerant and lubricants.

The evaporator is supplied with two refrigerant hoses. The larger hose (or suction hose, often 1/2in diameter) is easier to route in a truck, as there are fewer obstacles. It's still best, however, to plan the hose routing carefully before cutting holes in the firewall.

Once you have figured out the routing and cut the hoses, you need to tighten the fitting on the evaporator with the evaporator on the work bench. Be sure to use two wrenches, one on the hose fitting and one on the evaporator fitting. The expansion valve and the suction line leaving the evaporator will have to be wrapped with cork-lined tape too, before the evaporator is mounted into the car.

The routing you choose for the hoses as they run from the firewall to the compressor and condenser will depend on the truck, the location of those other components, and your personal taste.

Remember that the high-pressure hose coming into the evaporator (smaller diameter) should be kept cool and that the suction line that runs from the evaporator to the inlet of the compressor (larger diameter) can run close to the engine, where it will gain some heat. These two hoses can even be clamped together. On trucks, the hoses are often run together along the inner fender panel on the right side.

Be sure to leave enough "give" in the hoses near the compressor so the compressor can be pulled off the engine and over to the side with the hoses connected, just in case the engine needs to be removed from the car. That way you don't have to open the system (and later recharge it) every time you pull the engine.

When the system is installed, it's a good idea to have it evacuated and leak tested by a professional before you put all the shielding and the interior back together.

Cooling Fans and Insulation

Because many of these trucks are truly old, the comments made in an earlier chapter about checking the condition of the radiator bears repeating. The air conditioning will tax even an oversized cooling system like that found on many

All four hoses pass into the F-100 through this bulkhead plate making for a neat installation. Note that the liquid and suction lines are tied together with tie-wraps. Vintage Air

old trucks. If the radiator looks a little shady, send it out to be boiled and checked by the radiator shop.

Comments made earlier about cooling an early truck apply to more modern vehicles as well. Moving enough air across the radiator is most easily done with a large, belt-driven fan with a few extra blades. If Ol' Blue didn't come with a shroud, install one.

These old trucks are much like the cars of the same period, with one important exception: Where cars built after the war were rather well sealed and insulated, trucks often got only rudimentary sealing and often no insulation.

If the weather stripping around the doors is gone or torn, it is essential that you replace it. Be sure that all windows and doors seal at least as well as they did when the truck was new. If your truck is old enough, there may be no insulation, except maybe a little on the firewall. After looking at chapter 9, take the time to insulate your truck; it will absolutely do wonders for the effectiveness of the air conditioning.

Ultimately, how well the air conditioning works on your truck depends on how well you did the installation and also how well you covered the details. It's those little things that make the difference between a great installation and one that's just OK . Pay attention to detail questions like how neatly are the hoses run? Are there wires hanging down below the dash? Is the fan always on high because there's so much hot air coming in and so much cool air going out?

A good installation is more than just a matter of installing the components—it's a compete job, and includes the planning, the actual installation, and the little extras, like installing the correct insulation.

Chapter 8

Installing A/C in Kit Cars

Kit cars come in all shapes and sizes, from V-8 powered "Lamborghinis" to air-cooled dune buggy type vehicles. Some have the engine in front, some have it in back—and the engines can be water cooled or air cooled.

We have divided these cars into two groups here, air cooled and water cooled. Air conditioning needs a condenser and that condenser needs a mounting location where it gets maximum fresh air. Air-cooled cars seldom have a good natural location (such as in front of the radiator) for the condenser. The discussion regarding buying and mounting each component will include separate considerations for each group of cars.

Before jumping into the air conditioning, owners of kit cars need to consider the large role played by body fit and sealing in the effectiveness of the air conditioning system. You may

The size of compressor you use on your kit car depends a great deal on the size of the condenser. Don't assume you need a big compressor just to achieve a lot of cooling. This VW has a Sanden 505, which is plenty of compressor for a small car with a relatively small condenser.

first want to review chapter 9 and take time to be sure that doors and glass fit tight and that all seams are sealed by weather strips or sealants. The glass area (often large on a kit car) is also a big contributor to heat gain. Tinting the glass will help enormously to reduce the work the air conditioner must do to cool the car.

Buying and Mounting the Components

Compressor

Choosing a compressor for your car will depend on the same guidelines laid down in earlier chapters for other groups of vehicles. Owners often mount a compressor much too large for the job, working on the assumption that "it's better to be too big than too small." Not true. With a compressor it's better to be just right, or even a bit too small. Compressors that are too large create too much internal pressure, which means that it takes more horsepower to turn the compressor. A big compressor requires a big condenser—one that is often too big for the space available.

What works best in kit cars are the same two compressors discussed in earlier chapters: The Sanden/Sankyo 508 or, for smaller cars like a VW Bug, the model 505.

Mounting the compressor requires a stout bracket, and the bracket you choose will depend on the engine in the car. If your vehicle is powered by a Chevy small-block V-8, then the choice of brackets is almost endless. Air-cooled cars with VW power are more limited in bracket options, though there are brackets available (suppliers such as Vintage Air make such a unit) to mount a 505 compressor on one of these engines.

VW air-cooled engines with multiple carbs sometimes run into trouble with the support bracket for the main compressor bracket. Jack Chisenhall of Vintage Air has solved the problem by cutting a small slot in the fan housing at the back of the motor and running a support bracket through the fan housing to one of the engine mounting bolts.

Mounting of the bracket and compressor should follow all the common-sense guidelines. Be sure to use at least a grade five bolt on all brackets and mounting bolts. Fine-threaded bolts

Compressor mounts for the air-cooled VW engine are available and make the little baby Sanden look right at home.

are usually stronger unless the bolt is screwed into cast iron or aluminum. Because of the vibration, you need good lock washers or self-locking nuts.

Condenser

Choosing the size of the condenser is easy—if you're installing a complete air conditioning kit from a quality supplier. If you're putting the system together from individual pieces, then it can be more difficult. On a medium-sized car with a 508 compressor, you probably need a two-row, tube-and-fin type condenser of about 220 square inches (in a CFC-12 system). Before deciding to add a bigger compressor, consider that a compressor that's ten percent larger will require a condenser about twenty percent bigger.

Smaller cars—VW size—with the model 505 compressor need as much condenser as possible because there is often no good place to mount the condenser so it gets a good supply of cool air.

Jack Chisenhall recommends a minimum of 200ci of three-row condenser for VWs and cars based on a VW chassis. The three-row, tube-and-fin condenser packs more cooling capability into the space available.

Because air-cooled cars use the fresh air to cool the condenser—and not the radiator—they need less total airflow for good condenser operation than would a similar car with a water-cooled engine. For example, a small car powered by a VW air-cooled engine only needs 1200cfm of good, fresh air for good condenser operation.

Most aftermarket air conditioning manufacturers recommend that the condenser be twenty-five percent larger in mass than the evaporator. Thus a 200ci evaporator needs a 250ci condenser (for a tube-and-fin type of condenser in a CFC-12 system).

Situations where space is tight, such as on air-cooled cars without a good location for the condenser, might benefit from the increased efficiencies of serpentine or parallel flow condensers.

The biggest problem with kit cars might not be *which* condenser, but where to mount the condenser. Any car with a radiator (whether the engine is in front or back) should have the condenser mounted on front of the radiator. This is the location with the largest amount of the

This VW has the evaporator mounted in the front trunk with duct work used to feed the cool air to vents on the dashboard. The condenser is underneath, above the front axle. (There is no really good place to put a condenser on one of these cars.)

coolest air available.

Remember what was said in an earlier chapter: The condenser's job is to cool the refrigerant sufficiently so it condenses from a gas to a liquid. The condenser can't do its job if it is located in a dark, hot corner of the engine compartment with no fresh airflow.

Unusual and creative condenser locations should be saved for cars that absolutely require them. You don't want any heat transfer from the radiator to the condenser, so avoid letting the radiator touch the condenser. It's a good idea to insure that there is at least 3/16in of clearance between the condenser and the radiator. Remember too that the tubes must run horizontally to avoid having the oil settle in the "low" spots that are created when the tubes run vertically (in CFC-12 systems).

Air-cooled cars seldom have a "natural" location for the condenser. In fact, they seldom have any kind of acceptable location at all. In trying to make the best of a bad situation, stick with the basics: Expose the condenser to as much fresh air as possible, keep it as cool as possible, and try to provide air that is free of road debris.

Air-cooled VWs, for example (and cars based on this chassis), really have no good location for the condenser. Jack Chisenhall suggests mounting the condenser up above the front torsion bar tube. He feels that this works better than the area above the transaxle as the air in front is cooler. People have tried putting the condenser in the front, where the spare tire would go, but that requires eliminating the spare tire and louvers in the hood.

In cases where two condensers are used, the second one (farthest from the compressor) should have the coolest air supply.

Receiver-Drier

Receiver-driers are not all the same. In particular, polished aluminum receiver-driers are available if you want the installation to be neat as a pin. If you buy a polished housing, buy a full-flow, rebuildable receiver-drier, so the desiccant bag and filter can be replaced whenever the system is serviced or opened up to the atmosphere.

There are two basic things you have to remember about mounting the receiver-drier. First, if it was meant to be mounted vertically

Nifty aluminum vents are used to direct air into the VW's interior. The flat dash lends itself to this style of vent.

(most are); mount it that way and don't lay it on its side. Second, mount it where it can get some fresh air so the refrigerant leaving the cannister remains a liquid.

If possible, mount the receiver-drier up front with the condenser and run the liquid line from the receiver-drier to the evaporator. Always remember to leave the receiver-drier capped until you are ready to install it in a nearly finished system—in order to preserve the capacity of the desiccant.

Evaporator

Most kit car owners will have to adapt a universal type of condenser to fit their particular car. Choices begin with the two basic styles: In-dash or under-dash. In-dash evaporators tend to be much neater and more professional looking though they are a lot more work to install.

Sizing the evaporator can best be done by calling a manufacturer and discussing the size of your interior and the capacity of the various evaporators that are available. Though most kit cars don't have large interiors, some have a lot of glass area, something to consider when choosing an evaporator.

Air-cooled VWs and similar cars end up with the evaporator in the trunk or an area on the other side of the firewall and dashboard. These installations can be very neat, using nice aluminum vents mounted in the dash and connected by ducts to the evaporator. Always use all three of the outlet vents on the evaporator case, even if one just dumps air in under the dash. Blocking off one outlet tends to disturb the airflow within the case, reducing airflow and causing the fan to cavitate.

The air exiting the evaporator must blow directly on the driver and passenger for maximum cooling effect. Evaporators that vent under the front or rear seats often deliver disappointing results.

The evaporator creates cool air—cooler and heavier than the other air in the car—so try to keep the housing and vents high rather than low to create good air circulation in the car. Most evaporators are available with heaters and defrosters, something to keep in mind as you plan—if it's water cooled.

Kit cars are no different that other cars and pickup trucks in this sense: The things that get

Any round vents you use should be at least 2in in diameter in order to move enough air.

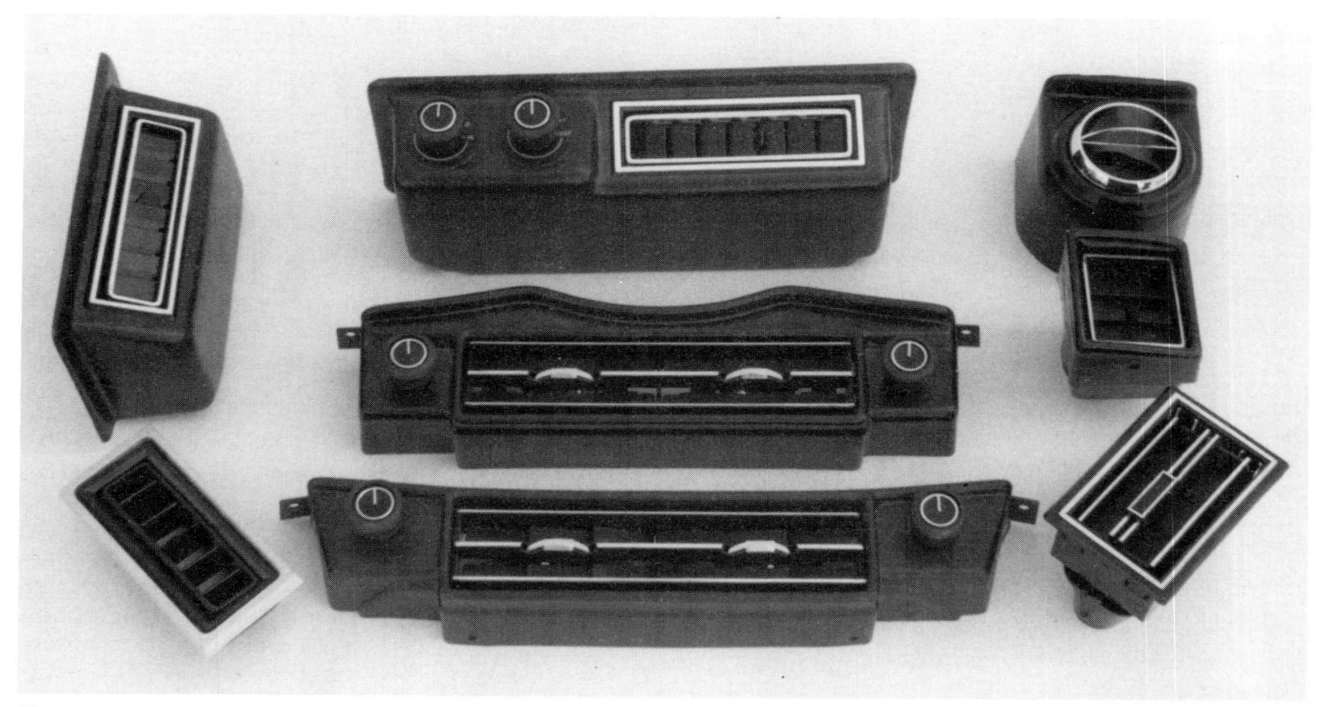

This is just a sampling of what's available in the way of vents. Some are designed to be used in-dash while others mount below the dash.

Installing air conditioning often means changing to new pulleys—why not change to trick new pulleys like these from Milodon?

in the way of an installation tend to be the gauges and the wiring, both of which should be kept on the driver's side, if possible.

Hoses and Fittings

Kit cars must follow all the normal guidelines for routing air conditioning hoses, though there are a few extra do's and don'ts due to the extreme length of the hoses in rear-engine cars.

The flexible hose you use, whether this is a CFC-12 or HFC-134A system, should be "barrier" hose. (Use "J51 AII" hose for HFC-134A systems.) Each hose should be routed according to the condition of the refrigerant inside that hose. The high-side hose (discharge line) leaving the compressor and running to the condenser should be kept cool, as you want the refrigerant in this hose to condense into a liquid. In a rear-engine car this discharge hose runs all the way from one end of the car to the other. Be sure to keep it away from heat sources, in the airstream if possible—but secure from rocks and debris if it runs under the car along the frame rail. Considerable cooling of the refrigerant can occur in these long discharge hoses, taking some of the load off the condenser.

Note: Rear-engine cars, because of the extra long hoses, need extra oil to compensate for the extra refrigerant in the system. As a rule of thumb, use two additional ounces of oil for an extra 10-12ft of hose. (Most rear-engined cars require an extra 10-12ft of hose compared to front-engined cars.)

The liquid line leaving the condenser and running to the receiver-drier and then to the evaporator should be kept cool as well. If your car has the engine in front, try to keep this line away from engine heat.

In some cases you can route two air conditioning hoses next to each other to save space and improve the system's efficiency. The liquid line that goes to the evaporator and the suction line that leaves the evaporator can be tied together. The cool suction line will help keep the refrigerant in the liquid line in a liquid state, and the hotter liquid line will help to vaporize the refrigerant in the suction line going to the compressor.

The other two lines that can be tried together (likely in cars with a rear-mounted engine) are the discharge line (leaving the compressor) and the suction line (the one going into the compressor). Again, this will save space and it will actually aid the operation of the air conditioning system. The discharge line is full of hot refrigerant that needs to be cooled and the suction line is filled with cool vaporous refrigerant that must

Some of the same installation accessories designed primarily for the street rod market can be used to good advantage on any kit car. These billet bulkhead fittings provide a nice clean way to get the hoses through the firewall.

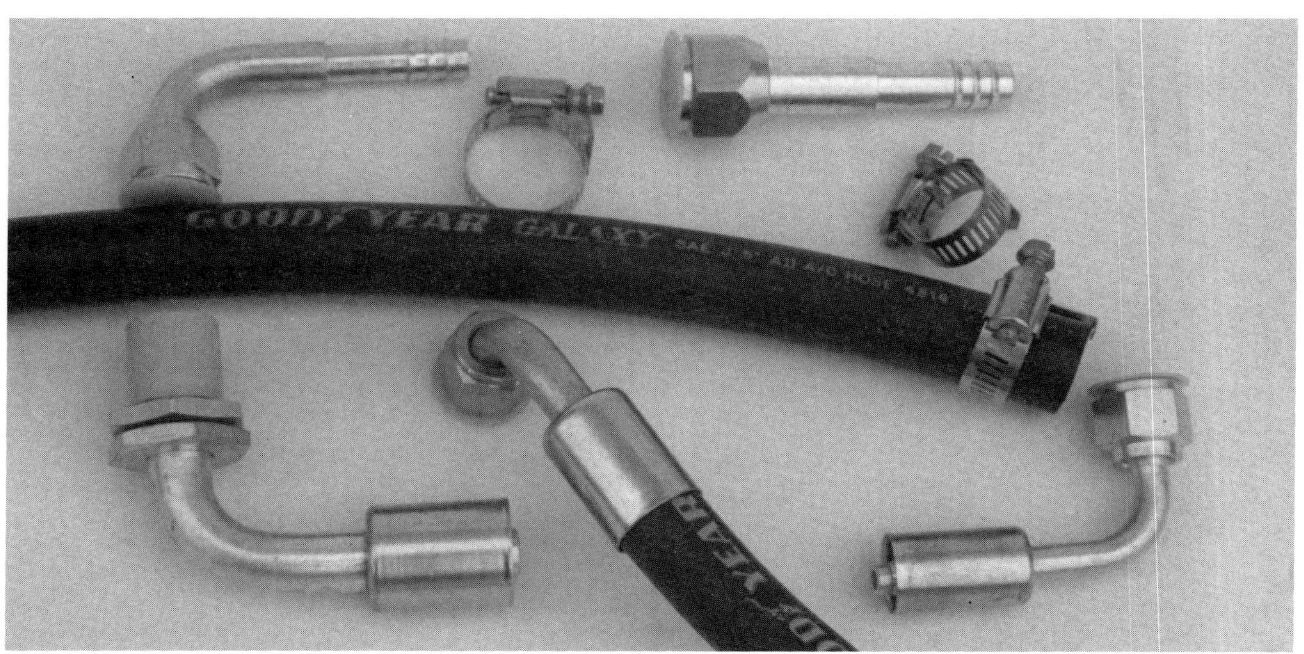

Any hose used on air conditioning—CFC-12 or HFC-134A—should use a liner to stop seepage through the hose. Fittings on all systems should be O-ring style. Hoses and O-rings used with HFC-134A must be compatible with the new refrigerant and the new oil.

This electric fan features its own ring style shroud and an adjustable bracket to fit many different applications. Electric fans may not move as much total air as a large belt-driven fan but offer other advantages.

remain in a vapor form so the compressor pumps a vapor and not a liquid.

A few more do's and don'ts:

•Do not run the liquid line (from drier to evaporator) alongside the discharge line from the high-side of the compressor.

•The suction line can be routed close to the engine, where it will gain heat. This hose contains vaporous refrigerant and you want it to remain a vapor so you don't feed liquid refrigerant to the suction side of the compressor.

•Try to keep the discharge and the liquid lines cool.

•Be sure to push rubber hoses all the way onto the barbs of the fittings.

•Avoid the use of hydraulic hose and don't use braided steel line with flare fittings. Flare fittings are no longer considered good enough, even for a CFC-12 system, so use O-ring fittings throughout the system. The clamps you use can be compression or crimp-style but don't use worm-gear clamps on the new barrier hose.

•At the firewall, you need to either run the hoses through the body with a grommet or use a bulkhead fitting designed for air conditioners to neatly get the hoses inside the car.

•Once you've got the hoses inside the car, remember that anything cold will condense water and drip it on the floor. Always wrap most of the expansion valve (see pictures for more detail) and the suction line with black cork tape. The tape acts as an insulator and helps stop moisture from condensing on the cold lines and fittings. The lines must be clean and dry when you do this or the tape won't stick.

•The suction line is the larger of the two hoses inside the car. Because of the size, this line isn't very flexible and is hard to route neatly. This is another case where it pays to take your time and plan the exact location of the evaporator housing and the routing of the suction line so everything ends up looking as neat as possible.

•Be sure to do the final tightening of the fittings on the back of the evaporator with the evaporator housing sitting on the bench. Use two wrenches to avoid twisting or damaging the evaporator itself.

Cooling Fans and Switches

Many kit cars have a rear engine, thus they must use electric fans to pull air over the radiator. Electric fans are a topic in themselves and anyone using electric fans to cool the radiator

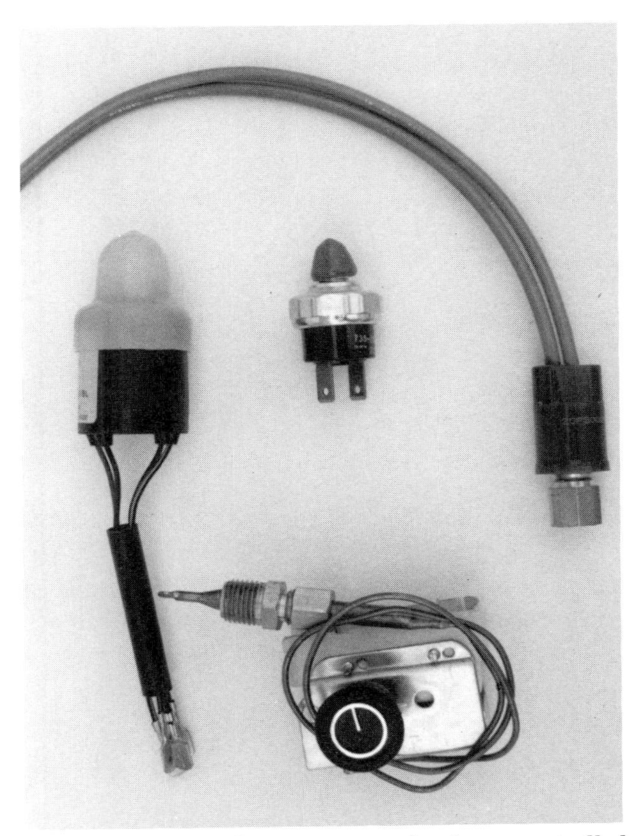

Electric fans and the compressor clutch are controlled by a variety of electric sensors like these. You need the fan to come on when the radiator gets too hot, or when the high-side pressure gets too high. Single- and multi-purpose switches can take care of all these little chores.

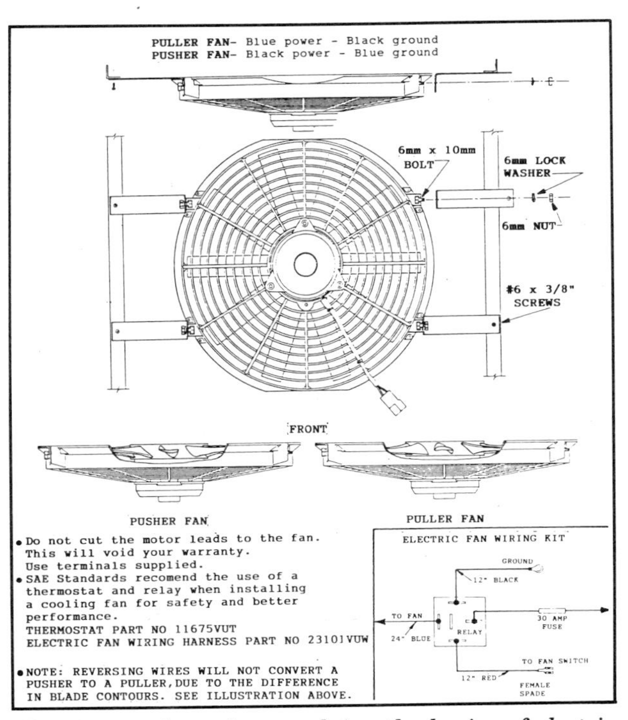

This instructions sheet explains the basics of electric fan installation. Note the use of a relay to power the fan and the fact that pushers and pullers are different fan designs. (It's usually better to pull whenever possible.)

and the condenser should read chapter 9.

In general, a larger fan is better than a small one. That may seem too obvious, but as the diameter of the fan blade increases, the tip speed increases dramatically—and the tip is where most of the work is done.

So use the largest fan (or fans) you can and be sure to integrate the function of the electric fan into the operation of the air conditioning. The fans need to come on when the high side pressure gets too high (about 350psi) and go back off at about 290psi. Some new cars run sophisticated circuitry for the fans, running one electric fan all the time the air conditioning is on and saving the other for situations when the high-side pressure goes too high or the radiator temperature sensor registers too high a temperature.

Unless you're real good with D.C. electricity, it seems easier to run the two electric fans together. They should come on with a signal from the radiator or a signal from the high-side sensing switch.

In addition to the high-side fan switch, you need another fail-safe high-side switch to kill the power to the clutch when the pressure goes too high—over 375psi. You should also run a low-pressure switch that cuts power to the clutch if the pressure drops too low, indicating a loss of refrigerant and, more importantly, a loss of oil. A triple-function switch (high-side fan, high-pressure cutoff, and low-pressure cutoff) can simplify the installation and is available from suppliers such as Vintage Air. This multi-function switch and any high-side sensing switches should be placed in the liquid line, preferably between the receiver-drier and the evaporator, since the pressures in this line tend to be very stable.

Summary

Kit cars are unique vehicles built from a collection of pieces. Seldom is there a provision made by the manufacturer for air conditioning, and never is there a kit made specifically to air condition a specific kit car. You are installing and adapting "universal" parts and your job is to make them fit neatly and work correctly.

Because of the adapting that goes on here, it's extra important that you truly understand how air conditioning works so you can buy and correctly install the right equipment.

Chapter 9

Keeping Your Cool

Cooling your car or truck may not be as simple as installing a good air conditioning kit. If the vehicle is unusual or old, installing the air conditioning may not be enough—by itself—to ensure a cool interior and trouble-free operation.

There are three types of problems that sometimes accompany the installation of air conditioning: Problems caused by a lack of planning for the installation, problems with the engine's cooling system, and problems with a lack of body sealing and insulation.

Planning the Job

Planning the installation of an air conditioning system is especially important for someone who is building an entire car, like a street rod, a full custom, or a new kit car. For these individuals, the air conditioning must be integrated into

Engine placement in the frame is critical to cooling system performance as it affects the location of the fan and how much room there is for the radiator and condenser. Always put a fan on the engine and double-check the location of the radiator before finalizing the engine location.

the design of the car and the placement of the other components.

Engine placement affects the placement of everything else, such as the radiator, condenser, fan—the list goes on and on. You need to install the engine (in a conventional drivetrain layout) so you leave room for an adequate radiator, condenser, and fan.

Street rodders in particular must pay attention to engine placement. Some of these cars have very short engine compartments. In addition, many builders place the engine very low in the chassis. While this may create a nice low center of gravity, it puts the water pump snout pretty low in relation to the radiator. The water pump snout is of course the mounting point for the belt-driven fan, with the snout real low you can only run a small diameter fan.

By paying particular attention to engine position when you're building the car you can make sure you get the engine high enough and that you get it back far enough to make room for the fan, radiator, condenser, and possibly a shroud.

Jack Chisenhall of Vintage Air encourages builders to mock-up the engine position with a fan on the engine and the radiator and front sheet metal in place. "Sometimes if these guys would just take a little notch out of the firewall they could move the engine back a few inches—enough to get the room they need for the right radiator and condenser—enough room so the final product is a 'real car,' one the owner can drive anywhere and anytime because it doesn't overheat and the air conditioning works great."

Jim Petrykowski, a long-time street rod builder and owner of Metal Fab in Minneapolis, Minnesota, offered advice regarding the height of the engine in the chassis: "A lot of these cars have the through-bolt on the motor mount (GM-style mount) only about 1in higher than the top of the frame rail. Besides putting the fan way down on the radiator, it leaves the headers and the oil pan hanging pretty low—down where they're more likely to get caught on bumps in the road.

"By having the motor mount through-bolt positioned 3 to 4in above the frame rail, the engine is high enough so everything clears and you can

Installation of air conditioning puts an additional load on the cooling system. The engine works harder and creates more heat, yet the airflow to the radiator is often reduced in volume while its temperature increases, due to the effect of the condenser.

run a decent-sized, belt-driven fan."

Your planning will also help determine the style of evaporator you buy and install. If you're building a car or truck, then the air conditioning—and especially the evaporator placement—should be planned early. Installing an in-dash evaporator housing and the duct work isn't too tough if the entire interior and perhaps the dashboard are already out of the car. But to put one in after everything else is finished can be a lot of work.

If you're going to use an in-dash evaporator, remember to plan the dashboard and interior to accommodate the evaporator. Gauges and wiring should be kept on the driver's side of the vehicle to make more room for the evaporator housing. The radio can tend to get in the way—ask yourself if it would be simpler to put it in an overhead pod or maybe in a console between the seats. If the car or truck has a factory heater, it might be simpler to discard the heater to make room for the evaporator housing and then use an air conditioner with both heat and cool.

It's a lot like building a house: An extra outlet in the kitchen can be installed very easily during construction, but putting the same outlet in after the house is finished can take a whole day (or more).

When you make plans to build a car or truck, plan the air conditioning, too. Leave room for the evaporator and fan; install the evaporator when you do the rest of the interior work; allow for sufficient airflow through the radiator; and insulate the vehicle (we'll talk more about insulation and airflow later).

Avoid Cooling System and Airflow Problems

The Cooling System

Keeping your car cool under the added stress of air conditioning can be a challenge. It requires a good radiator with enough capacity, a cooling system that moves adequate amounts of water through the radiator, and enough airflow over the fins of the radiator to remove the engine heat.

First, let's talk about the radiator and the liquid part of the cooling system. Because the ad-

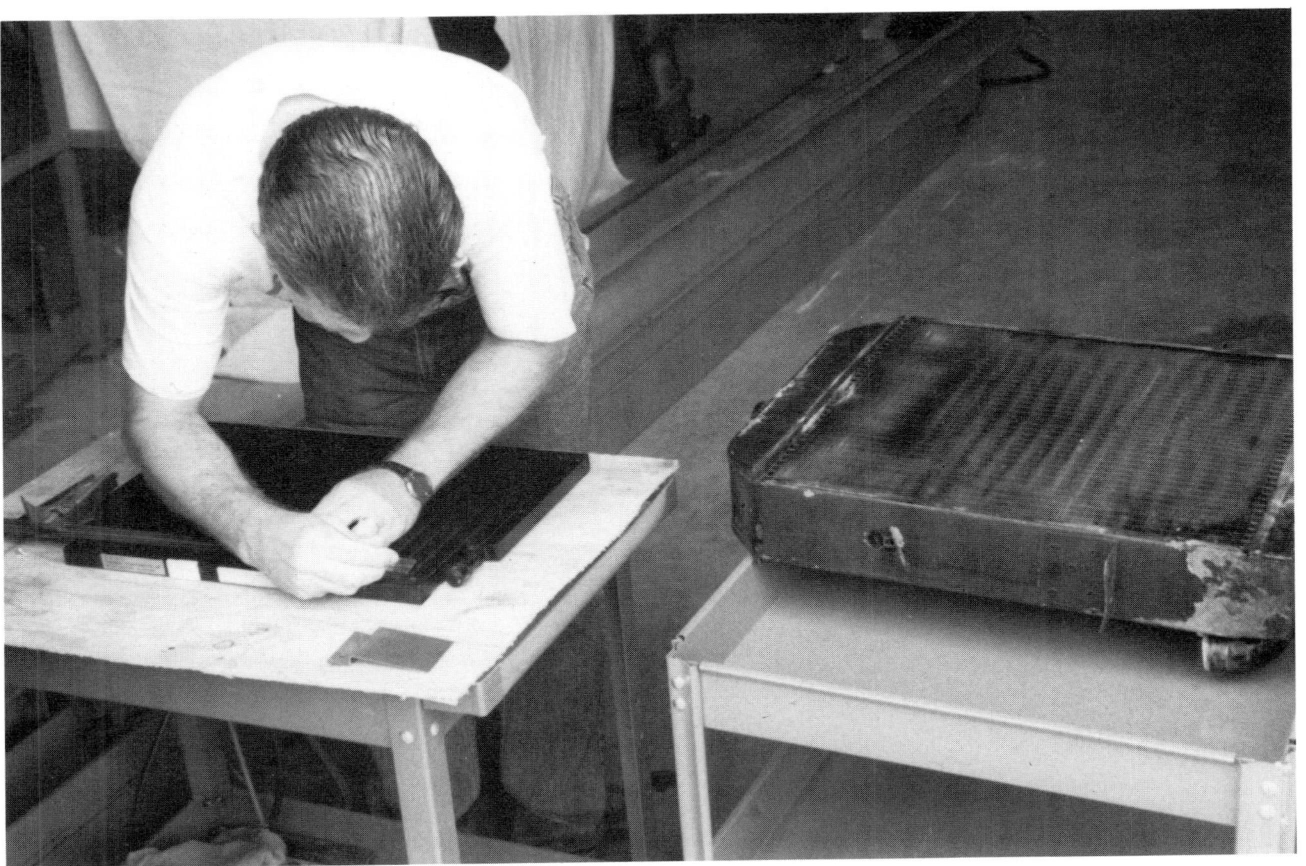

By adding air conditioning and putting a condenser in front of the radiator you make the radiator's job much more difficult. If the radiator looks old and tired, send it to the radiator health spa and follow their advice for getting it back in shape.

dition of air conditioning puts an extra heat load on the cooling system, the radiator must be in good condition with enough capacity to handle the extra heat. The best advice regarding the size you need comes from a quality aftermarket radiator manufacturer like Walker or a quality air conditioning manufacturer like Vintage Air.

If you have any doubts about the condition of the radiator, have it checked at the local radiator shop. If it's pretty dirty with considerable buildup inside the tubes, they may want to take off the tanks and rod out the core. At the very least, they will probably recommend boiling it out and a good pressure test.

Moving the coolant to and through the radiator is the job of the water pump. Not all water pumps are created equal. Chevy small-blocks have been equipped with both long and short versions of water pumps over the years. Nearly everyone in the aftermarket recommends the short version, which saves about 1 1/2in in length compared to the longer one.

Big-block Chevy engines use short and long water pumps as well. The shorter version was used on some Corvettes during the late 1960s and can save you the room you need to run a bigger fan.

Jim Petrykowski's advice regarding Chevrolets? "Some of the Chevy small-block trucks and heavy duty applications use a better water pump," he said. "This heavy duty pump uses a 3/4in shaft (instead of 5/8in) and a double roller bearing. This pump is a good idea for anyone running a big fan or a big fan and a clutch hub—all of which puts more load on the water pump bearings and shaft."

Jim also recommends a water pump with a cast iron impeller, rather than the stamped one, if you can find one. He warned that some small-block water pumps designed for new cars with serpentine belts will actually run backwards when converted to regular V-belts.

Special, high-rise water pump housings are available for small-block Chevy engines where the engine ends up very low in the chassis. The housing uses a six-cylinder Chevy water pump with plenty of capacity to move water through the V-8 water jackets. You can run a water pump with or without fittings for heater hoses, depending on your situation. The big advantage is that the water pump snout is now 4 or 5in higher, so you can run a nice big fan that pulls air over the whole radiator, instead of pulling air from just a small area at the bottom of the radiator.

High-rise water pump housings are available for cars (like '28 Fords) where engine placement makes it hard to run a large, belt-driven fan. These housings accept a six-cylinder Chevrolet water pump.

Here you can see how a high-rise housing puts the fan hub right in the center of the radiator—where it should be. The only thing missing on this installation is a radiator shroud. Vintage Air

In the interest of having only the very "best" on their street rods, some owners use fancy billet water pumps designed for oval-track race cars. These pumps might look great, but they're designed for cars turning 5000rpm and won't move enough water when used on a street car. Problems also arise from using the wrong head gaskets—such as a 350 gasket on a 400 application (the water passages aren't the same).

Some final words of wisdom for the water part of the cooling system include the old adage to always run a thermostat. Remember that the new tuned port injection (TPI) engines rely on the temperature sensor to determine the fuel mixture, so be sure to run the thermostat that the factory recommends. High-flow thermostats are available if you're concerned about the total flow. These open to leave an unobstructed hole for water to pass through, instead of making the water move past and around the valve, as in a conventional thermostat.

The coolant must be a mixture of antifreeze and water for three good reasons: the mixture has a higher boiling point, it won't freeze when the heater hose runs next to the cold A/C line, and because it contains rust inhibitors.

The radiator and coolant don't remove all the heat from your small-block. A considerable amount of cooling happens between the block surface and the air moving through the engine compartment. Painting the engine might make it beautiful, however, the many layers of primer you put on to make it look really finished will act as an insulator and make it harder for the engine to shed its heat load.

Smoothing off the block might seem better, until you realize that by removing all the little lumps you radically reduce the surface area of the block. It's like filing the fins off a motorcycle cylinder. Grinding the block smooth is probably a better idea (in a thermal sense) than ten coats of primer followed by finish paint. The best idea is a block that's clean and painted with only one or two layers of paint.

Airflow

An efficient cooling system is only as good as its ability to give up heat to the air moving through the radiator. Some cars (street rods in particular) have trouble with moving enough air over the radiator. First, we need to discuss airflow and as part of that discussion, we should talk about fans (again).

Good airflow is more than just a matter of presenting the full face of the radiator to the air

A variety of fans, belt-driven and electric, are available for your car. Many of the cooling system problems that crop up after installing air conditioning can be avoided with good planning.

in front of the radiator or grille. As stated earlier, the air won't move through the radiator unless the pressure on the back side is lower than the pressure on the front of the radiator. Street rods with smooth-sided hoods are among the worst offenders at restricting airflow. Often there is no good way for the air to exit the engine compartment, no matter what you do with the fan or fans. The final result is a lack of airflow over the radiator and a car that runs hot.

We aren't saying you can't run smooth hood sides, just that the hood and hood sides need to be part of the overall plan for the vehicle. If the air can't exit the side of the hood, it must exit below the engine compartment. Sometimes a simple air-dam near the front axle can effectively create a low pressure area behind the radiator and solve an overheating problem by moving more air through the engine compartment.

The fan you use is obviously part of the airflow discussion. The fan options are belt-driven or electric, and some situations dictate one or the other. A kit car with a mid-engine and the radiator in front of the car calls for electric fans. In a conventional engine layout, a good belt-driven fan operating with a properly designed shroud will move more air than one or two electric fans—all other factors being equal.

A belt-driven fan should be 17 or 18in in diameter and nearly 2in thick, with at least five blades. A shroud improves the efficiency of a fan (any fan) enormously. Think of it as a funnel, making it possible for the 18in fan to pull more air more evenly over the entire surface of the radiator. Even a simple "ring" shroud will improve airflow across the radiator and provide a significant improvement in overall airflow.

Fan clutch hubs are often installed as a means of helping the fan pull with maximum effect at low speed yet minimizing the horsepower drain at higher speeds where you don't need the full effect of the fan. A hydraulic clutch fan hub can be added to nearly any belt-driven fan to achieve these goals. Thermostatically controlled clutch hubs (often used from the factory) should only be added to a cooling system when all the components—radiator, shroud, fan, and condenser—match the factory components. These

Electric fans are helpful in situations where space is very tight because they fit in places a belt driven fan won't fit. They should always be installed to pull rather than push, and should be connected to automatic temperature and air conditioning controls.

hubs are calibrated for a particular set of conditions, and if you change any of those conditions, then the hub can become a disadvantage rather than an advantage.

Electric fans have the advantage of coming on only when they are specifically needed and drawing no power and no horsepower when they're not needed. Though they may not move as much total air as a good belt-driven fan, electric fans will often fit in places much too tight for a conventional fan.

Electric Fans and Thermostats

The first rule of electric fans is to pull the air, don't push it. Pusher fans obstruct the airflow all the time, whether they're working or not. The second rule is to always run fans off the thermostat, not off a manual switch, because it's too easy to forget to turn the fan on in a traffic situation, and you can cook the motor.

The simplest electric fan setups (in a car without air conditioning) use a thermostat in the radiator to sense the coolant temperature. When the coolant passing through the radiator is too hot—meaning it wasn't cooled sufficiently during its pass through the radiator—the sensor turns on the fan. The fan draws air over the radiator and cools the liquid passing through the radiator. The sensor can be used as the direct switch for the fan, or it can be used to control a relay—running the power circuit for the fan through the relay.

When an electric fan (or fans) is used on a car with air conditioning, it must be integrated with the air conditioning as well as the cooling system. On a hot day, sitting at idle with a cold engine and the air conditioning on, pressure on the high side of the air conditioner (CFC-12 system) can rise very rapidly. The high-side pressure can go as high as 400 or 500psi, enough to rupture a hose. You need a high-side switch that turns on the fan(s) at about 350psi, thus moving fresh air over the condenser and lowering the pressure. (Remember, temperature and pressure are closely related here.)

When buying an electric fan, buy one with a sensor that goes into the lower radiator tank (the one on the discharge or outlet side); sensors that clamp on the outside aren't as dependable or con-

The Modine Radiator Company did tests on air conditioned cars with and without shrouds. They found that the addition of a shroud and larger fan dropped the radiator temperature 15 degrees F at highway speeds.

These sheets of 1/4in urethane are ready to insulate a street rod. The coloring is spray adhesive used to glue the panels inside the car.

The key to a good insulating job is to cover all the inside surfaces—after filling any holes, of course. Use a material that can be easily cut to shape and don't skip anything.

sistent. An adjustable sensor is a nice feature.

The high-side switch can be a single function switch that turns on the fan, or it can be a multifunction switch like that from suppliers such as Vintage Air. These multi-function switches have three functions:

1. They act as a high-side fan switch.
2. They function as a high-side cutout, cutting power to the compressor clutch if for any reason the pressure goes above 375psi.
3. They also act as a low-pressure cutout, cutting power to the clutch when the pressure gets very low, meaning a loss of refrigerant and lubricant as well.

The fan you buy should be the biggest one that will fit your particular application. The blades near the hub of a fan don't move much air—nearly all the work the fan does is done near the tips of the blades. As the blade gets longer, the percentage of blade surface out away from the hub increases and the speed of the blade tip increases—resulting in a fan that can move significantly more air than one with short blades. Some of the newest designs incorporate their own ring-style shroud, a nice feature that will improve the fan's ability to move air.

Occasionally a car calls for both a belt-driven and an electric fan. A street rod like a '34 Ford with the engine very low in the chassis is a good example. With a stock water pump, only a small diameter belt-driven fan can be used and that won't draw any air over the upper, and hottest, part of the radiator. The answer might be an electric fan on top controlled by a thermostat high-side sensor and the belt-driven fan below.

Sealing and Insulating Your Vehicle

When winter comes we put our street rods away (at least in the Great White North) and put on our jackets and long johns. The jacket keeps your body heat in and the cold out. Pretty simple stuff, but when men and women build cars, they seem to forget all about the basic idea of insulation. Insulating your car is nothing more than putting a jacket on the car, only the jacket goes on the inside instead of the outside.

No matter how wonderful the output from the evaporator on your new ride, it isn't going to be large enough to cool the interior if there's tremendous heat gain from the outside environment or if the heat leaks in and the cool air leaks out through big gaps in the door and firewall.

The importance of sealing the car against heat gain from outside can't be overstated. Your sealing and insulating should include sealing all the holes, insulating the body panels, and installing tinted glass (or tinting the existing glass).

Old cars and trucks are full of holes—the firewall especially and the floor too. It might seem like the seal where the steering column goes through the firewall is "good enough," but it probably isn't. Holes in the firewall are especially troublesome as they allow the very hot underhood air to enter the car.

Clear or black silicone seal is the answer for the small holes, Use it liberally in combination with the correct grommets to seal all the holes in the firewall and floorboards.

Insulating the car can be done in a variety of ways, obviously it's a heck of a lot easier to do a good job when the interior is torn out of the car. The material you use will depend on your budget and what's available. The ideal insulation material would provide a perfect barrier, holding the heat outside and the cool air inside. This material would not trap water (to avoid problems with mold and mildew) and would cut easily into small sections that could be glued into place in your vehicle.

A perfect insulator doesn't exist. The two close runners-up are polyurethane and a space-age material from 3M called Y-370. The Y-370 is hard to find without the right connections (it helps if your uncle works for NASA). We mention it here because there was a time when companies like Metal Fab in Minneapolis could buy it as surplus, cut it into smaller sheets and sell it to street rodders.

Polyurethane is probably your next-best candidate. High-density polyurethane in sheets 1/4in thick are often available from a local vinyl top supplier or auto upholstery shop. This is a closed cell material. The closed cells means that it will not wick up and hold water. It also means that air can't move easily through it—the essence of a good insulator. This material can often be found in sheets 1/4in thick. It's easily cut and can be glued to inner body panels with a spray adhesive.

There are other materials that work in cars too. Some building supply stores have fiberglass similar to what you use in the house, only it's been rolled down to a sheet about a 1/4in thick and coated with paper or a plastic material on one or both sides. Rolled wool type material, similar to what is often used under the carpet of new cars can often be found as well. Some of these materials don't insulate as well as polyurethane and have more of a tendency to hold water than does polyurethane.

When you buy insulation, buy material with the best insulating values (or R rating) combined with attributes already mentioned.

Insulation is important, but to avoid heat gain, you need to install tinted glass (or have the existing glass tinted) and to replace or repair any bad weatherstrip at the doors and windows.

Sheets of polyurethane can be easily cut and glued to the inside of the body panels. Be sure to do a good job when gluing the material down, especially the sheets that go on the floor, so no water will seep underneath to grow into interesting life forms later. High-heat areas like the firewall and the floor should probably get more than one layer, or thicker sheets if they're available. Be sure to apply insulation to the entire inner surface of the car or truck—your air conditioner will be glad you did.

Tinted Glass

If you're gong to insulate the car to avoid heat gain, you should also install tinted glass, or at least have the existing glass tinted. Anything you do to darken the glass will help to keep the heat out. How, and how dark, you tint it depends on the car, whether or not it's disassembled, and your budget.

Tinted glass can be cut to fit nearly any street rod. Obviously the glass used in the windshield will be different than that used in the side glass. How dark the side glass can be differs from one state to another. Some traffic laws limit how dark the tint can be on windshields and side windows, so please be aware of these laws before you tint your windows.

Every town or area seems to have a glass shop or two that specialize in street rods and unusual cars. You probably want to find the best local glass shop and discuss your options with them. If your budget is tight, have the glass tinting done by a specialty shop, or do it at home with a kit.

If we're going to encourage you to plan your car or truck to make optimum use of your air conditioning, we also must urge you to consider the color of both the car and the interior. Before painting it black, think about it!

How Much Radiator?

The following formula can be used to determine a reasonable starting point for radiator volume for a given vehicle.

Start with 2 cubic inches of core for every cubic inch of engine. Increase or decrease that ratio by the following factors:

ADD:

.1 for a vertical radiator core
.1 for an inline engine
.1 for small trailer towing
.1 for three-row radiator
.1 for double evaporators
.2 for outside temperatures over 105 degrees Fahrenheit
.2 for medium trailer towing
.2 for a small engine in a heavy car
.2 for fan diameter less than 90% radiator core's smaller dimension
.3 for air conditioning
.3 for no fan shroud
.3 for an antique car with small engine compartment
.4 for large trailer towing
.6 for a diesel engine

SUBTRACT:

.1 for remote transmission cooler (not in the radiator)
.1 for standard transmission
.1 for single-row radiator
.1 for a V-6 engine
.2 for a pickup truck engine compartment
.2 for outside temperatures less than 90 degrees Fahrenheit
.2 for a full fan shroud
.2 for a horizontal-flow radiator
.3 for large engine in light vehicle

To check the formula against a late-model car, we checked a Mustang with a 302ci engine and air conditioning. The basic formula says 2 x 302=604ci of radiator core. But the formula must be factored for air conditioning (add .3), temperatures over 105 degrees (add. 2), and a horizontal-flow radiator (subtract .2). The corrected formula would be 2.3 x 302=698ci of radiator core. The actual core (not the radiator but the core dimension) on the Mustang measures 18 x 24 x 1.5in or 648ci of core.

The formula may not be perfect (should we allow for a large engine in a light vehicle?), though as you can see, it's a good starting point.

Chapter 10

Service and Repair

This chapter is intended for those of you who have succeeded in installing the system in your street rod or pickup truck, and you now need to fill it with refrigerant. This chapter is also intended for anyone having trouble with the air conditioning in their vehicle.

The chapter first deals with necessary tools, then moves on to charging techniques, service procedures, and finally to troubleshooting problems. Before you can service or troubleshoot your system, you need a few basic air conditioning tools.

CAUTION: Because of high liquid pressures and other specific hazards, the procedures detailed herein should be performed only by those persons suitably experienced and properly

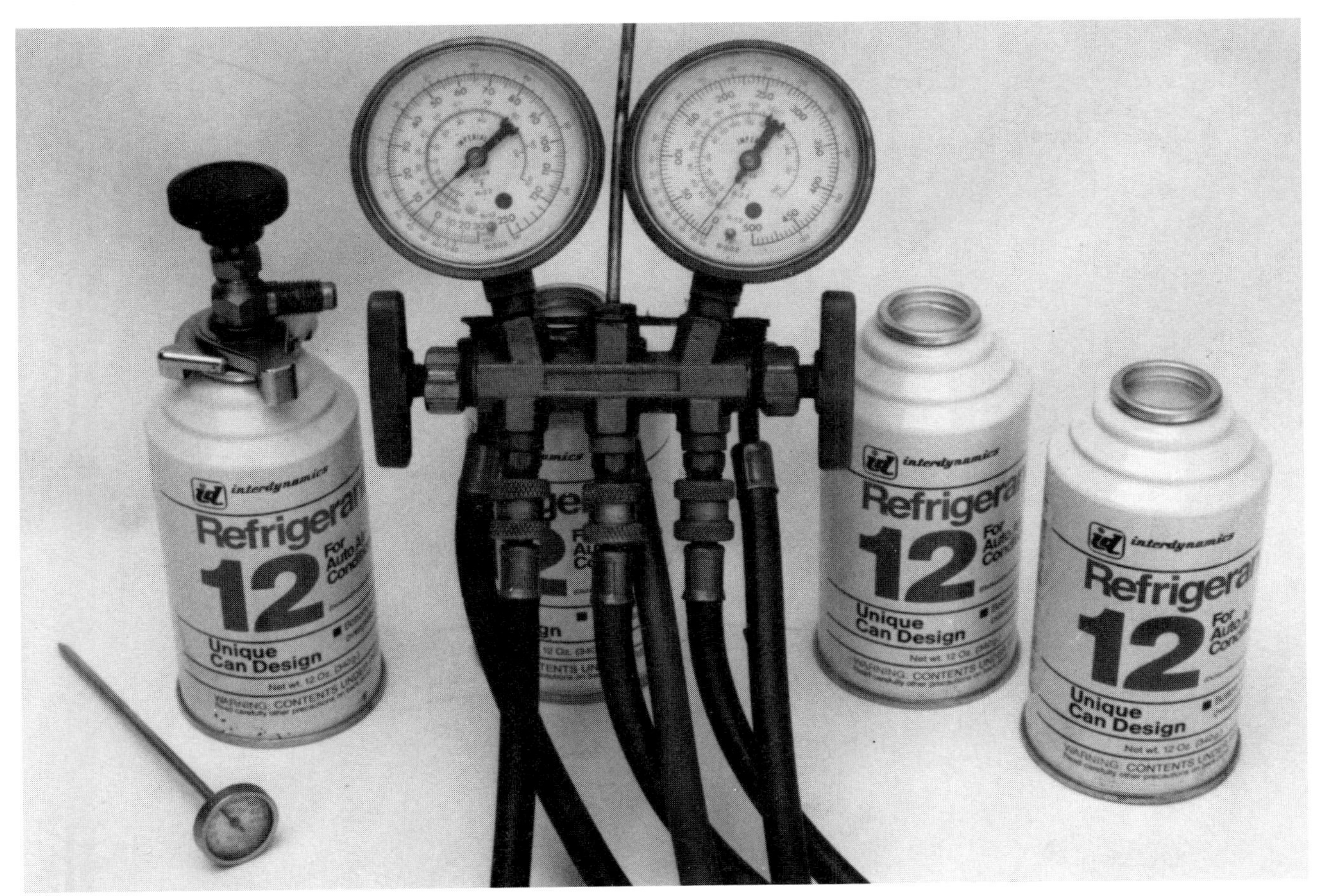

This is your basic air conditioning tool kit, CFC-12 (the small cans are no longer available), a set of manifold gauges, and a thermometer.

equipped to service automotive air conditioning systems. Further, it's best to remember that both CFC-12 and HFC-134A freeze anything they come into contact with. Always wear goggles to protect your eyes and avoid letting the refrigerant contact your skin. CFC-12 that comes into contact with a flame becomes Phosgene, a deadly gas.

Remember too that if you don't know what you're doing, you run the risk of wasting a lot of refrigerant, and our goal is to minimize the amount of the CFC-12 we vent to the atmosphere—an atmosphere that by all accounts has already collected far too much CFC-12 and related chemicals. There's nothing wrong with installing the system and then taking it to a professional for the evacuation and recharging.

Your Air Conditioning Tool Kit

Servicing and repairing air conditioning requires a few specific tools. They aren't cheap, meaning you might want to borrow some or perhaps take the option of allowing the professional shop to fill the newly installed system with refrigerant. The tools required include:

1. A standard two-gauge set of air conditioning gauges with 60in hoses. This set will contain one high-pressure and one low-pressure gauge.
2. A GE (General Electric) H10A leak detector.
3. A brand-name refrigeration vacuum pump, capable of drawing 29.5in of vacuum at sea level. This reading will drop by 1in of vacuum for each 1,000ft of elevation.
4. A large shop fan to place in front of the radiator and condenser to simulate airflow on a moving car.
5. A pocket air conditioning thermometer.

That should be enough special equipment for nearly anyone, professional or non-professional.

We should note here that, as discussed in chapter 3, the world of air conditioning and air conditioning service is changing as this book is written. The basic thrust of the new rules and regulation is to prevent the venting of CFC-12 to the atmosphere. By the time you read this book,

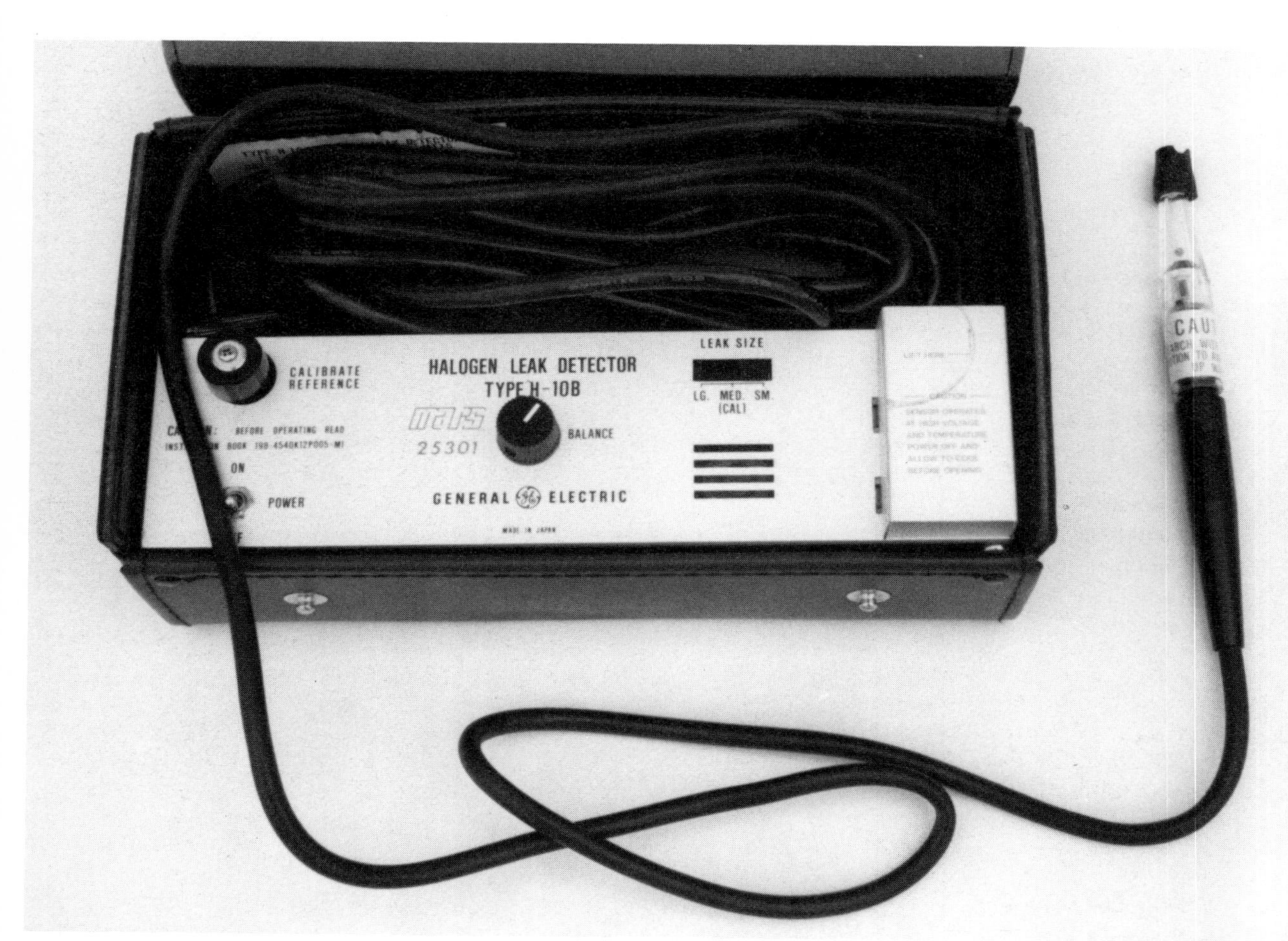

Finding leaks is becoming more and more important—what was considered acceptable seepage is no longer acceptable—thus the need for sophisticated leak detectors like this one from General Electric (GE).

CFC-12 will no longer be available in the small, 1lb cans.

So while we have included this service and repair chapter, it is becoming increasingly difficult for individuals to service their own air conditioning components. If you don't have ready access to CFC-12 (or HFC-134A for the most modern systems) then there isn't much point in buying the tools and equipment needed to service automotive air conditioners. Unless otherwise noted, the information in this chapter refers to air conditioning systems designed to operate with CFC-12 refrigerant.

Individuals who continue to service and repair automotive air conditioners at home need to stop venting CFC-12 into the atmosphere. In service situations where the system must be opened, take the car to a certified shop and have the CFC-12 sucked into a recycling machine—before taking it home to do the repair.

We stand by our earlier comments that only certified air conditioning technicians should service air conditioning systems. We present the service and troubleshooting information here for the benefit of those individuals, and so readers are as well informed as possible. Regardless of who actually services the air conditioner, the owner should know the basics of air conditioning service to ensure he or she gets what was paid for.

Use of the Gauge Set

The air conditioning gauge set is very important, an integral part of a serious air conditioning tool kit. Like most tools, this one can be abused and misused. The results of incorrect use range from incorrect diagnosis to the venting of more CFC-12 into the atmosphere.

The gauge set has a high pressure and a low pressure gauge, a manifold with two valves and (usually) three hoses. The low-side pressure gauge reads from 30in of vacuum to 120psi. It should read zero at whatever altitude it is being used. The high-side gauge reads from 0 to 500psi.

Each gauge is connected to a color-coded hose: High pressure is the red hose and red gauge while low pressure is normally a blue hose and blue gauge. The hoses are always open to the individual gauges; if you attach the low-pressure hose to a system that's full, the gauge will read the pressure, regardless of the position of the valve.

The valves open the central port of the manifold to the low- or high-pressure hoses and valves. When you charge an older CFC-12 system, the low-side valve is opened, allowing refrigerant to flow from the yellow hose through the low-side valve, down the low-side hose and into the system.

When you evacuate the system, both valves are open, allowing you to better evacuate the entire system.

The gauge set is connected to the air conditioning system through the two service ports or valves. Each valve is equipped with a Shrader valve, which looks like a tire valve. Small depressors are fitted to the ends of the low- and high-pressure hoses so the Shrader valves are opened as you screw on the hoses.

Most air conditioning systems have two service ports or Shrader valves, one for the high side and one for the low side. Many aftermarket systems have the service ports on the compressor. Otherwise the high-side service port is between the compressor and the condenser while the low-pressure service port is between the evaporator and the suction side of the compressor.

The important things to remember about your gauge set are: Always be sure you're connecting the right hose to the right side of the gauges, and always be sure the high-side gauge

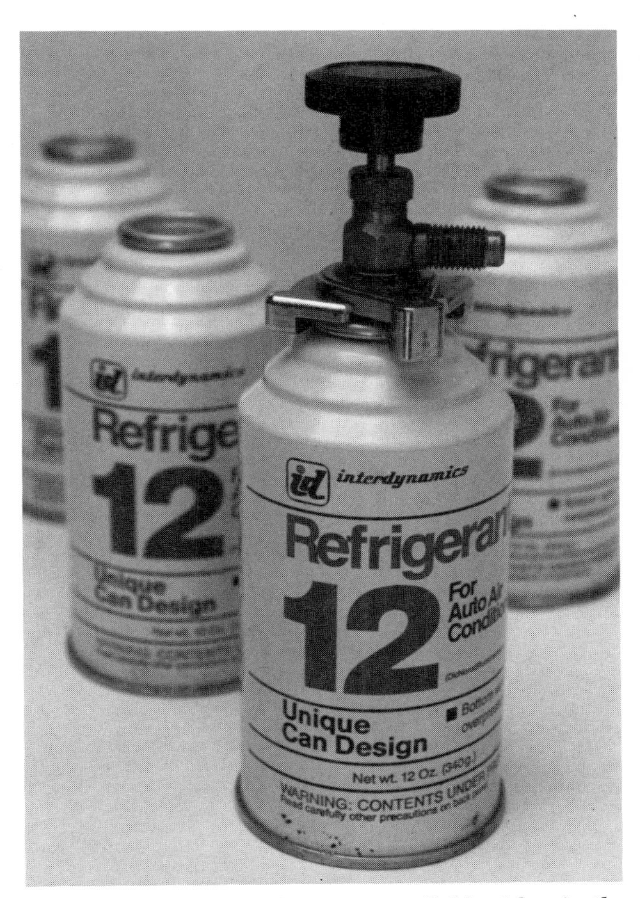

Up until late 1992 CFC-12 was available either in the small, 1lb cans, or larger cylinders for commercial shops. The small cans are no longer sold to nonprofessionals.

valves are closed whenever the system is operating. Though we have long charged CFC-12 systems through the low side, some manufacturers are recommending HFC-134A be charged through the high side while the system is at rest. Don't try this at home, kids!

Correct pressures for your new air conditioning system should be: 12-18psi for the low side and 180-250psi for the high side (CFC-12). Higher ambient temperatures will raise the high-pressure side approximately 20 or 30psi for each 10 degrees above 80 degrees Fahrenheit (this is another of Jack Chisenhall's rules of thumb).

Evacuation and Recharging

Before moving on to troubleshooting, it might be best to describe a basic evacuation and recharge cycle. This is the operation that must be performed after installing your new air conditioner, or any time the system has been opened for repair. Evacuation (or purging) will remove air, moisture, and other impurities in the system.

Every system has a high-side service port and a low-side service port. Each gauge set has a low- and a high-side gauge. Charging CFC-12 is usually done through the low-side port. (Check manufacturers' recommendations.)

Evacuation requires a good vacuum pump attached to the central hose on your gauge set. Once all the refrigerant in the system has been sucked into a recycling machine (or maybe the charge was lost due to a ruptured hose) and there is no pressure on either side of the system (a reading of 0), the vacuum pump can be turned on and both service valves opened fully.

The vacuum pump you use should be good enough to pull 29.5in of Mercury within five minutes. If you don't have at least 28in of Mercury after five minutes, you either have a leak or a bad vacuum pump. The system should be warm, at least eighty-five degrees Fahrenheit for good evacuation, because the moisture won't boil below that and if it won't boil, you can't do a good job of evacuating the system. If it's a cool day, warm up the system or warm up the shop to ensure that evacuation is complete.

Let the vacuum pump run for at least thirty minutes to be sure you've pulled all the moisture and impurities out of the system. Because moisture is one of the major enemies of an air conditioning system, it makes good sense to be thorough in the evacuation.

After allowing the vacuum pump to run long enough, close both gauge valves and watch for a change in the vacuum reading. A decrease in vacuum (an increase in pressure) of more than 1in in every four or five minutes indicates a leak.

Assuming the vacuum gauge holds steady after you close the valves, it is time to charge the system with refrigerant.

Start by connecting the central hose to the source of refrigerant. Refrigerant should always be charged according to the manufacturer's recommendations. Remember, some charge through the high-side and some through the low-side.

As you open the low-side gauge valve—to allow CFC-12 into a standard system that charges from the low side—the sight glass will get cloudy and you can actually watch the vaporous refrigerant as it passes through the receiver-drier.

There are two ways of knowing how much refrigerant is enough, or when the system is correctly charged. First, each manufacturer states the capacity of its system—most aftermarket systems require 2lb of refrigerant for a full charge. Second, the sight glass in a CFC-12 system will go from "cloudy" to "clear" when the system is properly charged.

If everything is installed correctly and your system has a capacity of 2lb, the sight glass will clear up just as the second pound of refrigerant goes into the system. The sight glass has become clear because the receiver-drier has filled with liquid refrigerant past the bottom of the pickup tube.

Liquid refrigerant is separated from the gaseous refrigerant in the receiver-drier—only liquid refrigerant passes out of the receiver-drier, past the sight glass, and onto the evaporator.

If you have a gauge set, it should have an extra valve on the end of the high-pressure hose. Otherwise there's a messy venting of refrigerant to the atmosphere every time you disconnect the high-side hose. Sixty inches of hose "charged" with 200psi of refrigerant makes quite a mess when it's suddenly disconnected from the system. By closing the valve at the end of the hose first, you can avoid the mess and the venting of CFC-12.

If this is the first charge in a new system, be sure to do a good visual inspection after the initial charge. Check all the fittings for bubbles or signs of leakage. Check the belt for tension; check all the bolts and brackets for lose bolts. Be sure that all the hoses are routed neatly away from things like exhaust manifolds and sharp metal edges.

Troubleshooting Your Air Conditioning System

Given Murphy's law, some of the newly installed systems are going to fail to cool after the initial charge. For these individuals and for those who are having trouble with an older system, we offer this troubleshooting section. Even though this section is directed toward the CFC-12 system, Jack Chisenhall's experience with HFC-134A leads him to believe that servicing is the same, except where noted.

The problems of an air conditioning system can be broken down to either internal or external problems. External problems may include air that's not cold enough because of poor air flow over the condenser caused by debris or by a defective cooling fan. Internal problems could, for example, include no cold air due to a restriction in a refrigeration line.

We should probably define "cold." Actually, for our purposes, "cold" is a relative term. Your air conditioner should produce air (measured at the duct) that is:

- 39 to 46 degrees F at 70 degree ambient

How cool the air feels coming out of the vents is a very subjective thing—the temperature should always be measured with a good air conditioning thermometer and results checked against charts that factor in the ambient temperature.

temperature.

- 40 to 48 degrees F at 80 degrees ambient temperature.
- 42 to 52 degrees F at 90 degree ambient temperature.
- 44 to 55 degrees F at 100 degree ambient temperature.

External problems are usually easy to identify, internal problems are more difficult to locate. Gauges are one way of looking into your system to find out exactly what the internal conditions are. If you learn how to read a set of gauges, the mystery of automotive air conditioning will be on its way to vaporizing.

Pressure is measured in pounds per square inch (psi). The weight of the atmosphere exerts 14.7psi at sea level. The low-side pressure gauge reads from 30in of vacuum to 120psi. It should read 0 (zero) at whatever altitude it is being used. The high-side gauge reads from 0 to 500psi.

Each service port (on CFC-12 systems) has a Schrader valve that looks much like a tire valve. The valve is opened by the depressor contained in the fitting for the hoses to the gauge set. The low-side fitting on this factory Ford installation is on the compressor (where the suction line comes in from the evaporator), while the high-side is on the high-side line where it leaves the compressor on its way to the condenser.

The gauges connect to the system by way of service ports at different locations. On aftermarket systems, these service ports are typically found on the compressor—one for the high-pressure side (always between the compressor and the condenser), and one for the low-pressure side (always between the evaporator and the compressor).

Each service port has a small valve that looks like a tire valve. These are known as Schrader valves and they prevent refrigerant from flowing into or out of the system unless the valve tip is depressed.

Refrigeration gauges are often misused. Inexperienced individuals may drain off significant quantities of CFC-12 while connecting and disconnecting the gauges. For these reasons the gauges should only be connected after a thorough visual inspection has been completed and you're sure you actually need them. Also be sure that before you connect the gauges you fully understand their use.

To prepare for diagnosis, run the engine at 1500 to 1800rpm, with fan and temperature controls on maximum cool, and check the general performance. If there is no cool air, first check that the compressor clutch is engaged and that the evaporator fan is blowing. If the compressor and fan are operating, check the refrigerant. Nearly all aftermarket systems contain a sight glass in the top of the receiver-drier or somewhere in the liquid line.

Cloudy Sight Glass

A cloudy sight glass indicates a system that is only partially full of refrigerant (with a few exceptions). A perfectly clear sight glass (use a light to get a good look) means the system is either full or empty. Note, with HFC-134A the glass appears milky when properly charged, though there should be no bubbles in the sight glass.

Now it's time to connect a set of gauges. You will likely get either no reading (meaning the system is empty) or a normal reading, meaning the system is full and you need to look somewhere else for the problem.

Correct pressures for your new air conditioning system should be: 12-18psi for the low side and 180-250psi for the high side. Higher ambient temperatures will raise the high-pressure side approximately 20 or 30psi for each 10 degrees above 80 degrees Fahrenheit. Note the correct pressure for HFC-134A: low side at compressor, 7 to 10psi; high side at compressor, 180 to 250psi.

An Empty System

If the system is empty, the search for leaks

Soldering 101—a simple repair of a copper line. The first principle is cleanliness. Be sure the objects to be soldered are free of dirt, grease, and oxidation.

A good brush-on flux will help to further clean the material and aid in obtaining a good, solid, soldered joint.

should begin with a good visual check. Is it a fast leak or a slow leak? When was the system last charged. If it's a newly installed and filled system, then look for obvious leaks like a screw in a hose or a loose fitting. (See the recharge and leak testing section for hints on charging new systems.)

CFC-12 leaks can be very tough to find. CFC-12 is colorless, odorless, heavier than air, and it evaporates as soon as it hits the atmosphere. The only helpful thing about it is the fact that the oil is carried with the refrigerant, so any sizable leak will leave a trail of oil at the offending hose or fitting. It will often just be a dark area, and the amount of oil might be slight. But if you find an air conditioning fitting with an oily residue, and the area around it is dry, you've probably found your leak. A good electronic detector can verify your visual diagnosis.

Because the system carries the oil in suspension with the refrigerant, any sizable leak will leak oil as well as refrigerant. Very slow leaks will usually only vent refrigerant and not oil, but a fast leak like a ruptured hose or a very loose fitting, will leak the refrigerant so fast that the oil is carried out of the system as well. If your system has suffered a major leak, be sure to check the oil level in the compressor before refilling the system.

Note that the industry doesn't yet have enough experience with HFC-134A and the tendency of oily spots to indicate refrigerant leaks. Our advice is to get the very best leak detector you can for the new refrigerant.

If you're lucky and the leak is an easy one to find, all that's left is the repair followed by evacuation and recharging. If your leak is slow, the normal procedure is to partially charge the system and then go over it, first with soapy water and then with an electronic leak detector, to find the leak. The trouble with this old scenario is that the partial charging and evacuating vents a lot of CFC-12 to the atmosphere.

So unless the leak is a big one and easy to

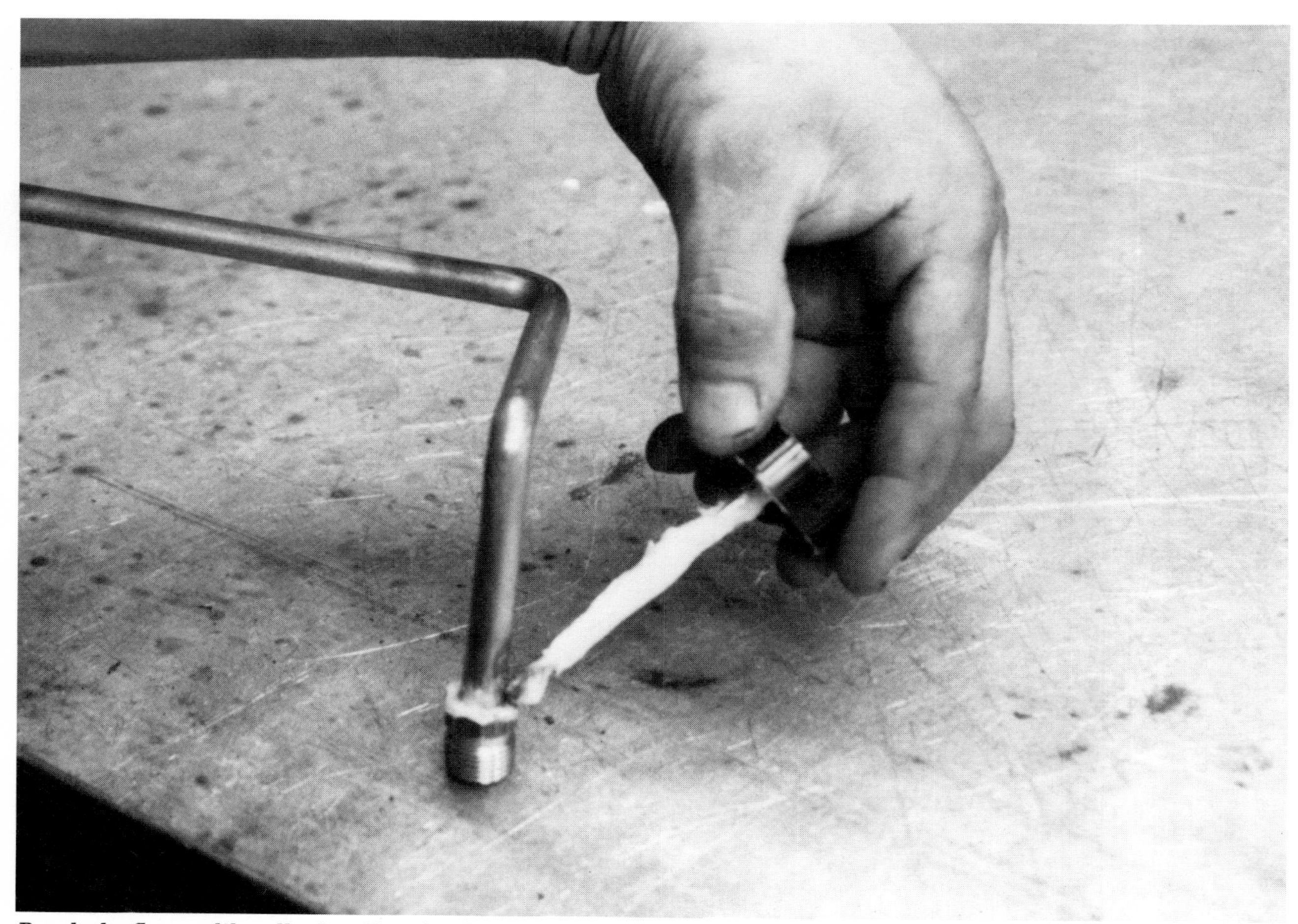

Brush the flux on liberally. It will melt when you hit it with the torch—flushing the area before the solder starts to melt.

find, you're probably better off to simply take the car to a good air conditioning shop.

A System Full of Refrigerant

First, you should double-check all the obvious things. The compressor clutch, the belt tension, and the operation of the evaporator blower. Next, establish some baseline conditions for your testing: engine running at 1500–1800rpm, high blower and coldest thermostat setting, doors and windows closed, ambient temperature of 70 degrees F or above.

Situations do occur where the system is full of refrigerant, yet the sight glass remains cloudy. The first thing to consider is whether the receiver-drier is installed backwards. Be sure the line from the condenser goes to the port marked "in" on the receiver-drier. The other condition that might give you a cloudy glass (on a full system) is a restriction in the liquid line from the condenser to the receiver-drier. On some new receiver-driers the filter screen could be pushed up so the bottom of the screen is blocking the liquid pickup tube. You will have to cut open the receiver-drier to confirm your diagnosis.

You should test next for a system that is overcharged. If the sight glass is clear, but both the high- and low-pressure gauge readings are high (300 or more on the high side, 50 or more on the low side), disconnect the compressor clutch. (Note that on HFC-134A systems, milky is the normal look for a correctly charged system.) The refrigerant should foam and then settle away from the glass in less than forty-five seconds. If the sight glass remains clear for more than forty-five seconds you have an overcharged condition and will have to have part of the charge sucked into a recycling machine.

Troubleshooting

If your troubles are not the rather obvious ones outlined above, you will need to go through a more thorough diagnosis. The following chart of fourteen problems and their symptoms will aid in finding the trouble with your air conditioning system.

1. Trouble: Excessively low refrigeration charge

Symptoms:

This is an acetylene torch, but a small propane torch has enough heat for most soldering operations like this one. The solder needs to be a high-quality, solid-core solder with a small percentage of silver.

No cooling
Low-side gauge pressure too low
High-side gauge pressure too low
Receiver-drier sight glass clear
Warm air in air conditioning ducts

Cause: The system is excessively low on refrigerant, probably caused by a serious leak.

Correction: Find and fix the leak. Be sure to check the compressor oil (oil is often lost with the refrigerant). Evacuate and recharge the system.

2. Trouble: Low or partial refrigerant charge

Symptoms:
Insufficient cooling
Low-side pressure too low
High-side pressure too low
Receiver-drier sight glass shows a stream of bubbles
Air in ducts only slightly cool

Cause: The system is low on refrigerant, probably caused by a leak.

Correction: Find and fix the leak. If there was a loss of oil, be sure to check the compressor oil level. Evacuate and recharge.

3: Trouble: Excessive air in the system

Symptoms:
Insufficient cooling
Low-side pressure too high
High-side pressure too high
Receiver-drier sight glass shows occasional bubbles
Air in ducts only slightly cool

Cause: The refrigerant is contaminated by large amounts of air and/or moisture.

Correction: Drain the system of refrigerant. Replace the receiver-drier (or the filter and desiccant bag if it's a rebuildable receiver-drier). Evacuate the system (at length) and recharge with fresh CFC-12.

Note: With HFC-134A systems there should be no occasional bubbles except after the compressor cycles. The sight glass should be milky with no bubbles.

The finished product, a leak-free joint. With a little polishing or paint, this could look just like new.

4. Trouble: Excessive moisture in the system

Symptoms:

Insufficient cooling during hottest part of the day or during extended driving

Low-side pressure normal, though it may be too low or even a vacuum

High-side pressure normal, though it may be low—at the same time low side is low

Receiver-drier sight glass may show tiny bubbles (**Note:** This could be a tough call with HFC-134A since the sight glass is always milky.)

Air in the ducts is usually cold, but becomes warm when pressure readings drop

Cause: Excessive moisture in the system. The drying agent in the receiver-drier is saturated with moisture, which is released to the system when outside temperature increases. Moisture in the system collects and freezes on the expansion valve, stopping the flow of refrigerant.

Correction: Suck all the CFC-12 from the system. Replace or rebuild the receiver-drier. Evacuate and recharge.

5.Trouble: Air and moisture in the system

Symptoms:

Insufficient cooling

Low-side pressure normal, but does not drop when the clutch cycles

High-side pressure slightly high

Receiver-drier sight glass shows occasional bubbles (Note again that with HFC-134A the sight glass should be milky when the system is fully charged.)

Air in ducts only slightly cool

Cause: Refrigerant contains non-condensible in the form of air and moisture.

Correction: Leak test, watch for bad compressor seals. Drain the system. Repair leaks as needed. Replace or rebuild the receiver-drier. Check the compressor oil. Evacuate and recharge.

6. Trouble: Compressor malfunction

Symptoms:

Insufficient cooling

Low-side pressure too high

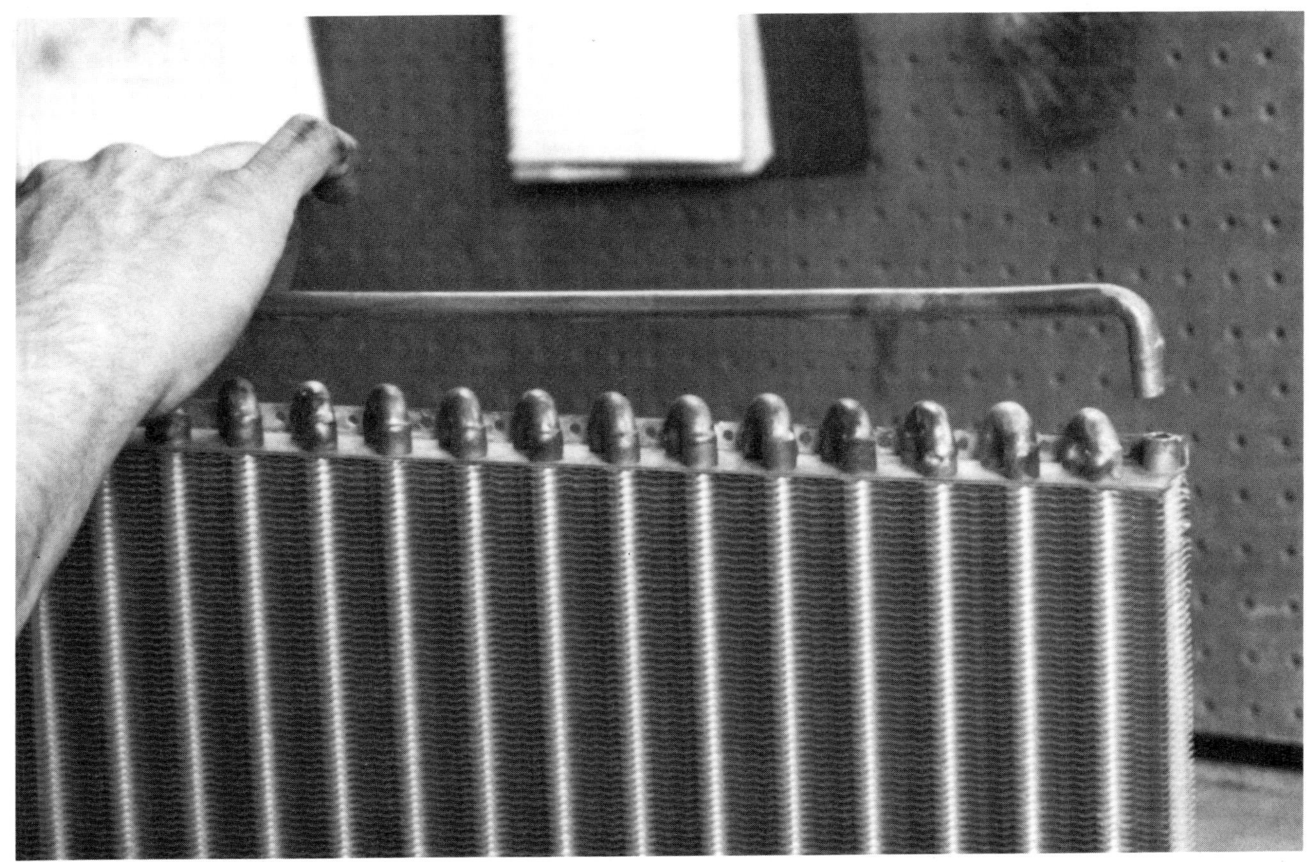

Another simple repair procedure. Part of the beauty of tube-and-fin type condensers is the ease with which they can be repaired and modified. Here a different inlet tube will be soldered into a condenser. Again, the first thing to do is clean the area before doing any soldering.

High-side pressure too low

Pressure readings do not change considerably when the engine speed is increased

Receiver-drier sight glass is clear

Air in ducts only slightly cool

Cause: Compressor is leaking internally. The reed valves or head gasket are leaking. Piston rings or cylinders may be excessively scored or worn.

Correction: Pull the refrigerant out of the system with a recycling machine. Replace the compressor. Evacuate and recharge the system.

7.Trouble: Clutch malfunction

Symptoms:

No compressor engagement—no cooling

Cause: No power to compressor clutch

Correction: Check to see if clutch engages when supplied with direct battery power. If yes, then controls are the problem. Check high-pressure, low-pressure, or cold-control switch—check switch operation with a voltmeter or test light.

8. Trouble: Condenser malfunction or system overcharge

Symptoms:

No cooling

Low-side pressure too high

High-side pressure too high

Receiver-drier sight glass may show occasional bubbles

Liquid line very hot

Air in ducts is warm

Cause: The condenser is not functioning properly because of high head pressure. System may be overcharged. Compressor and condenser may not be sized correctly.

Note: Technicians will have to be especially careful to avoid overcharging HFC-134A systems. Because the sight glass is hard to read and the volume for a given system is slightly lower with HFC-134A, overcharging is more likely with one of these new systems.

Correction: Check drive belts for tension and wear, and repair as needed. Check condenser for obstructions to air flow, and repair as needed. Check engine cooling fan for proper operation, and repair as necessary. Check engine overheating for possible impact on air conditioning system.

After liberal doses of flux, Jack Chisenhall applies the heat, slips the pipe in place, and melts solder into the joint. The key is the use of enough heat to do a good repair—without damaging any other joints nearby.

The finished product, a condenser with the right outlet for the job, one that looks like it came from the factory this way. All it takes is a little practice.

Individuals interested in a very neat air conditioning installation may be interested in the stainless steel line kit available from Vintage Air. The kit allows the builder to cut and bend lines to the exact dimensions needed.

If you suspect an overcharge, drain off some of the refrigerant into a recycling machine and then recharge until the sight glass goes clear. If you feel the condenser is plugged internally, you will have to pull all the refrigerant from the system and inspect the condenser before evacuating and recharging the system.

9. Trouble: High-side restriction
Symptoms:
Insufficient cooling
Low-side pressure too low
High-side pressure too high
Receiver-drier may show frost of condensation
Condenser hot on inlet side, cool on outlet side
Air in ducts only slightly cool
Liquid line may be to cool to the touch
Cause: A restriction in the high side of the system, probably in the liquid line, or the receiver-drier or condenser.
Correction: Pull the system down and disassemble and inspect receiver-drier, expansion valve, and liquid line.

10. Trouble: Low side restriction.
Symptoms:
Insufficient cooling
Low-side pressure too low
High-side pressure too low
Receiver-drier sight glass clear
Air in ducts only slightly cool
Suction line may be frosted
Cause: There is a restriction in the low side of the system, probably in the suction line. Refrigerant cannot leave the evaporator fast enough, and the expansion valve restricts the flow.
Correction: Pull the refrigerant out of the system, disassemble and inspect the components.

11. Trouble: Expansion valve stuck open
Symptoms:
Insufficient cooling
Low-side pressure too high
High-side pressure normal or slightly low
Receiver-drier sight glass clear or occasional bubbles
Air in ducts only slightly cool

First, the stainless line is cut to length, then an O-ring end is silver soldered on each end. Before the actual soldering, the stainless end is liberally coated with the same white flux used to solder copper.

Suction hose and evaporator coil suction tube show heavy condensation

Cause: Expansion valve is open too far, allowing excessive refrigerant flow into the evaporator, causing a flooded condition.

Correction: Test expansion valve as follows—remove temperature sensing bulb from suction line and pack bulb in ice, and low-side pressure should decrease. Next, warm the bulb with your hand, and low-side pressure should increase.

If the test indicates the expansion valve is operating properly, clean the surfaces of evaporator suction tube and temperature sensing bulb and reclamp bulb to tube and insulate.

If the test indicates a bad expansion valve, the system will have to be pulled down so the expansion valve can be replaced, followed by evacuation and recharging.

12. Trouble: Expansion valve malfunction, valve stuck closed

Symptoms:

No cooling

Low-side pressure very low

High-side pressure too low

Receiver-drier sight glass clear

Air in ducts only sightly cool

Expansion valve inlet may show frost or heavy sweating

Cause: The expansion valve is restricting the refrigerant flow through the evaporator. The cause may be a clogged filter screen, stuck valve, or kinked or broken sensing bulb.

Correction: Test the expansion valve per item 11 in this list of troubles. Clean and reclamp the bulb to the suction line if necessary, or draw down the system and replace the expansion valve.

13. Trouble: Temperature control switch malfunction, rapid cycling

Symptoms:

Clutch engages and disengages too rapidly

All other conditions normal

Cause: Temperature control switch feeler bulb is mislocated in evaporator coil or defective

Correction. Check location of feeler bulb in

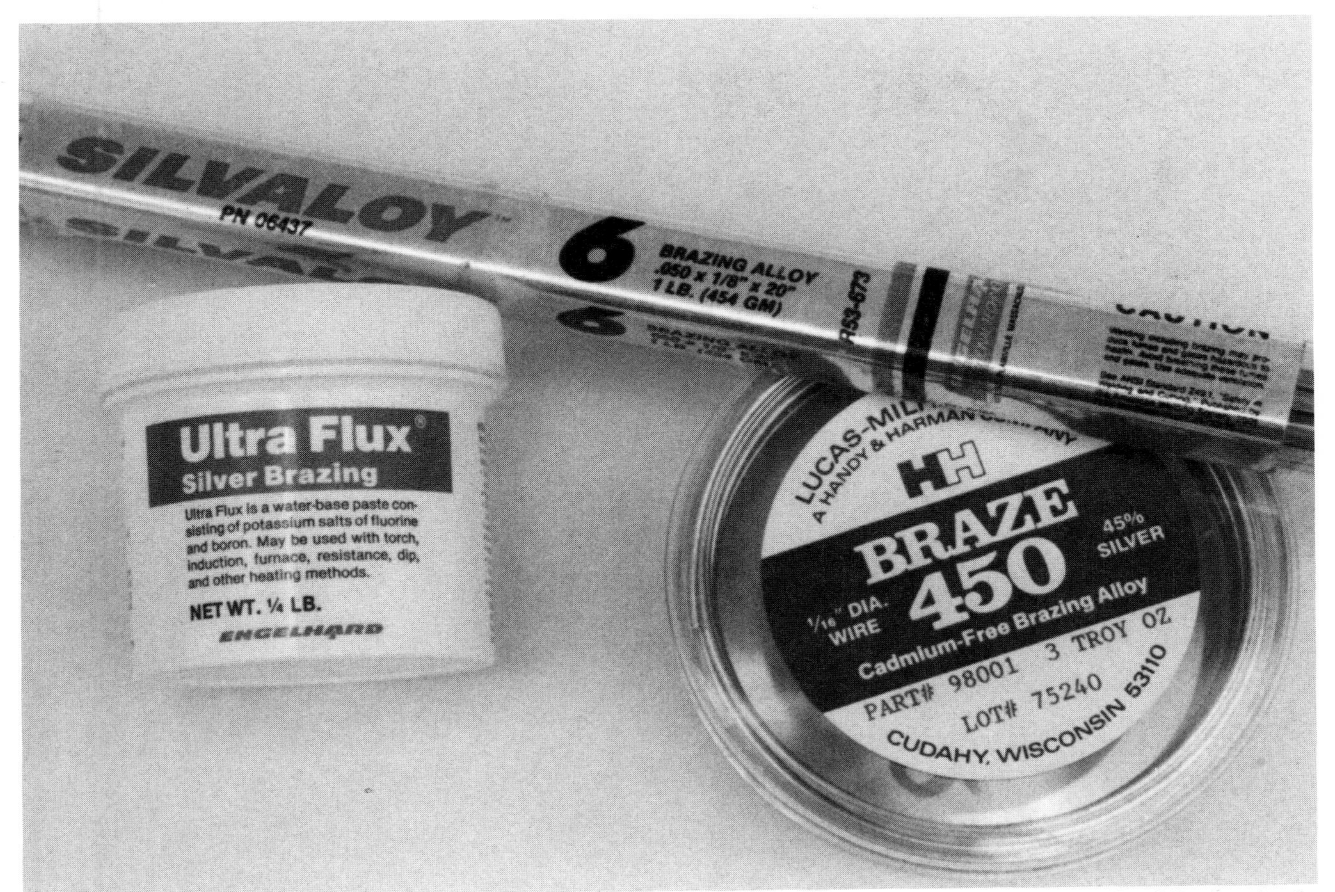

Braze 450 is the solder used for the stainless tubing and contains 45 percent pure silver. This product is also known as a brazing alloy. The Silvaloy is the solid-core solder used in soldering the copper tubing.

evaporator coil. Relocate as necessary. If is correctly located, replace the switch and check the operation of the system.

14. Trouble: Temperature control switch malfunction, slow cycling

Symptoms:

Clutch engages and disengages compressor so slowly that cab interior warms up during off cycle

All other conditions normal

Cause: Temperature control switch is out of calibration. Replace switch and test the system.

If your particular problem is difficult to pinpoint, find a way to run the gauges inside the cab of the car without crushing the hoses. Drive your car while a passenger monitors the readings. This is a very effective procedure—sometime's it's the only way you can get an air conditioning system to act up.

Compressor Oil Level Testing

As we said, any sizable refrigerant leak means the possible loss of refrigerant oil. Follow the following procedure to check the oil level in the compressor. First, determine the mounting angle with gauge #32448 set across the flat surfaces of the two front mounting ears. Center the bubble and read the angle.

Remove the oil filter plug, and rotate the clutch plate to position the internal parts to the position shown in the illustration. This is necessary so the dipstick will clear any internal parts when inserted into the compressor.

Insert the dipstick to its top position (see the illustration). The point of the angle must be to the left if mounting angle is to the right. The point of the angle must be to the right if the mounting angle is to the left. The bottom surface of the angle, in either case, must be flush with the surface of the oil filter hole.

Remove the dipstick. Count the increments of oil. Refer to the illustration to determine the correct oil level for the mounting angle of the compressor.

If the increments read on the dipstick do not match the table, add or subtract oil to the midrange value. For example, if the mounting angle on your 508 compressor is ten degrees, and the dipstick increment is three, add oil in one fluid ounce increments until seven is read on the dipstick.

Here Jack Chisenhall applies heat to the pipe and O-ring end while feeding solder to the connection.

This is what the new line-end looks like immediately after the repair. Yes, it's ugly but Jack isn't finished yet.

Install the O-ring and oil plug. Be sure the O-ring is clean, and if in doubt, replace the O-ring. Tighten the plug to 6-8lb-ft—never more.

When You Can't Fix It at Home

If you do decide to take your problems to a professional air conditioning service technician, you might want to bring this book along because it constitutes a good manual for aftermarket types of air conditioning systems. Here are a few pointers to pass along to the technician of your choice:

- A good automotive air conditioning mechanic shouldn't have any problems with the aftermarket air conditioning in your car.
- Make sure the technician is aware of whether your system is a mix and match, swap meet special, or a complete kit from a single aftermarket air conditioning company.
- If you have a wiring diagram for your car, bring it along and share it with the technician.
- Describe your problems in writing and point out the things to which the technician should pay special attention.

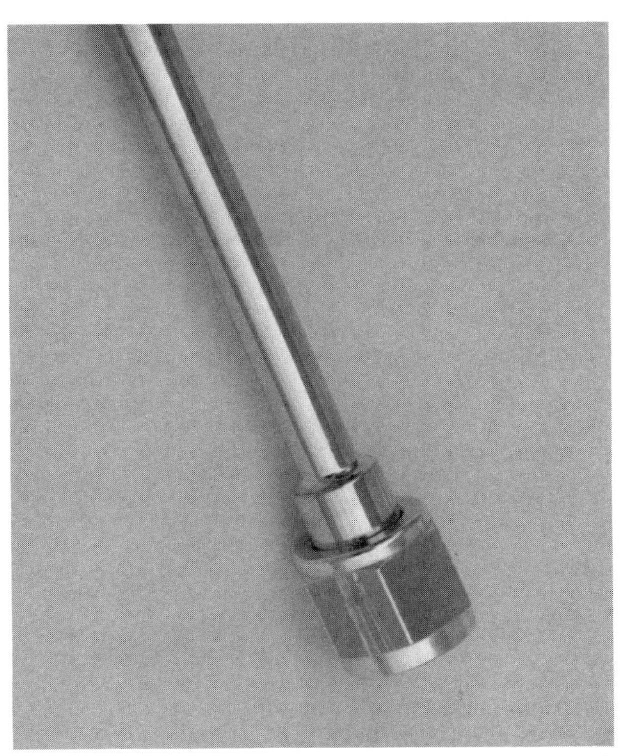

The finished product is a thing of beauty—with no evidence of the soldering. Much more attractive than those big, black hoses!

A little work on the polishing wheel will do wonders for that ugly area on the end of the stainless line.

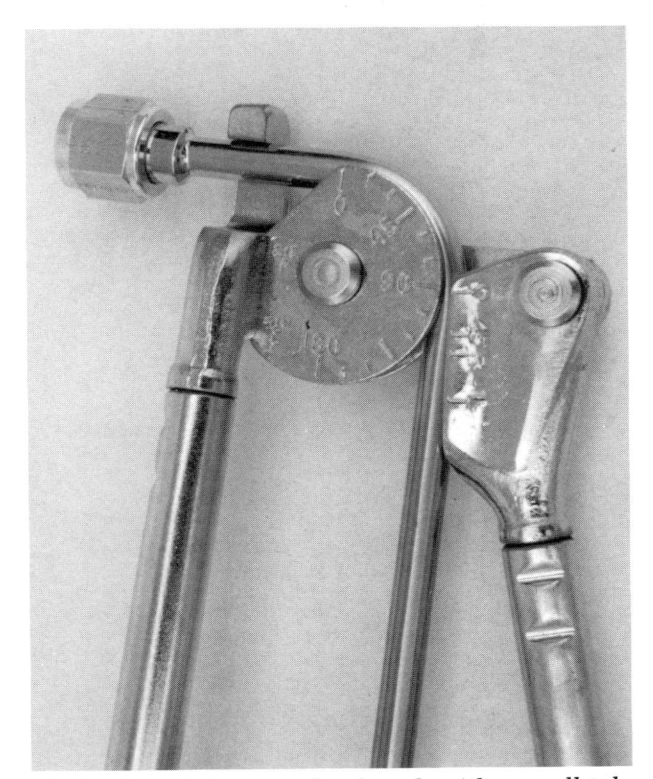

The final touch is a neat bend made with a small tubing bender like this one.

Sources

Steele Rubber Products
1601 Hwy 150 East
Denver, CO 28037

Vintage Air
10305 I-35 North
San Antonio, TX 78233

Walker Radiator
694 Marshall Street
Memphis, TN 38103

Alan Grove Components
Route 2, Box 5B
Louisburg, KS 66053

Zipps Water Pump Housings
1206 Seventh Street
Trafford, PA 15085

Glossary

Absolute Humidity: the mass of water vapor present in a unit volume of moist air.
Absolute Pressure: pressure measured from absolute zero in a perfect vacuum, or 29.92in of Mercury.
Accumulator: a refrigerant reservoir/drier located at the low-pressure outlet from the evaporator.
Air Conditioner: a device used in the control of the temperature, humidity, cleanness, and movement of air.
Air Conditioning: the control of the temperature, humidity, cleanness, and movement of air.
Air Inlet Door: a moveable door in the duct system that permits the selection of outside air or inside air for both heating and cooling systems.
Air Outlet Door: a moveable door in the duct system that directs airflow into the heater core or into the duct work that leads to the evaporator.
Ambient Temperature: temperature of the surrounding air, outside air temperature.
Ambient Sensor: a sensor used to prevent air conditioner operation by interrupting the electrical circuit to the compressor when ambient temperatures fall below a predetermined point.
Ambient Switch: a switch used to prevent air conditioner operation by interrupting the electrical circuit to the compressor when ambient temperatures fall below a predetermined point.
Ammeter: an electrical tester that measures current in amps.
Amplifier: a device used in ATC systems to amplify electrical signals from temperature sensors in the system.
ATC: abbreviation for automatic temperature control.
Atmospheric Pressure: air pressure at a given altitude. At sea level, atmospheric pressure is 14,696psi.
Automatic: a self-regulating system.
Automatic Temperature Control: an air conditioner control system that automatically maintains passenger compartment temperature at a level selected by the operator.
Axial Compressor: a compressor characterized by pistons that are arranged horizontally around and parallel to the crankshaft axis or center line.
Back Seat (Service Valve): position of a hand shut-off valve obtained by turning the valve stem counterclockwise as far as possible. The position for normal system operation.
Barrier Hose: refrigeration hose that has a nitrile rubber barrier liner inside to contain the HFC-134A refrigerant.
Bead Lock Fittings: new fitting type most suitable for barrier hoses.
Belt: a V-belt used to power the compressor or another accessory.
Bimetallic: two layers of different metals fused together. When temperatures change, the metal strip bends to trigger a switch.
Bimetallic Thermostat: a thermostat that uses bimetallic strips.
Bleeding: slowly releasing pressure by drawing off some liquid or gas.
Blower: an electrical motor and fan assembly used to move air.
Blower Relay: an electrical device used to control the function or speed of a blower motor.
Blower Resistor: an inline resistor that reduces voltage to the blower motor to provide different blower speeds.
Boiling Point: the temperature at which a liquid changes to a vapor.
Bowden Cable: a wire cable inside a metal or rubber housing used to open and close a valve or door in the duct system to provide operator control.
British Thermal Unit (Btu): the amount of heat necessary to raise 1lb of water 1 degree Fahrenheit.
Bulkhead Fitting: a fitting that attaches to and passes through a hole in a panel and seals mechanically to prevent air leaks.
Calorie: the smallest measure of heat energy. One calorie is the amount of heat energy required to raise 1 gram of water 1 degree Celsius.

Can Tap: a device used to pierce, dispense, and seal "one-pound" cans of refrigerant.
Capillary Tube: a small tube that transmits pressure to a sensing bulb to activate a valve. Commonly used with a thermal expansion valve to connect the TXV to a temperature sensing bulb located at the evaporator outlet.
Celsius: a temperature scale using the freezing point of water as zero. The boiling point of water is 100 degrees C.
Charge: a specific amount of refrigerant or oil by volume or weight required by a system.
Charging: the installation of refrigerant or oil in the system.
Charging Hose: generally used to describe any of the special hoses used to connect a manifold gauge set refrigerant supply, a charging station, or a vacuum pump to an air conditioning system.
Charging Station: a console housing a refrigerant supply and gauges plus other service equipment such as a vacuum pump. (See recycling/recharging station.)
Check Valve: a valve that allows a one-way flow of refrigerant only.
Circuit Breaker: a bimetallic device used instead of a fuse to protect a circuit.
Clean Air Act: an action by the US Government to curtail use of CFC-12 after December 31 1995.
Clutch: the device located on the compressor drive-shaft that transfers power from the belt drive to the driveshaft.
Clutch Armature: that part of the clutch that is pulled in when engaged.
Clutch Coil: See "Clutch Field."
Clutch Field: wire windings fastened to the front of the compressor. Current applied to the field sets up a magnetic field that pulls the armature in to engage the clutch.
Clutch Rotor: the grooved, rotating assembly in which the drive belt rides.
Cold: the absence of heat.
Compound Gauge: the "low-side" gauge. It registers pressures up to 150psi and also vacuum readings below zero psi.
Compressor: the pump that draws low-pressure refrigerant from the evaporator, compresses it, and forces it to the condenser.
Compressor Discharge Pressure Switch: a pressure-operated electrical switch that interrupts the electrical circuit to the clutch if internal pressures rise to dangerous levels. Not included in all systems.
Compressor Shaft Seal: springs, snap rings, O-rings, shaft seal, seal sets, and/or gaskets mounted on the compressor crankshaft to prevent refrigerant from escaping at the crankshaft
Condensate: water taken from the air; forms on the exterior surface of the evaporator and collects inside the evaporator case.
Condensation: the process of changing a vapor to a liquid.
Condenser: the component of a refrigeration system in which high-pressure refrigerant vapor is changed to a high-pressure liquid by removing heat.
Contaminants: anything other than refrigerant and refrigeration oil in the system.
Control Head: the operator control panel assembly.
Convection: the transfer of heat by the circulation of a vapor or liquid.
Cutoff Switch: electrical or mechanical switch used to interrupt system operation by opening the electrical circuit to the clutch.
Cycling Clutch System: a system which uses a thermostatic or pressure switch to turn the compressor on and off as necessary to keep the evaporator from freezing.
Desiccant: a drying agent used in refrigeration systems to remove excess moisture. May be a gel or crystals housed in the receiver-drier or accumulator.
Diagnosis: the procedure followed to locate the cause of a malfunction.
Dichlorofluoromethane: Refrigerant 12. Also known as R-12 or Freon (a DuPont brand name).
Discharger: bleeding some or all of the refrigerant from a system by opening a valve or connection and permitting the refrigerant to escape slowly. Systems must be fully discharged before removing any components in the refrigerant system.
Discharge Air: conditioned air as it passes through the outlets and enters the passenger compartments.
Discharge Line: the refrigeration line leading from the compressor to the condenser.
Discharge Pressure: pressure of the refrigerant being discharged from the compressor; also known as the high-side pressure.
Discharge Side: that portion of the refrigeration system under high pressure, from the compressor outlet to the evaporator inlet. Also known as the "high side."
Double Flare: a flare on the end of a piece of tubing; the tubing is folded over to form a double face.
Drier: a device containing desiccant; used to absorb moisture in the system.
Drive Pulley: a V-pulley attached to the crankshaft of an automobile; this pulley drives the compressor clutch pulley through the use of a belt.
Drying Agent: desiccant.
Duct: a passageway for the transfer of air from one point to another.
Engine Idle Compensator: a thermostatically controlled device on the carburetor which pre-

vents stalling during prolonged hot weather periods while the air conditioner is operated.
Engine Thermal Switch: an electrical switch designed to delay the operation of the system in cool weather to allow time for the engine coolant to warm up.
EPR: valve used on some Chrysler systems to control evaporator pressure. Located in compressor inlet.
Equalizer Line: a line or connection used to balance the pressure reading POA/STV at the evaporator outlet with that at the evaporator inlet to ensure that the expansion valve meters the correct amount of refrigerant to the evaporator.
ETR: valve used on some Chrysler systems to control evaporator temperature. Located at compressor inlet.
Evacuate: the removal of air and moisture from a system using a vacuum pump.
Evaporator: the coil assembly in the passenger compartment where refrigerant vaporizes and compartment where refrigerant vaporizes and absorbs heat.
Evaporator Control Valve: any of the several types of evaporator suction pressure control valves used to regulate the evaporator temperature by controlling the evaporator pressure.
Evaporator Core: the tube-and-fin assembly located inside the evaporator housing.
Evaporator Housing: the case that contains the evaporator core, doors, duct outlets, and blower.
Evaporator Pressure Regulator: see EPR.
Evaporator Temperature Regulator: see ETR.
Expansion Tube: a metering device, used in the inlet of some evaporators, to control the flow of liquid refrigerant into the evaporator core. Also known as an orifice tube.
Expansion Valve: see Thermostatic Expansion Valve.
Fahrenheit: a thermometer scale using 32 degrees as the freezing point of water.
Field: a wire coil located behind the clutch rotor. Current passing through this coil sets up a magnetic field and causes the clutch to engage.
Filter: a device used in the drier or as a separate unit to remove solid contaminant from the refrigerant.
Flare: a flange or cone-shaped end applied to a piece of tubing to provide a means of fastening to a fitting.
Flooding: a condition caused by too much liquid refrigerant being metered into the evaporator.
Flush: to remove solid contaminants from the components in a system.
Freeze up: failure of a unit to operate properly due to the formation of ice at the expansion valve or the formation of ice on the surface of the evaporator.
Freon: registered trademark of E.I. Dupont for refrigerant R-12.
Freon 12: Refrigerant 12.
Front Seat: closing of the compressor hand shut-off valves by turning them as far as possible in the clockwise direction. Isolates compressor from the rest of the system.
Fuse: an electrical device used to protect a circuit against accent overload or unit malfunction.
Gas: a vapor.
Gauge Set: two or more pressure gauges attached to a manifold and used for taking system pressure readings.
Genetron 12: registered trademark of Allied Chemicals Company for R-12.
Global Warming: some gasses contribute to global warming by acting like a greenhouse. Greenhouses are warmed by the sun because the glass allows the radiant heat from the sun to enter the greenhouse, but prevents the radiant heat of the earth from leaving. Because they have that same capability as glass to pass or block radiant energy from the sun on earth, these gasses have become known as greenhouse gasses.
Halide Leak Detector: a flame-type leak detector using propane gas and a search hose. Color of flame changes to indicate presence of a leak.
Head Pressure: the high-pressure reading taken at the compressor.
Hg: chemical symbol for mercury (used to identify a vacuum).
High-Pressure Cutout Switch: a protective switch that interrupts the electrical circuit to the compressor when very high pressures occur in the system. Not found on all systems.
High-Pressure Lines: the refrigerant lines from the compressor outlet to the expansion valve inlet.
High-Pressure Relief Valve: a "pop-off" valve that vents refrigerant into the air to relieve high pressures. Not on all systems.
High Side: see "Discharge Side."
High-Side Service Valve: the service port located in the high-pressure portion of the system.
H.N.B.R.: Hydrogenated Nitrile Butadiene Rubber. A rubber compound used for O-rings & seals in HFC-134A systems.
Idler: a pulley device that keeps the tensions of the drive belt that powers the compressor. The idler is used to tighten the belt.
Idler Eccentric: a device used with the idler pulley as a means of tightening the belt.
In-car Sensor: a sensor used in automatic temperature control units for sensing the in-car temperature. Visually located in the vehicle dash.
Inches of Mercury: a unit of measure when referring to a vacuum.

In-duct Sensor: a sensor used in automatic temperature control units for sensing the in-duct return air temperature.
Insulation Tape: tape used to wrap refrigeration hoses, lines, or a thermal expansion valve temperature sensing bulb.
Isotron 12: a trademark of Penn Salt Company (Refrigerant 12).
Latent Heat: the amount of heat required to cause a change of state of a substance without changing its temperature.
Leak Detector: a device used to identify the sources of leaks in a system.
Liquid Line: a refrigerant line from the condenser outlet to the evaporator duct.
Low-Head Pressure: the high-side pressure is lower than normal due to a malfunction of the system.
Low-Pressure Cutout Switch: a switch that interrupts the electric circuit to the compressor clutch to prevent system operation if internal pressures are very low.
Low Side: the low-pressure section of the system between the evaporator inlet and the compressor inlet.
Low-Side Service Valve: the service port located in the low-pressure portion of the system.
Low-suction Pressure: pressure lower than normal in the low-pressure portion of the system due to a malfunction of the unit.
Magnetic Clutch: a coupling device used to turn the compressor on and off electrically.
Manifold: the metal assembly to which the pressure gauges are attached. Includes hand shut-off valves and service hose connectors.
Manifold Gauge: a pressure gauge.
Manifold Gauge Set: a manifold complete with gauges.
Micron: a unit of measure; 1,000 microns = 1 mm = 0.03937in of mercury.
Molecular Sieve: a drying agent.
Montreal Protocol: a global action ratified by sixty-eight nations called for extensive international effort to reduce and eventually eliminate the CFCs that damage the ozone layer. Ozone-damaging CFCs include CFC-11, 12, 113, 114 and 115.
Mount and Drive: pulleys, mounting plates, belts, and fittings necessary to mount a compressor and clutch assembly on a vehicle.
Muffler: device used in the refrigerant line to minimize compressor noise transmitted to the inside of the car.
Oil Bleed Line: an external line that bypasses an evaporator pressure regulator, to insure positive oil return to the compressor at low compressor speeds and under a low charge or clogged system condition.
Oil Bleed Passage: internal orifice that bypasses an expansion valve, evaporator pressure regulator, or bypass valve to insure a positive oil return to the compressor.
Overcharge: too much refrigerant or refrigeration oil in the system.
Ozone Layer: a layer in the stratosphere that shields the earth from harmful ultraviolet radiation.
P.A.G. Oil: Polyalkalineglycol, the oil used in most new HFC-134A systems as a lubricant.
Performance Test: readings of the temperature and pressure under controlled conditions to determine if an air conditioning system is operating properly.
Pickup Tube: a tube extending from the outlet of the receiver almost to the bottom of the tank to insure that 100 percent liquid is supplied to the liquid line or expansion valve.
POA/STV Valve: a valve located in the refrigerant line at the evaporator outlet to maintain evaporator pressure in the 28-32psi range by regulating the amount of refrigerant leaving the evaporator. General Motors calls the valve a POA. Ford's similar valve is an STV.
Polyester Oils: an ester-based lubricant considered an alternative to P.A.G. oils as a lubricant. Early testing indicates favorable compatibility with HFC-134A and mineral oils used in CFC-12 systems. Polyester oils are being used in some early release OEM retrofit procedures; it may simplify the retrofit of many cars. Follow compressor manufacturers specifications.
Potentiometer: a rheostat type operator temperature control.
Power Servo: a servo unit used in an ATC system which is operated by a vacuum or an electrical signal.
Pressure Drop: the difference in pressure between any two points; a pressure drop may be caused by a restriction or friction.
Pressure Switch: an electrical switch that is actuated by a predetermined low or high pressure. A pressure switch is generally used for system protection.
Primary Seal: a seal between the compressor shaft seal and the shaft to prevent the leakage of refrigerant and oil.
Programmer: the part of an automatic temperature control system that controls the blower speed, air mix doors, and vacuum diaphragms.
Propane: a flammable gas used in the halide leak detector.
Psi: abbreviation for pounds per square inch.
Psia: abbreviation for pounds per square inch, absolute.
Psig: abbreviation for pounds per square inch, gauge.
Pumpdown: Evacuation of a system.
Ranco Control: a trade name used when refer-

ring to a Ranco Thermostatic control.
Ram Air: air that is forced through the condenser coils by the movement of the vehicle or the action of the fan.
Receiver: a container for the storage of liquid refrigerant.
Receiver/Dehydrator: a combination container for the storage of liquid refrigerant and a desiccant.
Recovery: Removing refrigerant.
Recovery/Recycling/Recharge Unit: refers to a single piece of equipment that performs recovery, recycling, and charging of an air conditioning systems.
Recycling: Processing (cleaning and drying) the refrigerant for reuse.
Reed Valves: thin steel leaves located in the valve plates of automotive compressors; these leaves act as suction and discharge valves.
Refrigerant: the chemical compound used in a refrigeration system to produce the desired cooling.
Refrigerant 12: the refrigerant used in automotive air conditioners. The chemical name of Refrigerant 12 is dichlorodifluoromethane. The chemical symbol is $C\ C1_2F_2$.
Refrigeration Cycle: the complete cycle of the refrigerant from a liquid to a vapor and back to a liquid.
Refrigeration Oil: highly refined oil free from all contaminants.
Relative Humidity: the actual moisture content of the air expressed as a percentage of the total moisture that the air can hold at a given temperature.
Relay: an electrical switch device that is activated by a low-current source and controls a high-current device.
Resistor: a voltage dropping device, usually wire wound, which provides a means of controlling fan speeds.
Restriction: a blockage in the system.
Retrofit: the upgrade of an air conditioning system from operating on CFC-12 to HFC-134A. Implies changing required components for correct operation.
Rheostat: a wire-wound variable resistor used to control blower motor speeds.
Rotor: the rotating or freewheeling portion of a clutch; the belt rides on the rotor.
Schrader Valve: a spring-loaded valve similar to a tire valve. The Schrader valve is located inside the service valve fitting.
Screen: a metal mesh located in the receiver, expansion valve, and compressor inlet to prevent particles of dirt from circulating through the system.
Sensor: a temperature-sensitive unit such as a remote bulb or thermistor.
Service Port: an access point where service hoses can be connected to the system.
Shaft Seal: see Compressor Shaft Seal.
Shaft Key: a piece of metal that fits into corresponding slots cut in the compressor shaft and the clutch end plate to prevent the end plate from turning on the shaft.
Short Cycling: a malfunction in which the air conditioner runs for very short periods. Also quick or fast cycle. Cycling clutch systems only.
Sight Glass: a window in the liquid line or in the top of the drier; this window is used to observe the liquid refrigerant flow.
Slugging: the return of liquid refrigerant to the compressor.
Solenoid Valve: an electromagnetic valve controlled remotely by energizing a coil.
Specific Heat: the quantity of heat required to change 1lb of a substance by one degree Fahrenheit.
Squirrel Cage Blower: a blower wheel that provides a large volume of air using vanes on the outside circumference of the wheel.
STV: Suction Throttling Valve.
Suction Line: the line connecting the evaporator outlet to the compressor inlet.
Suction Service Valve: Low-side Service Valve.
Suction Throttling Valve: a back-pressure-regulated device that prevents the freeze-up of the evaporator core; used by Ford and similar to POA valve.
Super Heat: adding heat intensity to a gas after the complete evaporation of a liquid.
Superheat Switch: an electrical switch actuated by an abnormal temperature-pressure condition (a superheated vapor); used for system protection.
System: all of the components and lines that make up an air conditioning system.

Tailpipe: the outlet pipe from the evaporator to the compressor. The suction line.
Temperature: heat intensity measured on a thermometer.
Ternary Blend: a mixing of compounds that produces a refrigerant that will function in a car air conditioner.
Tetrafluoromethane: chemical name for HFC-134A.
Thermal Fuse: a temperature-sensitive fuse link designed so that it melts at a certain temperature and opens a circuit. Used in 1972-77 General Motors systems. Also known as a thermal limiter.
Thermistor: a temperature-sensing resistor that has the ability to change values with changing temperature.
Thermostat: in cycling clutch air conditioners, a sensor used to cycle the clutch to control the rate

of refrigerant flow for the purpose of regulating evaporator temperature.
Thermal Expansion Valve: a valve at the evaporator inlet that regulates the rate of the flow of refrigerant into the evaporator.
Thermostatic Switch: see "Thermostat."
Time-delay relay: an electrical switch device that provides a time delay before closing (or opening).
Ton of Refrigeration: the effect of melting one ton of ice in 24 hours. One ton equals cooling 12,000 Btu per hour.
Transducer: a vacuum valve used to transfer the electrical signal from the amplifier into a vacuum signal. This vacuum signal regulates the power servo unit in an automatic temperature control unit.
Trinary Switch: a pressure switch that performs three functions: high-pressure safety compressor cutoff, low-pressure safety compressor cutoff, Fan operation.
Undercharge: less than the specified amount of refrigerant in a system. A condition that results in little or no cooling.
Vacuum: referring to a condition having less than atmospheric pressure; expressed in inches of mercury.
Vacuum Line: a rubber hose that carries a vacuum from one point to another.
Vacuum Motor: a device designed to provide mechanical control by the use of a vacuum.
Vacuum Pump: an electrical pump used to remove air and moisture from a refrigeration system.
Vacuum Reserve Tank: a metal container, resembling a large juice can, that is used to store reserve vacuum pressure.
Valves-In-Receiver (VIR): an assembly containing the expansion valve, suction throttling valve, desiccant, and receiver. Used in 1972-1977 General Motors systems.
Vapor: a gas.
VIR: Valve in Receiver.
Viscosity: the thickness of a liquid or its resistance to flow.
Water Control Valve: a mechanically or vacuum-operated shutoff valve that stops the flow of hot water to the heater core.
Woodruff Key: a shaft key that prevents the clutch end plate from turning on the compressor shaft. It has a rounded edge that fits into a corresponding cutout in the compressor shaft.

Green Technology

Safe Disposal and Recycling of Parts and Chemicals

One of the most difficult problems in repairing or restoring any vehicle is the question of what to do with the old parts and poisonous fluids you inevitably generate. Everybody knows these days that two of our largest environmental concerns are the related ills of landfill overuse and groundwater contamination. Unfortunately, our interest in environmental problems far outstrips our current ability to find answers to them.

While repairing or restoring your vehicle, there are several components and fluids that can actually be recycled, such as batteries, motor oil, electrical components, brake pads, and more. Take advantage of the recycling effort.

There are many more components and fluids that cannot be recycled, however. The best you can do with these hazardous wastes is to control the spread of the hazard. Check with your local pollution control agency or your county government for hazardous waste collection sites where you can dispose of these parts and fluids.

Parts

Actual pieces of mechanical junk are generally more of a pain than a danger to dispose of. Assuming that the pieces aren't filled with fluid or particularly greasy, metal parts will sit happily inert in a landfill and actually decompose over time—albeit a long, long time. Yet, some plastic and rubber pieces release a number of carcinogenic chemicals as they decompose. If possible, you should bring big metal parts to a local junkyard; often yards will accept these pieces for their scrap value and sometimes melt them down to be recycled.

Batteries

Old vehicle batteries are like environmental time bombs just waiting to explode. The average vehicle battery contains more than 18lb of toxic metals, and the chemicals inside can burst through the plastic shell or seep through cracks and leak onto your floor. And everyone has one or two old batteries laying around in a corner of their garage or workshop.

Fortunately, batteries are easy to dispose of and the cores can be recycled by the manufacturers to make new batteries. In many states, shops that sell batteries are required by law to accept old batteries free of charge and see to their safe disposal. Some responsible shops even reinforce this by giving you a rebate when buying a new battery if you bring in the old battery.

Tires

Tires are a well-known dumping hazard, and methods for their disposal have been well-developed in almost every state. In the past when you went to dispose of your old tires at a tire shop or landfill, the typical response was to say that you can't dump your tires there, which is ultimately the wrong answer, since many people just get frustrated and toss them by the side of the road or in vacant lots.

Most states today have mandatory tire buyback laws for dealers and shops. These laws typically have regulations that require tire dealers to accept used tires for disposal, usually with a small fee attached.

Electrical Components

Core parts of many electrical components can be recycled by the manufacturers to build new units. Alternators, generators, starter motors, and other electrical components fall into this category, and many shops will offer a rebate on your new part when you bring in the old one for recycling. Take advantage of such an arrangement.

Brake Pads

Brake pad cores can also be recycled by the manufacturers, and in many states, shops that sell pads are required by law to accept old pads free of charge and see to their recycling or safe disposal. This is especially important with nonmetallic, asbestos brake pads since asbestos is a powerful carcinogen.

When replacing asbestos pads, never blow away old brake dust with your face nearby as it simply provides you with easy-to-inhale airborne asbestos dust. Instead, use a moist cloth to wipe it away and dispose of the cloth.

Exhaust System Components

Not surprisingly, all of the exhaust system components that you route the engine exhaust through become caked with carcinogens and pollutants over time. The only way to safely dispose of used exhaust pipes, mufflers, and catalytic converters is to bring them to a hazardous waste collection site or to contact your local pollution control agency for other alternative sites.

Fluids

The best rule of thumb as you work with chemicals and fluids is to remember that if you can smell it, it's bad news. And the stronger the odor, the more dangerous it is—both to your immediate health and to the atmosphere and groundwater. Cleaners, paints, and all oil-derived liquids are the big things to watch out for. Dumped carelessly by the wayside, these toxic chemicals will quickly work their way into the water cycle and return to haunt us all.

The easiest solution, of course, is not to generate any more of these wastes than necessary in the first place. Except for motor oil, the greatest volume of volatile chemicals is generated by cleaning, not the actual changing of a car's fluids. It's best to start off with the mildest cleaners possible at first—soap and water can, in fact, do a lot of work—not just for the environment's sake but because these are also the easiest on the vehicle itself.

You will inevitably generate some hazardous material no matter what you do, however. Things like spray cleaners and naptha, for example—real health and environmental nightmares—are just too convenient to realistically swear off of completely. The trick is simply to catch as much of these fluids as possible after use, and to keep them tightly covered in plastic, glass, or metal containers until you can safely get rid of them. Leaving pans of cleaners uncovered sends these toxins directly into the atmosphere through evaporation, so keep them covered at all times.

Caked grease and ruined rags should also be kept tightly wrapped up in a cool place and disposed of along with actual fluids—they're simply volatiles that are currently trapped in solid form. And beware of the fire hazard of these rags.

All toxins should be kept separated since cross contamination simply makes the disposal issue more complicated.

Motor Oil

Used motor oil poses a great threat to the environment—and to yourself, as it contains carcinogens. Many states prohibit putting used motor oil in the trash or disposing of it in landfills.

Fortunately, however, motor oil can be recycled and used as fuel for ships, furnaces, and other things. In many states, shops that sell oil or provide oil changes are required by law to collect used motor oil for recycling.

Some counties offer curbside recycling of used motor oil, so check with your county government. These recycling programs sometimes have strict rules on how the used oil must be stored if they will take it for recycling; some want it stored only in plastic containers while others require glass jars, so be sure to ask.

You must also be certain to keep your used motor oil pure and not mix it with other fluids for disposal. If the used oil is contaminated with even minute traces of brake fluid or coolant, the entire batch in the collection tank will be ruined.

Antifreeze and Coolant

The main ingredient in antifreeze and coolants is ethylene glycol, a chemical that can be reconditioned in wastewater treatment systems. Small amounts of used antifreeze—1 gallon or so—can thus be safely disposed of in your home's sanitary sewer system when mixed with large amounts of water.

You should never dispose of antifreeze in storm sewers or septic systems as these do not run through the wastewater treatment system and the ethylene glycol will eventually contaminate the groundwater. Antifreeze dumped into a septic system will also destroy the bacteria in the system that septic tanks rely on to operate.

Parts Cleaners

The old-fashioned parts cleaner fluids that worked like magic in removing years of oil and grime from your vehicle parts also removed layers of your own skin and seeped directly into your liver, where they definitely didn't do you any good. When disposing of these old parts cleaners, first read the label on the container. If the product is labelled as being flammable, combustible, or contains any solvents such as petroleum distillates or aromatic hydrocarbons, then it must be disposed of at a hazardous waste collection site.

If the product is a liquid and does not contain any solvents, it can usually be disposed of in a sanitary sewer system after being mixed with large quantities of water. Never pour it down a storm sewer or into a septic system since the liquids will not be treated but will instead seep directly into our groundwater.

Today several alternative parts cleaners are readily available and easy on you and the environment while still scrubbing away all the oil and grease. Check them out.

There is also one other option: Never underestimate the power of hot water, soap, and scrubbing.

Gasoline

Gasoline is one of the most dangerous fluids around your house or workshop because it is extremely volatile.

Frequently, most waste gas is either contaminated or old. If it has been contaminated with paint or other soluble contaminants, it cannot be reconditioned. Check with your county for a hazardous waste collection site.

Stale gas can be used after adding one of the many reconditioning agents on the market. However, many people prefer not to risk their vehicle's engine and use the stale gas in a lawn mower or other small gas engine instead.

Index